Historical Consciousness and Religious Tradition in Azariah de' Rossi's Me'or ʿEinayim

Title page of Azariah de' Rossi's *Sefer Me'or 'Einayim*, Mantua, 1573.
Courtesy of the Library of the Jewish Theological Seminary of America

LESTER A. SEGAL

Historical Consciousness and Religious Tradition in Azariah de' Rossi's Me'or ʿEinayim

THE JEWISH PUBLICATION SOCIETY
Philadelphia New York Jerusalem
5749 1989

Publication of this book was made possible through a gift by the Pritzker Foundation.

First edition

Manufactured in the United States of America

Library of Congress Cataloging in Publication Data
Segal, Lester A.
Historical consciousness and religious tradition in Azariah de' Rossi's Me'or 'Einayim / Lester A. Segal.—1st ed.

p. cm.
Bibliography: p.
Includes index.
ISBN 0-8276-0316-9
1. Rossi, Azariah ben Moses de', ca. 1511–ca. 1578. 2. Jews—Historiography. 3. Rossi, Azariah ben Moses de', ca. 1511–ca. 1578. Me'or 'Einayim. 4. Aggada—History and criticism—Theory, etc. I. Title.
DS115.9.R66S44 1988 88-13058
909'.04924—dc19 CIP

Designed by Tracy Baldwin

To the memory of my father and teacher

Jonah Segal

ר׳ מרדכי יונה ב״ר נחמיה הלוי סג״ל ז״ל

and

To my mother

Sylvia Segal

מ׳ צביה בת ר׳ אברהם אליעזר ז״ל סג״ל

Contents

Preface

The now widely accepted idea of an early modern stage in European history, beginning in the fifteenth century, cannot be employed without qualification in the study of Jewish experience. For the Jews, the end of the Middle Ages was far more protracted than in general society, and cultural continuity tended to predominate far longer. Still, even in Jewish society there are clear indications of the interaction of traditional modes of belief and thought with new or modified ones, which is so significant a feature of the early modern period.

The resurgence of Jewish historical interest in the sixteenth century—while in part symptomatic of such new developments—proved to be largely compatible with traditional Jewish perceptions, with one notable exception. Only the work of Azariah de' Rossi differed both substantively and methodologically from the rest of this new body of literature; it was so discontinuous with tradition as to arouse strong opposition among some leading contemporaries and long thereafter. Azariah's thinking, conditioned in part by the authoritative continuity of classical Jewish juristic (halakhic) teaching, was also historically oriented with respect to other fundamental components of Judaism. It has been my purpose to examine the direction of Azariah's inquiry into those areas of Jewish tradition in which he gave historical considerations free rein and to assess his conclusions.

Of the modern scholarship on Azariah de' Rossi, special mention should be accorded the pioneering essays of Professor Salo W. Baron, the twentieth-century master of Jewish history. These essays can be found in his *History and Jewish Historians.*

I wish to express my appreciation to Professor Nahum M. Sarna, Academic Consultant on Judaica for the Jewish Publication Society, who saw fit to have it consider this work. I am also appreciative of the efforts and suggestions of the JPS editorial staff in facilitating publication. I am deeply indebted to Professor Marvin Fox, Director of the Lown School of Near Eastern and Judaic Studies at Brandeis University, for his early encouragement of the interests that led me to nurture the idea of doing this book. For its content, I alone am responsible.

My research was greatly facilitated by the library staff of the Hebrew College, Boston, to whom I am very thankful. I also had the forthcoming assistance of the interlibrary loan and reference departments at the University of Massachusetts in Boston. I wish to thank the Curators of the Bodleian Library, Oxford, for permission to cite de' Rossi manuscripts in their possession. In addition, Rabbi Abraham Shonfeld of Newton kindly allowed me the use of various volumes of medieval rabbinic responsa from his private library. Mrs. Margaret Allen of Belmont deserves my sincere thanks for her care and concern in preparing the typescript, which called for repeated demands on her time and skill.

For their great forbearance while this work was in progress I am deeply grateful to my wife and children. My wife, Ethel, lent her constant support along with the scrutiny of a perceptive lay reader and critic, often making for greater clarity in both broad statement and fine detail.

Lester A. Segal
June 1987

PART ONE

CHAPTER 1

The Sixteenth-Century Jewish Historiographical Scene: An Overview

An unusually abundant and diversified literature attests to a Jewish historiographical revival in the sixteenth century. While each of these works reflects its author's particular interest, taken collectively their concern is the contemporary crisis in Jewish society engendered by the expulsion of Spanish Jewry, a crisis compounded further by papal anti-Jewish policy of the Counter-Reformation. The shattering experience of the Spanish Jewish exiles and later of those Jewish communities subject to hostile papal policy generated a great deal of historical reflection on the perplexities of Jewish existence, usually with implications for their ultimate metahistorical resolution. What resulted were therefore essentially *pièces de circonstance*.

Solomon ibn Verga's *Sheveṭ Yehudah*, among the most sophisticated of these works, attempts, often through provocative if imaginary dialogues, to objectively investigate the realistic factors that led to hatred of the Jews in Spain—including those internal to Jewish society that might be detrimental to its well-being.[1] Although *Sheveṭ Yehudah* employs an empirical approach to historical phenomena and even an element of religious relativism and skepticism,[2] it is far from a detached historical analysis, since Ibn Verga is preoccupied with the destiny of the Jewish people and its continuing tribulations over the ages. Traditional religious concepts continue to inform his thinking about the Jewish condition as he recounts the past and reflects upon the aftermath of 1492, which he himself had lived through. His account of Jewish travail is intended to arouse a penitent mood among coreligionists and thus effect God's intervention on their behalf.[3] Although *Sheveṭ Yehudah* does not qualify as a conventional moralistic tract, the fundamental idea that God has imposed the trial of exile and that it is He who will effect redemption remains integral to Ibn Verga's thinking.[4] A circumstance that sheds further light on his religious posture is his apparent involvement, along with several qabbalists, in a risky but successful effort to take out of Portugal a unique anti-philosophical manuscript—especially anti-Maimonidean—called *Sefer ha-Emunot*, by the fifteenth-century qabbalist Shem Tov ibn Shem Tov. In Shem Tov's vehement, if not fanatical, expression of Jewish anti-rationalist sentiment, Jewish heresy and apostasy in Spain were directly related to the influence of Maimonides' philosophical speculation.[5]

The unusually precise and objective account of the papacy of Paul IV (1555–1559) by the little-known chronicler Benjamin Nehemiah ben Elnathan of Civitanova is, again, inspired by the concerns of the day growing out of the increasingly insecure Jewish political and religious situation. If it reflects an extraordinary awareness both of papal affairs and of the general political scene, the author nonetheless sees himself as one who "relates the misfortunes."[6] The detailed structure of this narrative, and the author's apparent realization that the Jewish situation is only to be understood within the larger context of papal politics,[7] differs substantially, for example, from the few pages that constitute a parallel contemporary account of Paul IV in Joseph ha-Kohen's *'Emeq ha-Bakhah*, written in Italy as well. The limitations of *'Emeq ha-Bakhah* are due neither to deficiencies in Joseph ha-Kohen's knowledge of general history—his earlier work on the kings of France and on the Ottoman Turks attests to his abilities—nor to his cursory coverage of the whole story of persecution since the Roman destruction of the Temple. Rather, his "valley of tears" approach, with its litany-like narrative periodically invoking God's intervention on behalf of his suffering coreligionists, gives this work a moralistic tone and leads to primary emphasis on Paul IV as the epitome of evil.[8]

Nonetheless, the chronicler Benjamin Nehemiah also asserts that his intent is not to commemorate the career of Paul IV but "only the calamities and sufferings that have befallen our people during his rule," a rule he characterizes as wicked. Almost predictably, this "account of misfortunes" is linked in the author's peroration with the anticipation of messianic redemption, the biblical conditions for which appear to him as virtually fulfilled in the great distress of his own generation. Such messianic concerns are so integral to the Jewish historiographical creativity of the period that they apparently also account for the interest in world history manifested in Joseph ha-Kohen's *Divrei ha-Yamim le-Malkhei Ṣarfat-u-Malkhei Beit Ottoman ha-Togar*.[9]

Even the rabbi of Candia (Crete), Elijah Capsali, who several decades earlier wrote a lengthy history of the Ottoman Empire and Venice, *Seder Eliyahu Zuṭa'*, did so primarily because he saw a relationship between this subject matter, Jewry in the post-expulsion era, and the ultimate destiny of the Jews. He incorporates aspects of specifically Jewish experience and also autobiographical material, especially as these relate to his years in Italy.[10] A main function of his historiographical undertaking, however, is to demonstrate divine providence at work in the non-Jewish affairs about which he writes, in particular, that the Ottoman Turks serve as God's agent in exacting punishment of those peoples "whose measure is full."[11] Capsali's analogy between the wisdom and counsel that the exoteric meaning of certain scriptural narratives provides and the knowledge and understanding that he believes is to be derived from his account of "the Gentile and Turkish kings" is apparently inspired by his view of the acts and dramatic conquests of the Ottoman Turks. He views them as directly related to the unfolding of the messianic drama and to the scheme of redemption as envisaged in Jewish tradition.[12]

Common and critical to these and other sixteenth-century Jewish historical works is their publicistic function.[13] They no doubt mirror in part the Renaissance resurgence of historical interest and historical writing and in part the gradual secularization of historical thought; some even mirror the influence of the Reformation in its use of history as a medium for religious polemic, as in Samuel Usque's mid-century pastoral dialogue *Consolation for the Tribulations of Israel*. For Usque, the ex-Marrano, neither accuracy of detail nor critical analysis of sources, regardless of their legendary elements, is of great moment. What is important for him is the theological message, notably the millennial significance resonating from within the Iberian Jewish catastrophe and such dramatic contemporary events as the schism within Christianity and the ascendancy of the Ottoman Turks.[14]

The extensive utilization of the historical mode of expression, however, is novel for Jews in this period as a means of addressing their troubled condition. Ibn Verga even notes the long-standing Christian interest in past events as a source of wisdom and counsel. His praise of this interest as a worthy cultural achievement apparently implies by contrast a failing in the long Jewish neglect of history.[15] But as perceived by the sixteenth-century Jewish authors, the real value of history is not to provide political and moral edification as understood by the Renaissance humanists. Its function instead is as a barometer of the present Jewish situation and as an intimation of the future one.

Whatever combination of narrative, inquiry, speculation, martyrology, messianism, or millenarianism this literature may exhibit, it neither exhausts the sixteenth-century range of Jewish historical interest nor addresses other than tangentially the substance of classical Jewish culture as a subject of inquiry. This is more properly the domain of the historian-antiquarian, personified in the sixteenth century by the Italian Jewish author Azariah de' Rossi, who displays some of the most novel features of the Renaissance understanding of the past: the growing awareness of historical change, development, and perspective and the increasingly critical approach toward evidence that results from close study of sources and comparative procedure.[16] Azariah's work of 1573, *Me'or 'Einayim*, is distinguished from that of the narrators, chroniclers, memorialists, and polemicists in that its historiographical objective, the "enlightenment of the eyes" as he suggestively entitles his scholarly enterprise, derives from a preoccupation with Jewish antiquity and, notably, from the attempt to elucidate certain well-known but nonetheless perplexing aspects of the classical tradition. The enterprise is at once his expression of a non-utilitarian intellectual quest and a concern to meet the needs of that type of coreligionist whom he describes as "he who drinks thirstily the words of our sages but who is [simultaneously] drawn by human reason"[17] and for whom the contemporary milieu has made this combination problematic and controversial. Azariah brings into play new methods of verification, frequently extraneous to the tradition itself, that outrage conventional Jewish opinion and even distress those authoritative Jewish voices who have a cultural affinity with him.

Notes

1. *Sefer Sheveṭ Yehudah*, ed. A. Shohet (Jerusalem: Mosad Bialik, 1947), e.g., 30f., 32, 40, 45, 47, 95, 127f., 151.

2. Ibid., Intro., esp. 12–15, for Yitzhak Baer's characterization. The following passages in the text are illuminating: pp. 29, 36f. (religious relativism and tolerance); pp. 21, 80 (futility of religious coercion); p. 31 (criticism of the

talmudists, suggesting they have distorted the meaning of scripture). Baer (p. 15) finds an "Averroistic" attitude toward religion in the *Sheveṭ Yehudah* typical of certain Italian Renaissance circles. See too Baer, *Galut*, trans. R. Warshow (New York: Schocken, 1947), 77–82; and idem, "He'arot ḥadashot le-Sefer Sheveṭ Yehudah," *Tarbiz* 6 (1935): 152–179. Baer's view of Italian Renaissance influence on Ibn Verga has, however, been challenged on the grounds that Ibn Verga apparently never settled in Italy. See Meir Benayahu, "Maqor 'al Megorashei Sefarad be-Portugal ve-Ṣetam aḥarei Gezerat Rasa"v le-Saloniki," *Sefunot* 11 (1971–1977): 249ff.

3. *Sheveṭ Yehudah*, 19.

4. Ibid., e.g., 74, 120, 141, regarding divine retribution and redemption; and see Baer's analysis in *Galut*. In his "He'arot," (p. 178), Baer observes that just as Christian Averroism of the Renaissance period did not break with the authority of tradition, so too and in even greater measure the indications of religious faith in the *Sheveṭ Yehudah* are far more pronounced than any suggestions of heresy. This suggests, in short, that the process of secularization progressed slowly in the sixteenth century. See below, p. 76ff., regarding the cultural climate of the sixteenth century.

5. See the discussion in Yosef Hayim Yerushalmi, *The Lisbon Massacre of 1506 and the Royal Image in the Shebet Yehudah* (Cincinnati: Hebrew Union College Press, 1976), 51, and n. 127. Regarding Shem Tov ibn Shem Tov, see Julius Guttmann, *Philosophies of Judaism*, trans. D. W. Silverman (London: Routledge and Kegan Paul, 1964), 251f.; and *Encyclopaedia Judaica* (1972), s.v. "Ibn Shem Tov, Shem Tov."

6. *Divrei ha-Yamim shel ha-Apifyor Paulo Revi'i*, in *Mi-Paulo ha-Revi'i 'ad Pius ha-Ḥamishi*, ed. Isaiah Sonne (Jerusalem: Mosad Bialik, 1954), 19–93, and see 64, 91. Regarding the new papal policy that commenced with Paul IV and the efforts to promote mass conversion, see Kenneth R. Stow, *Catholic Thought and Papal Jewry Policy, 1555–1593* (New York: Jewish Theological Seminary of America, 1977), esp. 3–59.

7. See Sonne, *Paulo ha-Revi'i*, 3ff.

8. Joseph ha-Kohen, *'Emeq ha-Bakhah*, ed. M. Letteris (Cracow: Faust's Buchhandlung, 1895), 133–138, 140ff. Stow, *Catholic Thought*, 40, and n. 146, sees ha-Kohen's very brief reference to papal conversionary policy (*'Emeq ha-Bakhah*, 131) as proof of Jewish "anxiety and reticence in expression" at the time, noting that *'Emeq ha-Bakhah* remained unpublished until the nineteenth century.

9. Sonne, *Paulo ha-Revi'i*, 49, 90ff. Sonne (pp. 8f.) refers to the apparent influence of the medieval Jewish historical work *Josippon* in the Italian Jewish chronicler's concluding emphasis on redemption. Like *Josippon*, the author's intent is thereby to link his work with scripture rather than to leave it in the realm of purely profane narrative. Regarding Joseph ha-Kohen's general history, see Yosef Hayim Yerushalmi, "Messianic Impulses in Joseph ha-Kohen," in *Jewish Thought in the Sixteenth Century*, ed. B. D. Cooperman (Cambridge: Harvard University Press, 1983), 460–487.

10. *Seder Eliyahu Zuṭa'*, ed. A. Shmuelevitz, S. Simonsohn, and M. Benayahu (Jerusalem: Ben-Zvi Institute and Diaspora Research Institute, 1975), 2:251–259.

11. Ibid. 1:10.

12. Ibid. The messianic meaning with which Capsali endows the history of the Ottoman Turks and their famous sultans as well as the redemptive implications of the 1492 expulsion is discussed by Charles Berlin, "A Sixteenth-Century Hebrew Chronicle of the Ottoman Empire: The Seder Eliyahu Zuta of Elijah Capsali and Its Message," in *Studies in Jewish Bibliography, History, and Literature in Honor of I. Edward Kiev*, ed. Charles Berlin (New York: Ktav, 1971), 26ff., 31f., 39f.

13. The publicistic thrust of this historical literature is described by Moses A. Shulvass, "'Al ha-Hitraḥashut ha-hisṭorit veha-Maḥshavah ha-hisṭorit," in *Bi-Ṣevat ha-Dorot* (New York: Ogen, 1960), 208f. Cf. Salo W. Baron, "Azariah de' Rossi's Historical Method," in *History and Jewish Historians* (Philadelphia: Jewish Publication Society, 1964), 423 n. 4: "In contrast to Azariah, most of his Jewish confreres too, sought to teach, move, or fortify the reader."

14. *Consolation for the Tribulations of Israel*, trans. M. A. Cohen (Philadelphia: Jewish Publication Society, 1965), 10, 18f., 25, 27. In none of these Jewish works is there yet anything resembling that "methodical separation of a profane historical view of the history of mankind from the theological meaning of the universal historical context," associated especially with the sixteenth-century thinker Jean Bodin. See Adalbert Klempt, *Die Säkularisierung der universalhistorischen Auffasung. Zum Wandel des Geschichtsdenkens in 16. und 17. Jahrhundert* (Göttingen: Musterschmidt Verlag, 1960), 42.

15. *Sheveṭ Yehudah*, 21.

16. The subject is very usefully dealt with by Peter Burke, *The Renaissance Sense of the Past* (New York: St. Martin's Press, 1970); and see below, Chap. 3.

17. *Sefer Me'or 'Einayim*, ed. David Cassel (Vilna: J. R. Romm, 1864–1866; Jerusalem: Maqor, 1970), 1:217 (hereafter cited as *M.E.*). Vol. 3 of the Cassel edition includes de' Rossi's two shorter treatises *Maṣref la-Kesef* and *Ṣedeq 'Olamim*, some hymns and poems, and Cassel's annotated indexes. The two shorter treatises were first published from Azariah's manuscript by H. Filipowski (Edinburgh, 1854). The first (Mantua, 1573, with modifications and additions in the 1574–1575 printings) and subsequent editions of *M.E.* are discussed in Cassel's introduction (pp. iiif., xf.). In 1899 Z. H. Jaffe published another edition of *M.E.* with notes. For the apparent biblical inspiration of Azariah's choice of titles for his works, see the Hebrew text of Prov. 15:30—and cf. *M.E.* 4—and Prov. 27:21.

In the choice of title for his shorter treatise *Maṣref la-Kesef*, Azariah is apparently suggesting that the further validation and justification of his views—views already set forth in the *Me'or 'Einayim*—requires a refinement process comparable to the refining of silver. An analogy between testing for truth and the testing of silver is already used by the tenth-century R. Saadyah Gaon, based however on a different verse in Proverbs (10:20). See *Book of Doctrines and Beliefs*, ed. and trans. Alexander Altmann, in *Three Jewish Philosophers* (New York: Harper Torchbooks, 1965), Prolegomena, 27f., 28 n. 1. See too *Maṣref la-Kesef*, p. 3., where Azariah comments on his choice of title.

On the purely artistic side, there is some unintended irony in the fact that the title page illustration in the 1573 Mantua edition of the *Me'or 'Einayim*, an ornate archway capped by the verse from Psalms, "This is the gateway to the Lord," is identical with that in the first Mantua edition (1558–1560) of the classic of Jewish mysticism, the *Zohar* (see the illustration of the *M.E.* title page on p. ii above; and cf. for the *Zohar*, Israel Zinberg, *Toledot Sifrut Yisra'el*, trans. and ed. S. Z. Ariel, D. Kenaani, G. Karu [Tel Aviv: Sifriyat Poalim, 1955–1960], vol. 2, following p. 452).

CHAPTER 2

Azariah de' Rossi: The Man and His Intellect

In his *Me'or 'Einayim,* Azariah de' Rossi, or Azariah Min ha-Adumim as he was known in Hebrew, identifies himself as a native of Mantua, "the joyous city," but notes that he presently resides in Ferrara.[1] Another source, which describes Azariah's 1576 poems occasioned by the death of Duchess Margarita of Savoy, identifies him as "Azaria alias Buonaiuto de' Rossi hebreo mantovano, habitatore in Ferrara"; Azariah himself, using this equivalent of his Hebrew name, signed several Italian letters addressed to Christians as "Buonaiuto de' Rossi hebreo."[2] Additional autobiographical information emerges from the often intricate course of his historical essays in the *Me'or 'Einayim.* Nonetheless, one would be hard put to reconstruct a complete, detailed account of his life. Although his ancestry in Italy undoubtedly went back numerous generations, we obviously cannot substantiate Azariah's report of "a tradition we have received from our ancients"—that the family Min ha-Adumim had been one of "the four noble ones whom Titus had exiled to Rome."[3] This piece of Italian Jewish lore regarding

Titus and the Jews first appeared almost a millennium ago[4] and in later centuries served the penchant to claim familial antiquity.[5] In the case of the de' Rossis, at least as early as the thirteenth century one of its members in Rome, Solomon ben Moses ben Yekutiel, already represented the family's tradition of Jewish learning and literary creativity through his polemical work *'Edut ha-Shem Ne'emanah.* Solomon's grandson Moses ben Yekutiel, though not an especially original writer, authored a handbook of Jewish laws and customs, *Sefer ha-Tadir.*[6] Despite the talmudic proscription of *sefarim ḥiṣonim,* that is, sources "outside" of the canonical Jewish scripture and tradition, Solomon de' Rossi considered knowledge of such sources—notably Christian scripture—a necessary prerequisite to engaging effectively in polemics.[7] For Solomon's sixteenth-century descendant, Azariah, the issue of this proscription became, as we shall see, much more complex and controversial.[8]

Exactly when the de' Rossi family settled in Mantua is unknown. It seems probable that there were some Jews in Mantua in the Roman period, but there is no reliable information for a Mantuan Jewish settlement before the twelfth century. And only by the end of the fourteenth century does the documentation become sufficiently abundant so as to permit a clearer picture of Mantuan Jewry.[9] By then the majority of Italian Jews resided in the north and in the papal states of central Italy. Mantua was among the most important of the large cities in which Jews were settling in growing numbers, and in the fifteenth century it could already boast such leading scholars as the rabbi Joseph Colon and the humanist Judah Messer Leon. Such Jewish settlements were typically small; by the end of that century the city of Mantua had perhaps some 150 to 200 Jews. Only in the early sixteenth century, by which time the Jewish population had further increased and become more diversified, did the Mantuan authorities accord its Jewry communal status. Close to the end of the sixteenth century the influx of refugees from the papal states, the duchy of Milan, and elsewhere, had brought its Jewish population to over fifteen hundred.[10] By the time of Azariah's birth, sometime after 1510, his family was undoubtedly long established in this city, and when in his mature years he speaks of "my land Mantua,"[11] it is certainly with an awareness of a long familial connection with it. The archival and literary sources reveal that the de' Rossis, along with other influential Mantuan Jewish families (including the Massaranos, the family of Azariah's wife) were active in communal, commercial, and cultural life.[12] Azariah's brother-in-law, Haim Massarano, was a Mantuan banker from a family associated with learning, and he possessed a manuscript of a medieval halakhic compendium that Azariah consulted. And from a dedicatory Hebrew verse inscription written by Azariah for a synagogue ark curtain, we see that Haim Massarano and his wife, Deborah, were benefactors of Jewish religious life.[13]

Azariah reports that he was about sixty years old in 1571 when he began the scholarly enterprise represented by the *Me'or 'Einayim.*[14] This would place his date of birth roughly in 1511. Yet according to information provided by the well-known Marrano physician Amatus Lusitanus, who treated Azariah in 1548 or 1549, he could have been born as late as 1514, since Amatus describes "Azariah, the Hebrew of Mantua," as being thirty-five years of age at the time.[15] Of Azariah's youth and early intellectual development we know virtually nothing. He was no doubt served well by the rich Jewish cultural environment that had taken shape in fifteenth- and sixteenth-century Mantua. Opportunities existed for Jewish-Christian intellectual exchange, mutual influences of Italian and northern Jewish learning and creativity abounded due to the influx of German, French, and Spanish refugee coreligionists, and Jewish culture was also enriched by the works printed in the important Mantuan Hebrew presses.[16] The spirit of the age in Italian Jewish life encouraged a broad education that combined traditional biblical and rabbinic learning with the study of Hebrew literary and philosophical works and general learning. Still, most of what is known regarding the actual trend and content of such education in sixteenth-century Mantua is essentially reconstructed from the attainments of individuals like Azariah himself or from occasional autobiographical statements or proposed courses of study.[17]

Even with these rich opportunities, Azariah could hardly have attained his high level of Jewish and secular learning without extraordinary diligence, lifelong persistence in scholarly endeavor, and the acumen so frequently displayed in the *Me'or 'Einayim.* He may have "conceived" the main part of his *Me'or 'Einayim* on the eve of Passover 1571 and then "begot" it, as he reports, some eighteen months later,[18] but the process of intellectual gestation by which he worked through the manifold issues contained in this product of his older age clearly had been in progress for decades.

Long before the publication of that work, he was already known to be, as Amatus Lusitanus attests, "a great scholar both in Hebrew and in Latin letters."[19] Azariah apparently had studied medicine as well and was a practicing physician. Amatus, in assessing Azariah's then troubled physical condition, refers to the fact that "he is extremely studious and zealously occupied with medical work"—an area of endeavor to which Italian Jews made significant contributions in that age.[20] Exactly how Azariah earned a living cannot be ascertained; for example, whether the practice of medicine was his primary source of income and whether it was adequate for his needs. Nor can it be determined from a brief, passing reference in the *Me'or 'Einayim* if his work at one time as a book censor also provided income.[21] His financial situation appears to have permitted him to purchase books and manuscripts; thus he reports that he acquired works from the estate of the recently deceased Jehiel Nissim da Pisa (d. 1574),[22] a well-known Jewish scholar and spokesman who had been a member of the Ferrara rabbinate. Only in his last years, and especially in connection with the problems surrounding the publication of the *Me'or 'Einayim,* are there indications that Azariah was experiencing financial difficulties.[23]

The physician Amatus describes a very slender and emaciated patient who "had long been afflicted with many and serious diseases." Amatus diagnosed Azariah as suffering from quartan fever, a dermatological disorder, digestive distress, chest constriction, melancholic insomnia, and various other maladies. For their treatment, he provided a comprehensive dietary, physical, and psychological regimen for a four-month period, "during which his strength increased to that of a boxer." Amatus had prescribed, among many other things, that "sadness, anger, sorrow and such like emotions must be avoided. Instead, his life must be filled with comfort, enjoyment, pleasure, which certainly contribute greatly to health."[24]

But this was not to be. The death of Azariah's beloved young grandson Benjamin,[25] added to the threatening conditions that led him and other Jews to flee from the papal territory of Bologna in the late 1560's,[26] the unsettling conditions of life, the economic hardships imposed in the wake of the 1570 earthquake in Ferrara,[27] and the controversy several years later regarding his *Me'or 'Einayim*, surely must have aroused precisely those emotions about which Amatus had cautioned him.

Amatus had insisted as well that Azariah "avoid foggy and moist weather," with which "Mantua and Ferrara are richly blessed";[28] and Azariah indeed seems to have resided some time thereafter in Bologna. But by the end of the 1560s Azariah was destined to relocate once again since, as he puts it, God rescued him "from the hand of the angel of destruction in the holy congregation of Bologna"[29]—no doubt a carefully veiled reference to the repressive, conversionary papal posture assumed by Pius V since 1566.[30] By 1568, when the Inquisition was incarcerating and torturing Jews in Bologna to extract confessions that rabbinic works had defamed Christianity,[31] Azariah might indeed be thankful that he had been spared such trials. A contemporary in Bologna, for example, Ishmael Haninah of Valmontone—who signed a declaration several years later as a member of the Ferrara rabbinate restricting the use of Azariah's *Me'or 'Einayim*—recorded the experience of interrogation and physical abuse to which he and other Jews had been subjected.[32] This description makes the reasons for Azariah's expressions of good fortune dramatically clear. He either managed to escape along with some other Jews during these dismal proceedings, when departure from the city had actually been prohibited,[33] or he fled Bologna in 1569 with Pius V's order expelling Jews from papal territories except for Rome and Ancona.[34] He established his new home in Ferrara, where he apparently had lived earlier and where the vast majority of the "Bolognese" now settled.[35] Although Azariah may have been more familiar with later sixteenth-century papal Jewry policy than he lets on, writing in the early 1570s under the much less restrictive conditions in Ferrara (a territory that would not come under direct papal control until 1597) he had good reason to be reticent in describing his experiences and his impressions of the deteriorating Jewish political situation in Italy.[36] As the Ferrara minute book (*pinqas*) reveals, Azariah participated in the Jewish communal arrangements of 1573 for the sustenance of the many refugees who, from 1569 on, fled from the oppressive conditions in Rome and Ancona to sojourn in Ferrara under the rule of the rather enlightened dukes of the house of Este.[37]

The period beginning in 1573 was one of great fulfillment for Azariah, whose unusual historical and scholarly talents came to fruition in the *Me'or 'Einayim*, which he saw through the press that year in Mantua.[38] Of this achievement a contemporary wrote: "I have heard it said that all those upon whom God has bestowed wisdom have brought this work of yours into their treasure-houses, they concurred in their high praise of it."[39] But since there were those who wished "to devour him without cause, to bury him while he was yet alive"[40] because of *Me'or 'Einayim*, Azariah's last years were marred. In addition to the controversy surrounding his book and what he described as the malevolence of some opponents, difficult financial conditions and family cares were also a source of distress.[41] In the years just prior to his death, toward the end of 1577, Azariah was also in a poor state of health. He notes his weak physical constitution in *Maṣref la-Kesef* (Refinement of the Silver) of 1575—a response to his critics that remained in manuscript until the nineteenth century. In a tone that seems to forebode ill, he reflects on man's mortality, which has led him to hasten the completion of this treatise.[42]

Azariah's description of the 1570 Ferrara earthquake yields additional biographical information. He refers, although not by name, to his wife and his children, including a married daughter, all of whom lived through these dramatic events with him; and tells too of a peculiar affliction from which his wife suffered at the time.[43] This account, which Azariah entitled *Qol Elohim* (Voice of God) and which he arranged as the first of three major divisions of the *Me'or 'Einayim*, is also his most extensive report of contemporary events. His description of what transpired during the earthquake—actually a succession of earthquakes—is detailed and graphic; it reflects the work of a contemporary Italian physician in Ferrara, Iacomo Buoni, as well as his own experiences. So strong were the two greatest tremors, Azariah reports, that they were felt over a distance of two hundred miles, from the outskirts of Pesaro to Milan, that is, to the south and north of Ferrara respectively, as verified by both travelers and inhabitants. But the destructive impact was experienced only in Ferrara and beyond its borders, within a radius of some ten miles.[44] The narrative sections of *Qol Elohim* provide, among other things, details of the great destruction, of the dislocation of people that followed in its wake, and of the many prominent Jewish communal leaders in Ferrara who extended themselves on behalf of the needy. Included among the leaders was Don Isaac Abravanel, grandson of the famous author and statesman of the same name. Azariah also reports that worship in the various synagogues of Ferrara did not cease throughout this entire period despite the critical conditions of life.[45]

In a more personal vein, Azariah notes that during these very difficult days he and many others relocated "on the other side of the river Po, southward." Here, an unidentified Christian refugee and scholar, obviously someone aware of Azariah's reputation and talents, engaged him in a discussion of the ancient *Letter of Aristeas,* a fanciful Hellenistic Jewish account of the translation of the Torah into Greek by seventy-two Jewish elders. In Azariah's day the author of the *Letter* was still generally believed to have been a Greek court official in Ptolemaic Alexandria who reported on the origins of this famous translation, known as the Septuagint. In the course of this encounter, the Christian, along with other "distinguished" individuals in Azariah's company, strongly urged him to prepare a Hebrew translation of the work in question. This was presumably the impetus for such a project undertaken by Azariah; under the title *Hadrat Zeqenim* (Glory of the Elders), the translation became the second section of the *Me'or 'Einayim.*[46] In relating this incident, however, Azariah reminds the reader that the subject of the book of Aristeas was one "that I had [previously] begun to speak of"[47]—that is, his scholarly interest in the *Letter of Aristeas* apparently had long preceded the Ferrara earthquake, as is obvious in his introductory remarks to the *Me'or 'Einayim*. The exchange with the Christian scholar on the outskirts of Ferrara perhaps furthered but did not necessarily initiate his concern with this work, which had fallen into virtual oblivion among Jews many centuries earlier. Still, according to his own account in *Qol Elohim,* that discussion led him to decide on a Hebrew translation of the *Letter,* for he thought it reasonable to assume that it "could not but be wholly acceptable to the intelligent [*la-maskilim*] among our people."[48]

Beyond the narrative in Azariah's account of the Ferrara earthquake, *Qol Elohim* begins to provide access to Azariah's speculative thought processes. His opening remarks, taken at face value, convey a belief that whoever experiences God's signs and awesome deeds is obliged by scriptural prescription to record them for the religious edification of posterity.[49] But on reading this section, one wonders whether he is not more motivated by theological reflection than by the several biblical proof texts he invokes.[50] Even by his own account earthquakes are phenomena that have transpired many times in the past,[51] whereas the wondrous occurrences referred to in the context of the biblical verses he cites—the plagues in Egypt, events in the days of the prophet Joel—are, by scriptural testimony itself, unique in the annals of the providentially directed course of events they describe: "Something that neither your fathers nor your fathers' fathers have seen from the day they appeared on earth to this day," and "Has the like of this happened in your days or in the days of your fathers?"[52]

In fact, the Ferrara earthquake becomes a point of departure for an investigation of the phenomenon of earthquakes per se, one that displays an intellectual frame of reference often echoed in Azariah's diverse historiographical essays. More specifically, since he introduces a good many talmudic and midrashic statements or descriptions attributing anthropomorphic acts to God, in this instance with respect to earthquakes, Azariah briefly sets forth the premise of their purely metaphorical intent in order to prevent any misunderstanding.[53] This entire issue of the status and meaning of aggadah, the nonlegalistic, narrative, or anecdotal element in rabbinic literature, is one that long predates Azariah, as his own passing reference here to earlier authorities is intended to remind the reader. But he elaborates it along novel lines in the body of his *Me'or 'Einayim.*

Broader issues of outlook come into play as well, for even though he designates this essay *Qol Elohim,* what is subsumed under that title does not quite fit the description. It is not that Azariah dissimulates in referring to the "voice of God"—a title inspired, he tells us, by scripture and by Pythagoras's usage of it[54]—but rather that the phrase is somewhat disarming. There are the references to God's mercy, fury, and anger[55] that one may expect from Azariah and his contemporaries as part of the response to a catastrophe of this kind; simultaneously, however, he introduces for consideration a range of naturalistic, rational explanations drawn from the ancients, who were the guides to rationalism for sixteenth-century authors and observers seeking a fuller understanding of the world.[56]

In addition to biblical and rabbinic texts that substantiate the supernatural origin and religious significance of earthquakes, Azariah brings supportive Christian opinion from the account of the physician Buoni and turns as well to authorities such as Aristotle, Seneca, Pliny, and Plutarch, also cited by Buoni. And from Plutarch, Azariah culls additional ancient naturalistic opinion in this matter, including that of Epicurus.[57] He grapples with the problem of whether earthquakes are purely God's doing or are at times the result of natural causes alone and appears unwilling to exclude either possibility. Although in general nature serves as the instrument of God's will, it is true, he concedes, that various natural phenomena are sometimes known to occur without any apparent moral or divine significance. Let us, says Azariah, avoid either extreme and assert that at times earthquakes stem from God, and at times from natural, accidental causes.[58]

Yet one senses in Azariah's overall discussion a decided preference for restraint with respect to the definition of the miraculous and its application to the manifestations of nature. He refers to God's works, inclusive of the established order of events in the universe, as extremely formidable and awe-inspiring, as the maskil, the intellectually perceptive individual so often addressed and praised in the *Me'or 'Einayim*, correctly realizes. According to Azariah, then, this is where the miraculous is truly to be found, and the merit of the maskil lies in the fact that he is profoundly moved precisely by these recurring phenomena of nature. Yet in the ordinary course of things, the *masses* are relatively unresponsive and insensitive to the grandeur of the regular, established order, unlike their reaction upon experiencing some sudden frightening and novel event—although in truth the latter is trifling in comparison with what is intrinsic to nature. Azariah observes that people tend to react more to what they physically experience, especially with the sense of sight, than to what reason dictates. He does not doubt that from one point of view, the earthquake he describes is not a miracle removed from nature's normal scheme of things, since earthquakes are an eternal phenomenon that has occurred many times in the past. Yet for the one who experiences any such troublesome, sudden occurrence, it is something "*close to a miracle*" and will thus stimulate man to a greater recognition of the divine power so that he may take it to heart.[59] Again, the devout note is not an afterthought or formality for Azariah. But one may venture that having reduced even so extraordinary an event as an earthquake to natural proportions, he finds it necessary to reassert his basic theological frame of reference. Within this theological perspective, however, Azariah puts no small premium on the capacity of the mature human intellect to discern the extraordinary in what the mind experiences routinely.

An issue remains, concerning how much of the miraculous may in fact inhere in that which is "*close to a miracle.*" In another context, in *Qol Elohim,* Azariah reports that as a result of the fright caused by the earthquake, his wife experienced a peculiar change of facial color and a subsequent, almost insatiable desire for salt. He suggests that there was perhaps some relationship between the "noxious salty vapor and its sulfurous mist" in the atmosphere as a result of the earthquake and the cure effected by the intake of salt. For as the desire for salt diminished, her appearance returned to normal "and this was a miracle." In citing this unusual cure, Azariah calls the discerning reader's attention to "God's work, the secrets of nature."[60]

Whatever the scientific merits or limitations of Azariah's analysis, the ostensibly miraculous nature of the cure he initially describes leads him to reflect momentarily on a possible parallel in the Bible: "And *who knows* if [perhaps] Elisha's miracle concerning the cure through water [i.e., the miraculous cure for leprosy accomplished by bathing in the Jordan, which Elisha recommended to the Aramean captain] followed a *somewhat* similar direction." This is a case of a controversial suggestion that Azariah felt obliged to revise, for in a subsequent annotation to the text of the *Me'or 'Einayim*, he reports that some scholars expressed reservations concerning his apparent naturalistic interpretation of a biblical miracle. Although Azariah notes that there are those exegetes who are known to have dealt with many scriptural miracles in this manner, he himself disavows any such approach. Indeed, he insists that, on the contrary, his explanation of his wife's cure had given miraculous meaning to a seemingly natural course of events—for no such cure had ever occurred, even to the greatest of the naturalists. But, he adds a qualification; since he "had not considered her cure a real miracle," he had taken great care when making the comparison with the prophet Elisha to be very reserved in his choice of words (i.e., "who knows," "somewhat," etc.) in order to distinguish between what had been a miracle in truth and "something that appeared to me *close* to it."[61]

Just as it seems that Azariah has finally said what he apparently means, his closing comment on the subject in this annotation leaves open the question of whether he indeed means what he has said. For he proceeds to point out that in addition to the clarification already provided, "one needs to consider that in truth, with respect to miracles affecting individuals it is the manner of the prophets, and Elisha in particular, *to bring them close to nature.*" To illustrate this prophetic effecting of miracles through a natural course of action, Azariah cites Elisha's reviving of the Shunammite woman's dead son; the cleansing of the Aramean captain Naaman from his leprosy through bathing in the Jordan; the account of Elijah and the Zarephath widow's jar of flour that did not give out; his reviving of the same widow's dead son by stretching out over the child; and Isaiah's healing of King Hezekiah's near fatal rash through the application of a cake of figs (*2 Kings* 4:34–35; 5:9–14; *1 Kings* 17:14–16, 21–22; *2 Kings* 20:7).[62] The note on which Azariah has ended this entire analysis is most significant, particularly insofar as it involves a class of biblical miracles. For he is very insistent on the divine authority and literal truth of scripture, with the exception of occasional comments on such features as the fairly frequent occurrence of certain round numbers in the Pentateuch and the prophets or observations that in the book of Ecclesiastes the words of the author Solomon "are not of divine and toraitic wisdom . . . but like a man speaking with the power of human wisdom alone."[63]

One might conclude that by the end of all the circumlocution in *Qol Elohim,* particularly his annotation to the text, Azariah has kept the miraculous designation of certain extraordinary natural events almost purely within metaphorical limits, albeit within the larger providential scheme of things to which he subscribes. But he has simultaneously diverted a range of scripturally designated miracles along naturalistic lines, including the one about which his critics had originally raised objections. An element of paradox and ambiguity thus accompanies Azariah's attempts to strike a delicate balance between the classical Jewish theological position and the limits of rational analysis. But for him the latter is a sine qua non of intellectual integrity both in *Qol Elohim* and in the main substance of his work, which is, after all, dedicated to the "enlightenment of the eyes."

Realizing the potentially controversial nature of such an undertaking, Azariah nonetheless chooses to make his particular contribution to the understanding of central facets of Judaism and the Jewish past. In an introductory apologia to *Imrei Binah* (Words of Wisdom), the third and main section of his treatise, Azariah informs us that God has moved him to leave this collection of useful historical and related essays to posterity. He is particularly so disposed as he reflects upon the fact that he is now about sixty years old and has no male offspring who, together with his good deeds, might otherwise perpetuate his name. Among the occasional autobiographical reflections, these are particularly insightful, for they reveal an interesting dimension both of his motivation in composing the

Me'or 'Einayim and of his self-perception. Readers of this work, Azariah continues, may derive some pleasure from it and will thus have occasion to make mention of the author whose aim, above all, has been to set forth the truth and that which is just. This, Azariah prays, will assure the everlasting endurance of his scholarly teaching, and his lips, as talmudic imagery puts it, will thus continue to speak forth from the sepulcher. Finally, he expresses the hope that his work will be comparable to that of Ben Bebai, a functionary in the ancient Temple of Jerusalem who performed a holy but minor charge: to superintend the preparation of the wicks.[64] In drawing this comparison, Azariah could hardly have failed to notice that the relevant passage in the Palestinian Talmud goes on to say that Ben Bebai, his function notwithstanding, was nevertheless counted among the most distinguished leaders of his time. Azariah's tone of humility, then, is rather disingenuous. He is clearly as convinced of the significance of his work as he is concerned with the perpetuation of his name.

Although one should not gainsay the element of religious conviction in Azariah's autobiographical sentiments, it seems clear that his wish to perpetuate his name (he even refers to the "everlasting title"[65] of his work *Me'or 'Einayim*) stems from a desire to find an enduring place in the annals of the Jewish people. This sentiment, not uncommon among Azariah's Jewish peers as well, reflects a general tendency of the Renaissance period. Immanuel of Rome, the contemporary Hebrew imitator of Dante, had in his rhymed prose already declared, "If I die, my works will yet live on." And in the generation after Azariah, Leone Modena says in his autobiography, "Here I will record several of the books that I have composed, especially those already published . . . and books in which my name occurs . . . since this will be a source of great comfort to me in that so long as the universe endures, my name will not be wiped away in Israel and the world, in spite of death and this evil time."[66] In his own way, Azariah expresses similar sentiments, and while he couches them in the idiom of classical Jewish piety, he chooses to realize eternality through an essentially nonclassical Jewish intellectual endeavor.

Notes

1. *M.E.* 1:1, 2:484f.; *Maṣref la-Kesef,* 122. See the 1575 Hebrew letter of Azariah to Isaac Finzi, now published by Abraham David, "Le-Toledot ha-Polmos saviv ha-Sefer *Me'or 'Einayim*," *Kiryat Sefer* 59 (1984): 641f. The response of Azariah's friend, Rabbi Judah Moscato of Mantua, to views expressed in *M.E.* is addressed "el he-ḥakham Min ha-Adumim be-Ferrara." See David Kaufmann, "Con-

tributions à l'histoire des luttes d'Azaria de Rossi," *Revue des études juives* 33 (1896): 81; and see below, pp. 73f. In addition to the works cited in the notes to this chapter, the specifically relevant biographical essays are those of Leopold Zunz, "Toledot Rabbi Azariah Min ha-Adumim," together with the annotations of S. J. L. Rapoport, reprinted and prefaced to de' Rossi's *Maṣref la-Kesef,* ed. I. Benjacob (Vilna: Finn and Rosenkranz, 1865), 1–30. This volume is part of Benjacob's 1863–1865 edition of *M.E.*; Cassel, *M.E.* 1:i–xii; Salo W. Baron, "Azariah de' Rossi: A Biographical Sketch," in *History and Jewish Historians* (Philadelphia: Jewish Publication Society, 1964), 167–173, 405.

2. The description of the poems and of Azariah is given in the Bodleian Library manuscript, cited by Joanne Weinberg, "Azariah dei Rossi: Towards a Reappraisal of the Last Years of His Life," *Annali della Scuola Normale Superiore di Pisa,* 3d ser., 8 (1978): 499. The manuscript is the same one from which Azariah's *Maṣref la-Kesef* was first published in 1854 (see chap. 1, n. 17 above; and see the description by Filipowski on his title page). See L. Modona, "Une Lettre d'Azaria de Rossi," *Revue des études juives* 30 (1895):316; and two other letters, published by Weinberg (p. 510). The Hebrew and Aramaic poems—not the Italian and Latin ones—occasioned by the duchess's death, are in Cassel, *M.E.* 3:149f. The Italian version of Azariah's name occurs too on the title page of the manuscript containing his exposition of passages from the Syriac text of the Gospels. See Weinberg, p. 495; and see below, p. 56.

3. *M.E.* 2:483.

4. Cecil Roth, *The History of the Jews of Italy* (Philadelphia: Jewish Publication Society, 1946), 13; Hermann Vogelstein, *Rome,* trans. Moses Hadas (Philadelphia: Jewish Publication Society, 1940), 156f.

5. Moses A. Shulvass, *Ḥayyei ha-Yehudim be Italyah bi-Tequfat ha-Renesans* (New York: Ogen, 1955), 37; Cecil Roth, *The Jews in the Renaissance* (Philadelphia: Jewish Publication Society, 1959), 32f.

6. *'Edut ha-Shem Ne'emanah,* ed. Judah Rosenthal, in *Meḥqarim u-Meqorot* (Jerusalem: Reuven Maas, 1967), 1:373–430; Vogelstein, *Rome,* 212f.; Roth, *Jews of Italy,* 149f. Concerning the de' Rossis, and especially Solomon, see too Hermann Vogelstein and Paul Rieger, *Geschichte der Juden in Rom* (Berlin: Mayer and Müller, 1896), 1:24f., 269f., 299, 395ff., and nn. 1–3. This volume contains the detailed notes and bibliographical references that Vogelstein omitted in his revised but shorter English work on the Jews of Rome.

7. Several manuscripts of *'Edut ha-Shem* read: "*ve-sheye'ayen ba-sefarim ha-ḥiṣonim*" (Rosenthal, p. 378 n. 7).

8. See below, pp. 54–58.

9. Shlomo Simonsohn, *History of the Jews in the Duchy of Mantua* (Jerusalem: Kiryat Sefer, 1977), viii, 2ff.

10. Salo W. Baron, *A Social and Religious History of the Jews,* 2d ed. (New York and Philadelphia: Columbia University Press and Jewish Publication Society, 1965), 10:294ff., 288ff.; Simonsohn, *Jews in the Duchy of Mantua,* 18, 190f., 322f. Roth surveys the gradual establishment and situation of Jews in central and northern Italian cities in *Jews in the Renaissance,* 3–20.

11. *M.E.* 2:480.

12. Simonsohn, *Jews in the Duchy of Mantua,* 518f.

13. Ibid. 217 n. 69, and 418–424, 719, regarding the communal activities of Bezalel Massarano and his son R. Samson Massarano; *M.E.* 1:212, n. 2, and the manuscript material published by J. Bergmann, "Gedichte Asarja de Rossi's," *Zeitschrift für hebräische Bibliographie* 3, (1898): 54, 56f.

14. *M.E.* 1:81.

15. The information on Azariah from Amatus's *Centuriae curationum* is given in Harry Friedenwald, *The Jews and Medicine: Essays* (Baltimore: Johns Hopkins Press, 1944), 2:391–403. Friedenwald's collected essays include two on Amatus himself (1:332–390).

16. Simonsohn, *Jews in the Duchy of Mantua,* 600f., 681f.

17. Ibid., 581–584.

18. *M.E.* 2:485.

19. Friedenwald, *Jews and Medicine* 2:393. Between 1547 and 1556 Amatus's home was in Ancona (Friedenwald 1:338ff.). From 1540 to 1547 he had lived in Ferrara, where he may have first made Azariah's acquaintance. Cf. Roth, *Jews in the Renaissance,* 318.

20. Friedenwald, *Jews and Medicine* 2:395; Roth, *Jews of Italy,* 201ff.

21. *M.E.* 2:475 and n. 5.

22. Ibid. 1:93, n. 1:93, n. 2. The Bodleian Library, Oxford, possesses a copy of the *Me'or 'Einayim* (Mantua, 1574) with numerous manuscript notes by Azariah. These include a manuscript interleaf, inserted between pp. 85b and 86a of this volume, in which Azariah refers to "the books from the estate of the late R. Jehiel Nissim da Pisa . . . *all of which* I purchased from his son R. Samuel here [in] Ferrara" (emphasis added).

23. See, p. 15, and n. 41.

24. Friedenwald, *Jews and Medicine* 2:393f., 400f., 403.

25. *M.E.* 2:484.

26. See, p. 14f.

27. *M.E.* 1, *Qol Elohim.* See discussion, pp. 15f.

28. Friedenwald, *Jews and Medicine* 2:398.

29. *M.E.* 1:21, and 2:475, for a separate reference to his presence in Bologna.

30. See Kenneth R. Stow, *Catholic Thought and Papal Jewry Policy, 1553–1593* (New York: Jewish Theological Seminary of America, 1977), 17f. Both Zunz ("Toledot Rabbi Azariah," 3) and Cassel (*M.E.* 1:ii) appear to take Azariah's statement to be a reference to a plague.

31. Stow, *Catholic Thought,* 38f.

32. Ibid. Stow cites pertinent sections from this document, the manuscript of which was published by Adolph Jellinek in *Ha-Shaḥar* 2 (1870). And see Kaufmann, "Contributions," 85, where, in the text of the 1574 ban against *Me'or 'Einayim,* "ha-qatan Yishma'el Ḥaninah . . . mi-Valmontono" appears among the signatories. Cf. *Ha-Shaḥar,* 17.

33. See Roth, *Jews of Italy,* 306.

34. Stow, *Catholic Thought,* 22, and, following a detailed analysis, the summary statement concerning the purpose to be served by expulsion (p. 58). Cf. Roth, *Jews of Italy,* 306f.

35. Sonne, *Paulo ha-Revi'i,* 222, 226, regarding the communal arrangement with the "Bolognese" for support of the refugee needy.

36. See Stow, *Catholic Thought,* 39f., 42f., 46–49, regarding the anxiety but also the ignorance of the actual specifics of papal Jewry policy, which conditioned the response of the other Jewish authors and spokesmen; and see pp. 190f., regarding the status of Jews in Ferrara.

37. Sonne, *Paulo ha-Revi'i,* 221, 223–227, 230.

38. See, e.g., *M.E.* 1:229. Azariah reports being in Mantua attempting to have his work printed but experiencing delays. His good friend in Mantua, the famous Jewish playwright Judah (Leone) de' Sommi, urged him to persist in his efforts and assured him success ("ki sifrekha zeh . . . yikra'u ki-feri 'eṣ hadar 'ad mel'ot sifqo shehu az matoq le-ḥiqenu").

39. See the manuscript material published by S. J. Halberstam "Sheloshah Ketavim 'al Devar Sefer Me'or 'Einayim," in *Festschrift zum achtzigsten Geburstage Moritz Steinschneider's* (Leipzig: Otto Harrassowitz, 1896), 7. Halberstam suggests (n. 1) that this letter may have been written by Rabbi Abraham Provençal of Mantua, mentioned several times in *M.E.*

40. Ibid., 8. This comment reporting contemporary sentiment occurs in a letter of another admirer of Azariah.

41. See Modona, "Une lettre," 314.

42. *Maṣref la-Kesef,* 121; and see Modona, *Une lettre,* 314ff. Regarding the year of Azariah's death, see Rapoport's notes to Zunz, "Toledot Rabbi Azariah," 23f. the Bodleian Library possesses, in addition to Azariah's manuscript of *Maṣref la-Kesef* that Filipowski published in 1854 (Ms. Mich. 308), a second manuscript of the same work acquired by the Bodleian in 1927 from the library of the scholar S. R. Driver (Ms. Heb. e. 153). I have come across some textual variations between the two manuscripts, for example: on the title page (cf. fol. 22v in the first manuscript with fol. 2v in the second one), and also in pt. 2, chap. 13 of *Maṣref la-Kesef* (cf. fol. 72v in the first manuscript with fol. 73r in the second; lines 1–2). The polemical reference to the Karaites on the title page is far more restrained in the Driver manuscript. In the other illustration I cite here, the order of the words differs in lines 1–2. Moreover, where Azariah notes his concern in these lines about the possible adverse reaction to his views from some Torah scholars ("qeṣat tofsei ha-Torah") the Driver manuscript refers more generally to "tofsei ha-Torah." Cassel, in his edition of *Maṣref la-Kesef,* apparently utilized a text similar to the Driver manuscript. He refers in fact to Filipowski's already printed version, but also to a transcription of *Maṣref la-Kesef* in his possession, which had been copied from a manuscript of that work by the contemporary Jewish scholar Z. H. Edelmann (*M.E.* i:xii).

43. *M.E.* 1, *Qol Elohim,* 5–23, esp. 20, 21; and see, p. 19., for the discussion of his wife's affliction.

44. *M.E.* 1:6–8, 17, 18–23. See the references to Buoni (*M.E.* 1:10, 16; Azariah renders his name in Hebrew "rofe' . . . mekhuneh ha-ṭov . . . ha-rofe' ha-ṭov); and see Cassel's discussion of Buoni's work in his note to this section of *M.E.* (pp. 24f.).

45. Ibid., 8, 20f.

46. Ibid., 22f., and 4, where he alludes to these circumstances. The text of *Hadrat Zeqenim* is on pp. 27–69, followed by Cassel's long note on the subject of Aristeas (pp. 69–76).

47. Ibid., 22.

48. Ibid., 23.

49. Ibid., 5, 6.

50. Ibid., 5. He quotes Exod. 10:2, Joel 1:3 (not 1:6, as the text of *M.E.* has it), Ps. 78:4.

51. *M.E.* 1:6.

52. Exod. 10:6, Joel 1:2, and even Ps. 78, to which he refers, recount the unique "marvels in the sight of their fathers in the land of Egypt" (78:12) and in the post-Exodus period. Biblical citations follow the new Jewish Publication Society translation.

53. *M.E.* 1:13 n., 16f.

54. Ibid., 16.

55. Ibid., 7, 9, 12f.

56. See, for example, the discussion in Lucien Febvre, *Life in Renaissance France,* ed. and trans. Marian Rothstein (Cambridge: Harvard University Press, 1977), 40.

57. *M.E.* 1:10f., 16.

58. Ibid., 13f. Azariah is certainly not prepared to abandon outright the traditional theological approach toward such events. Personal experience with the Ferrara earthquake may have made him even more sensitive to certain biblical descriptions; thus he attempts to explain some verses in Amos as an extension of the earthquake referred to in the opening verses of that prophetic book (see *M.E.* 1:8f.). Azariah's biblical exegesis here is problematic, but from his perspective one is still dealing in Amos with sacred prophecy not profane history. Whatever his perception of nature and natural causation may be, his understanding of the system of moral accountability still presupposes theological foundations. And since this understanding, to the extent that it applies to contemporary as well as biblical experience, is rooted in prophetic teaching, in dealing with Amos, Azariah has in effect made the biblical past illuminate the present rather than the reverse.

59. *M.E.* 1:5f.

60. Ibid., 20.

61. Ibid., 20, and 20 n.

62. Ibid., 20 n.

63. *Maṣref la-Kesef,* 11; *M.E.* 1:202; and see also *M.E.* 1:98, 114ff.

64. *M.E.* 1:81; and see J. Sheqalim 4:1, J. Pe'ah 8:6.

65. *M.E.* 1:4.

66. Cited in Shulvass, *Ha-Yehudim be-Iṭalyah,* 327f., and for the somewhat fuller quotation from Modena's autobiography as I cite it, see *Sefer Hayyei Yehudah,* ed. A. Kahana (Kiev, 1911), 42.

CHAPTER 3

Azariah's View of Historical Inquiry

Long before Azariah's time, the early Italian Renaissance humanists formulated an educational and cultural program based on the study of the classics. They looked to history and the Roman historians, Livy in particular,[1] for moral and political edification. A knowledge of the past, as Livy himself had declared, provided instruction applicable to the present. Since Roman history was especially valued as a source of moral philosophy, humanist educators such as the influential fifteenth-century Mantuan Vittorino da Feltre gave special attention to the study of Livy.[2] Inspired by such didactic as well as political considerations, a good many humanists themselves wrote historical works on postclassical times and places. In the process they contributed to the gradual growth of a more sophisticated sense of historical perspective, becoming more conscious of change and developing critical scholarly techniques for the handling of evidence. In the fifteenth century, scholars and antiquarians were also developing the auxiliary sciences of epigraphy, archaeology, and numismatics, as well as the art of printing which (especially by the sixteenth century) facilitated knowledge of these as well as of literary sources.[3]

The humanist preoccupation with drawing instructive examples from history hindered a fully realistic assessment of the course of human events. Nonetheless, the study of the past took on the characteristics of a genuine, almost self-assured branch of knowledge,[4] exemplified in the fifteenth century by Leonardo Bruni, one of a sequence of humanists who served as chancellors of Florence. As a statesman and scholar, Bruni sought lessons on civic liberty from Roman history and wrote his own work on the Florentine people in a consciously didactic manner.[5] Among the ancients who served as models for Bruni in matters of language, style, and form, Livy was especially important, although the thrust of Bruni's work on Florence is much more explicitly political than that of Livy on Rome. Especially important for Bruni was the utility of history. It taught prudence and political wisdom, and it revealed truth. Bruni helped to shape the criteria for attaining truth from history and like other humanists was disposed to accept the ancient historians at face value. But even he realized that someone like Livy was only as reliable as his sources.[6] By the time of the late Italian Renaissance, Gianmichele Bruto, a Venetian humanist and historian, had reached far more extreme conclusions about Livy. In his Florentine history published in 1562, he was very critical of the ancients and their emphasis on rhetoric and polished literary narrative, viewing Livy in particular as one who had falsified history. Still, Bruto looked upon contemporary historical works as worse yet because of their failure to ascertain the truth, and he subscribed, at least in principle, to the view of history as a source of lessons and a goad to virtue, using classical illustrations in abundance to demonstrate the point.[7]

Not surprisingly, Azariah also invoked Livy. For him, Livy was unmatched "to this day" among gentile authors in his masterful history of Rome from its origins to his own age.[8] If Azariah had any reservations regarding Livy he gave no evidence thereof. It would appear that he, like the early Renaissance humanists of the fifteenth century and much of the traditional opinion of the later sixteenth and early seventeenth centuries, viewed Livy's work as a kind of "canonical" history of Rome.[9] One can only speculate as to the conclusions Azariah might have reached had he addressed his own impressive critical talents to Livy's work rather than to areas of Jewish historical interest. The point, however, is that history in the Livian sense and in the humanist tradition—patriotically arousing, morally edifying, and politically instructive—is irrelevant for Azariah. Having briefly confirmed the widely accepted praise of Livy, Azariah then quotes the cultured Roman Stoic's affirmation of history's great didactic function, only to demonstrate that it is inapplicable to Jewry.[10]

Azariah would have us believe that Jews can dispense with history and the lessons it has to proffer, Livy's affirmations notwithstanding, because they find all the guidance they require in the divine commandments and in the narratives of scripture. The latter provide direction for all possible temporal eventualities that may be encountered in life. Yet Azariah's assertion—even as an ostensible defense of the self-sufficiency of scriptural teaching—that there is no need for profane history (this "excessive study that wearies the flesh") or for writers who in their plethora of words never cease to nullify one another[11] taxes the imagination if one considers his own intellectual endeavor. What is believable is that Azariah had substantially familiarized himself with many of the classical and Renaissance historiographical works that had become available in many editions since the fifteenth century.[12]

Even the Renaissance humanists and historians who looked to or wrote history to inculcate moral philosophy and wisdom were not all invariably enthusiastic about what history had to offer. Thus Poggio Bracciolini, Bruni's successor as Florentine chancellor and historian, acknowledged that history supplied moral lessons but saw in it primarily the negative and transitory side of the human condition. His interest in the subject was therefore essentially intended to substantiate that assessment. Nevertheless, despite such pessimism or resignation and the presumed inability to ascertain the meaning of the course of events, for Poggio, the utility of history lay in its edifying role. One hundred or so years later, in the 1530's, this pessimistic tone is equally obvious in the work of his fellow Florentine Francesco Guicciardini, generally viewed as the leading historian of the Italian Renaissance. At the very outset of his "masterpiece of national historiography" on Italy, written in the last years of his life in an age of a dismal Italian political situation, the shrewd statesman and realistic historian declares, "From the innumerable examples [of the last thirty years] it will be fully evident that human affairs are subject to the same instability as is the sea when stirred up by winds."[13] For Guicciardini, who found too little uniformity in human experience to provide useful examples, the purpose of history was to explain how the present calamitous political situation had come about and to instruct man regarding the strengths and limitations of the human condition.[14]

Azariah's stated critique of historians and their craft gives no evidence of that pessimistic strain so conditioned by the vagaries of Italian politics. (Politics, even the Jewish political situation, were hardly an area of historical inquiry for Azariah.) Nor are there any obvious grounds for linking his critique to the element of skepticism found in the later Renaissance writers, such as Guicciardini.[15] His own concern with the pursuit of truth is perhaps an issue that enters into his critique of historians.[16] But what he does criticize about historical works, namely, their presumably wearisome, overly wordy, and conflicting nature, rings somewhat hollow, since it is inconsistent with his own extensive efforts to reconstruct and clarify numerous aspects of the Jewish historical record. And in the course of these efforts, Azariah himself amply contributes to the plethora of words and more than once flaws his own line of inquiry by utilizing unreliable sources then current and accepted by some other historians and antiquarians.[17] The speciousness of his argument becomes obvious when one considers that it is enunciated far along in Azariah's assorted studies—despite the ostensible irrelevance of history, he nonetheless presses on with the investigation of historically problematic issues, even those as highly sensitive as the chronology of the creation era. If the study of history is so utterly dispensable and scriptural law and narrative so absolutely self-sufficient, then Azariah's own deep interest in the subject becomes absurd. Neither his dismissal of history nor his deprecation of secular knowledge can be taken seriously. For it is in the very "obscurity of human studies,"[18] as he describes it, that he again and again seeks information to illuminate the Jewish past, even if this sometimes means challenging the traditional record of that past. By the sixteenth century, one's—Azariah's—ability to delve into the past is greatly enhanced precisely by the extensive dissemination and proliferation of those "human" studies, both classical and more recent, to which he refers and by his receptivity to them.[19]

One may, in fact, assume that in disavowing Livy's didactic emphasis, Azariah's ultimate scholarly objective is not the seemingly Judeocentric one of proclaiming the superiority of the sacred sources and experiences as a guide to life. Rather, he seeks to advance the legitimacy of objective historical inquiry into the Jewish past by establishing the total adequacy of Jewish religious tradition for purposes of moral edification, independent of any outside sources. If, as he argues, he does not in the process of such historical inquiry intrude on the self-sufficiency and integrity of Jewish religious tradition, then he may hope to make his inquiry palatable to the learned among his coreligionists. As it turned out, he was not to be spared by the fact that his historical investigations were directed to intellectual enlightenment rather than to eloquent inspiration of right conduct.

In fact, Azariah's historical bent suggests a religious dilemma: immersion in the ostensibly useless study of history must inevitably lead to neglect of the study of the Law and thus flies in the face of the time-honored Jewish religious ideal of preoccupation with *talmud torah* (Torah study)—an ideal he enthusiastically endorses. But having pronounced that "indeed, the Torah, being our life and the length of our days, there is nothing that stands before it,"[20] Azariah does not allow this order of intellectual priorities to determine his own. It does not deter *him* from an avowedly detached investigation of Jewish annals and literature, one that is quite unconventional in both form and content. Intended more for intellectual enlightenment than conventional religious edification, it is hardly capable of being subsumed under the talmudic category of Torah study still so central in the Jewish society of his own day.[21]

For example, Azariah introduces his justification for a very controversial investigation of the traditional Jewish chronology by emphasizing its value as a pursuit of truth per se—a learned debate, not a practical religious application. If, in addition, it is even "more important that in the course of this investigation [of the chronology] you will see that we shall happen to understand the sense of some scriptural matters,"[22] this is a somewhat circuitous route to the Jewish classics and by no means certain to inspire positive religious sentiment. Here Azariah obviously does not propose to deal with biblical exegesis as such but rather wishes to enlist certain problematic aspects of biblical chronology—such as the uncertain duration of the First Temple period—in dealing with the larger issue of an erroneous chronology of the creation era. He follows with an analogy wherein even talmudic discussion of theoretical issues that have relevance only in messianic times is presently useful, according to the sages, either to explain aspects of scripture or to merit the reward of study for its own sake,[23] an argument that reinforces his original emphasis on the value of theoretical investigation. At the same time it significantly reduces the independent value that may derive from the understanding of "some scriptural matters." Indeed for Azariah this scriptural material is far less of an independent concern than it is a function of the pursuit of truth. This pursuit, moreover, is closely linked to another pressing concern: Azariah undertakes the study of the Jewish chronological system in response to the "not trifling" consideration that the "stumbling block" of messianic speculation was rife among his Jewish contemporaries. Azariah wishes to "remove the stumbling block from the path of our people" and thus help prevent widespread disillusionment by demonstrating that the widely assumed imminent coming of the Messiah—"according to the opinion of many, respected individuals"—rests on faulty chronological assumptions. This objective could hardly have seemed spiritually worthy in so highly charged a Jewish messianic climate as existed in his day.[24]

With Jewish society so conditioned to expect intellectual endeavors to serve the ends of religious practice and sentiment, Azariah feels compelled to account for the purely academic element of historical inquiry in his *Me'or 'Einayim.* Thus he interrupts himself and in an appropriately apologetic tone invokes the talmudic view that "what has been, has been," suggesting that the preoccupation with the past is pointless and that the very issues he addresses are, in fact, inconsequential from the point of view of what really counts, that is, Jewish law and religious practice.[25] But this rabbinic dictum by no means reflects his involvement with the past on its own terms. About to launch his critique of the chronology at the beginning of chapter 29 of the *Me'or 'Einayim,* Azariah anticipates that *the reader* may consider the undertaking irrelevant, for "what has been, has been." Here, Azariah *responds* to this negation of history and argues that thousands of scholars have engaged in far more theoretical studies because the pursuit of "truth itself" is so compelling an objective.

In other words, he justifies the study of history as an end in itself precisely *because* it exemplifies for him the search for truth as an intellectual ideal, one to which he attributes great spiritual worth, for truth is "the seal of the truthful God, the quality of the beautiful soul, and it is well that all pursue it."[26] Azariah makes a point of emphasizing that the understanding of aspects of scripture may be enhanced by certain of his historical investigations. Perhaps calculated to accommodate contemporary Jewish religious sensitivities, this move nevertheless hardly interferes with his own perception of the pursuit and exposition of truth as an inherently worthwhile objective,[27] a significant corollary of which is his firm rejection, even in "secular affairs," of consciously fabricated data.[28]

Azariah's emphasis on truth may also help explain his criticism of contemporary historical works, his own brief conventional praise of Livy notwithstanding. That praise of Livy is followed by such criticism may suggest that he sees the continuing contemporary perception of history as essentially a branch of rhetoric and pedagogy and as a detriment to the ascertainment of historical truth. Such a suggestion appears to be substantially strengthened when one considers that in his discussions of the pursuit of truth as a goal of historical studies, Azariah invokes no purely rhetorical claims like those of Cicero on history as "light" and "teacher" of truth or those of Quintilian on history as a form of poetry. Both of these ancients continued to be cited as standard authorities in sixteenth-century historical discourse, and Azariah himself refers to them, albeit for other purposes. Additionally, Azariah neglects to mention the work of influential humanists on the theory of writing history, such as that of the fifteenth-century Giovanni Pontano, who shared Quintilian's view of history as related to poetry. Ciceronian precepts or those from Lucian's "How to Write History," an equally popular ancient authority in the sixteenth century,[29] are irrelevant for Azariah. First, they address the art of narrative history, which is not his area of endeavor; second, they do not offer any critical methodological guidance.

Those who actually wrote history in the sixteenth century generally continued, unlike Guicciardini for example, to uphold its exemplar function even though they may have ignored it in practice.[30] Yet regarding the theory of history, there was no dearth of treatises that continued to emphasize its oratorical and edificatory purpose, especially in the second half of the century—the age of the Counter-Reformation's preoccupation with authoritative precepts, even in history. The notable exception to this trend was the work of the philosopher Francesco Patrizi *Della historia diece dialoghi* (*Ten Dialogues on History*), the import of which has been described as revolutionary in light of the then dominant current of historiographical thought. Patrizi's book, published in Venice in 1560, a little over a dozen years before the *Me'or 'Einayim,* rejects authorities like Cicero, Lucian, or Ponatano and challenges the idea that history is stylistic eloquence and a guide to life. And despite what the ancients like Cicero had written regarding "laws" pertaining to the truthfulness of history, Patrizi (essentially a philosopher) doubts that it is possible to achieve absolute historical truth. His position, however, is far less an argument for skepticism per se or for the worthlessness of history than for the need to ascertain how truth could best be apprehended.[31] In other words, Patrizi's doubts did not constitute historical Pyrrhonism, and even though he failed to formulate an applicable critical historical method,[32] for him "the apprehension of truth" was a principal goal of history.[33] Given his extensive reading, it is conceivable that Azariah was familiar with Patrizi's *Della historia* and that it helped shape his own reflections on the subject of historical truth.

Azariah's conviction regarding the theoretical value of historical investigation, the purpose of which is truth,[34] is especially evident from the more antiquarian topics encountered in the *Me'or 'Einayim*. He explicitly acknowledges, for example, the practical irrelevance of ascertaining the precise details of the Jewish priestly vestments of antiquity, yet in an inquiry that ranges over no fewer than five chapters, he goes so far as to provide the reader with illustrations. Although in this enterprise "we derive nothing concerning either the permitted or the forbidden," Azariah feels intellectually compelled, indeed delighted, to marshal every available source of evidence, Jewish and non-Jewish, that may shed light on doubtful or problematic aspects of the topic. For all the irrelevance of this inquiry he sees it as his function to benefit "that reader whose wisdom is enhanced by virtue of truth," and he therefore deems it "obligatory to inquire and probe and to make sense of the [relevant] scriptural texts to the utmost extent that our intellect permits."[35]

Azariah carefully notes that the rabbinic sages of antiquity paid little attention to history and were often imprecise in historical detail. Being primarily engaged in the exposition of the Torah, they were "frugal with their time that they not waste it acquiring knowledge of history which *for them* was useless"[36] (emphasis added). Azariah, by contrast, delves with obvious enthusiasm into various aspects of the Jewish past for its own sake. His historiographical perspective, therefore, is novel. It is not ancillary to the study of the Law in that it is no longer determined by halakhic considerations or by the desire to clarify the chain of rabbinic tradition and its expositors or even by the need to chronicle the main course of Jewish events and personalities.

In contrast to Azariah's historical concerns, unique even by the criterion of contemporary Jewish historiographical achievement, the sixteenth century begins on a conventional note with *Sefer Yuḥasin* (completed by 1509),[37] the work of the Spanish Portuguese expatriate Abraham Zacuto, and even ends rather conventionally with the *Ṣemaḥ David* (1592) of the German Jewish author David Gans. Despite new features, both chronicles continue to serve purposes or to reflect attitudes and methods that are far more traditional than those of Azariah. Zacuto's important work, intended for the scholarly talmudist, traces the genealogies of the talmudic and post-talmudic authorities. Although he apologizes for his efforts, which he describes as not very profound wisdom,[38] *Sefer Yuḥasin* is on the whole more comprehensive and better arranged than its predecessors. While Zacuto utilizes earlier methodological, literary, and polemical treatises on the history of Jewish tradition—especially Abraham ibn Daud's twelfth-century *Sefer ha-Qabbalah,* which he follows almost verbatim and to which he acknowledges his debt[39]—he has also carefully sifted through the vast corpus of talmudic literature in order to provide a detailed and precise account of the bearers of that tradition. Nevertheless, despite the careful scholarship, Zacuto's outlook and objectives are not significantly different from those evinced in the earlier works of this genre. He too emphasizes the importance of precise knowledge of the rabbinic sages in their proper chronological sequence in order to sustain the authority of the tradition and to render correct decisions in matters of Jewish law.[40] Zacuto's sense of historical reality often fails him when he is confronted with talmudic tradition, for in his opinion the latter can never give way to contrary views, well-founded though they may be;[41] he utilizes numerous sources, but none, least of all non-Jewish materials, can take precedence over rabbinic ones. In dealing with the history of issues of Jewish religious law and ideology in the manner of a critical talmudic dialectician, he nonetheless assumes the literal truth of all narrative accounts in rabbinic literature, including the most imaginary aggadic materials[42]—a point of view Azariah de' Rossi will vigorously dispute later in the century.

In the concluding section of *Sefer Yuḥasin,* Zacuto displays a wide knowledge of universal history but organizes the subject matter according to a catalog format. Despite a systematic chronological division—predictably beginning with Adam—Jewish and general events, including information on scientific research and a good deal of fantastic folklore, are unsystematically entwined.[43] Zacuto introduces this material with emphasis on the knowledge of all history to serve the greater end of religious utility, not because he views history as all of one piece and all events as being of equal weight. Rather, history should strengthen faith in God's power and providence and in other fundamental principles of the Torah, all of which are presumably subsumed in the scriptural mandate "to remember the days of old." With regard to non-Jewish historical works (which Azariah frequently consults and cites respectfully as a corrective to erroneous rabbinic accounts), Zacuto views them at best as a necessary evil to provide a fuller picture concerning events mentioned in the rabbinic literature. But his argument to justify even this narrowly circumscribed concession is itself rather circular, for he believes that those non-Jewish authors themselves relied on the *Jewish* one, "Joseph ben Gorion" (i.e., *Josippon*). Yet even though he unhesitatingly subscribes to the then standard view that the ancient historian Josephus had himself written the Hebrew book of *Josippon*—ostensibly a version of his Greek work—Zacuto does not necessarily accept its authority. He claims that the author resorts to exaggerations and arrogant language and "makes calculations which are other than the plain meaning of the Torah." This assessment becomes superfluous, however, since Zacuto has in advance enunciated that the non-Jewish sources "speak lies and attest to falsehood."[44] The anti-Christian sentiments expressed in the concluding section (which is in any event not an integral part of the *Sefer Yuḥasin*) make it apparent that he was primarily pursuing a polemical objective.[45]

Almost ninety years later the author of *Ṣemaḥ David* describes his "chronicle" (*sefer zikhronot*) as intended neither for the great scholars nor as a guide in matters of Jewish law, but rather for ordinary Jews. In his view, the latter require a brief, straightforward account of Jewish history and also long for an account of general history. The chronicle of general events is to serve Gans's coreligionists as a source of enjoyment, relaxation, and inspiration in the midst of the travail of exile. It is to enhance the Jews' awareness of the larger society in which they live and thus their relationship with the Christians with whom they come into contact.[46]

Jewish and general history are generally (but not always) treated separately in the *Ṣemaḥ David* in order to "distinguish the sacred from the profane . . . so that the words of the living God not be confused with those of men."[47] This suggests Gans's conviction that the history of other peoples must be dealt with separately from that of the Jews, for the Jewish sources—certainly the biblical and talmudic ones—are inherently superior and implicitly reliable because of their sacred status. Where there are discrepancies between the classical Jewish literature and non-Jewish sources, the former takes precedence.[48] And in cases of discrepancies between post-talmudic Jewish authorities themselves, Gans, no doubt in the interest of truth and enlightenment, sometimes leaves it to the reader to decide; that option then becomes "the sacred one."[49]

In his introduction to the section on general history, Gans stresses that any account of the distant past that is not divinely inspired cannot claim absolute certainty for what it reports, since even regarding contemporary events eyewitnesses differ in their accounts. While the latter half of this statement indicates Gans's awareness of the serious pitfalls in certain types of historical evidence, the first half suggests one of the inherent limitations of his approach to evidence. He affirms the principle, followed earlier by Zacuto, that should the information he cites from general sources conflict with talmudic aggadah in even the smallest detail, such information is to be rejected.[50] Azariah, who had challenged precisely this view some two decades earlier, had demonstrated it to be fallacious and unworkable. But his position was not congenial to pious Jewish sentiment of the later sixteenth century, and he was opposed on this very issue by one of the leading religious spokesmen of the age, Rabbi Judah Loew (Maharal) of Prague, the revered teacher of Gans. Gans, who otherwise frequently cites the *Me'or 'Einayim* (though he never mentions Azariah by name) seems to defer here as in some other religiously sensitive issues to the spirit of the Maharal.

There are strikingly new elements in Gans's careful and comprehensive chronicle. Notable are the author's keen awareness of the contemporary age with its novelty and ongoing change; his frequent willingness to spell out the details of certain controversial issues of the kind dealt with in *Me'or 'Einayim*, even where he challenges the conclusions implicit in them; and a trace of the secular, which runs through the section on general history. Also significant, given the intellectually insulated character of Ashkenazic Jewry and its continuing emphasis on the primacy of talmudic studies, is his utilization of secular erudition.[51] Yet Gans, almost a quarter of a century after Azariah's scholarly precedent, still finds it necessary to defend the use of non-Jewish authors. This is especially striking in light of his biography. He is after all not merely the first Ashkenazic Jew to produce a historiographical work but also a scientific author of note, an acquaintance of Kepler and Brahe, and a major figure in the enlightened Jewish circle of Prague that upheld the pursuit of secular intellectual interests. He nevertheless must defend his position and does so by citing the example of medieval Jewish philosophers and "recent" historical writers like Zacuto and Joseph ha-Kohen; but he omits reference to Azariah. Moreover, his arguments for the study of general history are couched almost exclusively in terms of its particularistic moral advantages and the religious lessons that Jews may derive from it.[52] In the face of "novel opinions" like Azariah's in matters of chronology Gans (while by no means unimpressed by Azariah's line of argument) chooses to uphold tradition, asserting that his predecessor's views are unsustained, "for we have only what our ancestors bequeathed to us, and the tradition and custom of our forefathers shall remain Torah for us . . . to all eternity."[53] Azariah holds to the general, virtually diametrically opposed principle that "it is not good to be partial to the ancients in speculative matters";[54] for him the facts warrant no other conclusion than that the creation era chronology is a relatively late innovation with no biblical or halakhic foundations.

By using the genre of the chronicle and avoiding causal analysis and historical interpretation, Gans further displays his traditionalist disposition. The chronicle is apparently also intended as a response to Azariah's reservations regarding the accuracy of the accepted chronology. Azariah's views, it seems, had unsettled the Jewish intelligentsia of Prague and had become a widely discussed issue in the community. Gans seeks to defend the established tradition. Having demonstrated, at least to his own satisfaction, that "his [Azariah's] words have been absolutely nullified and that they have neither basis nor essence," he adds that his only purpose in introducing them is "to dispel any doubts in the mind of the multitude about the years of creation."[55] It seems likely that Gans also defends the accepted chronology as an expression of a deeply felt imminence of messianic redemption,[56] whereas the thrust of Azariah's chronological studies is to deny the validity of all contemporary Jewish speculation and prediction regarding the year in which the Messiah might come.[57]

Notes

1. See Myron P. Gilmore, "The Renaissance Conception of the Lessons of History," in *Humanists and Jurists* (Cambridge: Harvard University Press, 1963), esp. the discussion of Petrarch's role in the development of a new historical consciousness that departed from the medieval view of the past (pp. 9f.), his appeal to Roman history and notably to Livy, and his simultaneous emphasis on the need to ascertain what the ancients had actually said by careful study of the classical sources (pp. 14, 16–19).

2. Ibid., 21ff.

3. The role of the auxiliary sciences and of printing in this period is noted, for example, by Bernard Guenée, *Histoire et culture historique dans l'occident médiéval* (Paris: Aubier Montaigne, 1980), 90f., 365.

4. See, for example, the discussion of Renaissance historical interest by William J. Bouwsma, *Venice and the Defense of Republican Liberty* (Berkeley and Los Angeles: University of California Press, 1968), 20f. The steady advance in Italian Renaissance historical method is discussed by Werner Goez, "Die Anfänge der historischen Methoden-Reflexion in der italienischen Renaissance und ihre Aufnahme in der Geschichtsschreibung des deutschen Humanismus," *Archiv für Kulturgeschichte* 56 (1974): 27.

5. Gilmore, "The Lessons of History," 20f.; Eric Cochrane, *Historians and Historiography in the Italian Renaissance* (Chicago: University of Chicago Press, 1981), 3–6. Guenée (*Histoire et culture historique,* 69), notes that from 1424 to 1494, five humanists served in succession as chancellors of Florence; four of them composed historical works. "Chancelleries," he observes, "were the crucible of national history."

6. Cochrane, *Historians,* 3–5; Arnaldo Momigliano, *Essays in Ancient and Modern Historiography* (Middletown: Wesleyan University Press, 1977), 85: "This mixture of uncritical repetition of ancient sources and of very critical awareness that the ancient authorities themselves were conditioned by their own sources is the real beginning of historical criticism." The distinctly political character of Bruni's history is noted by Donald J. Wilcox, *The Development of Florentine Humanist Historiography in the Fifteenth Century* (Cambridge: Harvard University Press, 1969), 34f., and 102ff., regarding aspects of Bruni's "advance in critical method over the previous [Italian] chroniclers."

7. Bouwsma, *Venice,* 173; Giorgio Spini, "Historiography: The Art of History in the Italian Counter Reformation," in *The Late Italian Renaissance, 1525–1630,* ed. Eric Cochrane (London: MacMillan, 1970), 117f. The defects in Livy's work have been discussed by P. G. Walsh, *Livy: His Historical Aims and Methods* (Cambridge: Cambridge University Press, 1961), e.g., 109.

8. *M.E.* 2:264.

9. The characterization is that of Arnaldo Momigliano, *Studies in Historiography* (New York: Harper and Row, 1966), 6f.; Spini ("Historiography," 123ff., 126) deals with the place of Livy in discussing "the return to . . . Counter-Reformation orthodoxy."

10. *M.E.* 2:264.

11. Ibid, 264: "u-vilti she-nistarekh 'od bekhmo eleh le-lahag harbeh shel yegi 'at basar uli-leshon 'et soferim asher be-rov divreihem lo yeḥdal zeh me'abbed et zeh." Cf. Salo W. Baron, "Azariah de' Rossi's Historical Method," in *History and Jewish Historians* (Philadelphia: Jewish Publication Society, 1964), 423 n. 4.

12. Cochrane, *Historians,* 256ff.

13. Felix Gilbert, "The Renaissance Interest in History," in *Art, Science, and History in the Renaissance,* ed. Charles Singleton (Baltimore: Johns Hopkins Press, 1967), 375; Cochrane, *Historians,* 28f., 305; idem, *Late Italian Renaissance,* 9.

14. Gilbert, "Renaissance Interest in History," 375f., 381; Gilmore, "The Lessons of History," 50f.; Cochrane, *Historians,* 298; Bouwsma, *Venice,* 22.

15. Bouwsma, *Venice,* 166.

16. See, p. 32f.

17. Azariah relied, for example, on the famous late-fifteenth-century forgeries of the Dominican friar Annio da Viterbo, even though by the mid-sixteenth century these invented "ancient" texts had already been exposed by some (see Cochrane, *Historians,* 432ff.; for Azariah's use of these materials, see *M.E.* 1:187, 242, 2:280, 455, 466; and see the remarks of Cassel, 3:162f.).

18. *M.E.* 2:264: "uve-ḥeshkat ha-limudim ha-enoshiyim yithalekhu."

19. Guenée, *Histoire et culture historique*, 109, 365.

20. *M.E.* 2:265ff.

21. Not even twenty years earlier Immanuel Benevento, a leading Italian Jewish qabbalist, had already complained of the preoccupation among his coreligionists with secular literature, including history, and the consequent neglect of Torah. The penalty for this, he believed, was the infamous 1553 burning of the Talmud in Rome and other Italian cities. See Moses A. Shulvass, *Ḥayyei ha-Yehudim be-Iṭalyah bi-Tequfat ha-Renesans* (New York: Ogen, 1955), 216; and see the long citation from Benevento's introduction to the medieval qabbalistic treatise *Ma'arekhet ha-Elohut* (Mantua, 1558) annotated by Isaiah Sonne, *Mi-Paulo ha-Revi'i 'ad Pius ha-Ḥamishi* (Jerusalem: Mosad Bialik, 1954), 127ff. Characteristically, one of Benevento's guiding considerations is total avoidance of the "opinions of Aristotle and his disciples and anything derived from the *brood of aliens*" (*yaldei nokhrim,* i.e., non-Jewish sources and the views derived from them. See Isa. 2:6; and see Sonne, 127, emphasis added). Sonne (p. 128 n. 6) considers it almost certain that Benevento's sardonic dismissal of the "chronicles of kings" as a substitute source of religious inspiration—in the absence of the Talmud—refers to Joseph ha-Kohen's *Divrei ha-Yamim le-Malkhei Ṣarfat u-Malkhei Beit Ottoman,* published several years earlier in 1554. Azariah formally upholds the traditional ideal of *talmud torah* and in appropriately stylized form also refers to the "brood of aliens" as useless for purposes of moral instruction for Jewry (*M.E.* 2:264). Yet he constantly invokes them in the *Me'or 'Einayim* and develops a line of historical

investigation that Benevento would have found infinitely more reprehensible than Joseph ha-Kohen's chronicle and as deserving of extirpation as other books, the publication of which he decried. See Sonne, pp. 127f. and n. 11. Sonne (p. 125) views Benevento as a primary example of that class of Italian Jewish spokesmen who had internalized the spirit of the Catholic reaction and sought to implement it in the Jewish community.

22. *M.E.* 2:275f.

23. Ibid., 276f. The religious respectability that Azariah no doubt also seeks through this analogy is less easy to achieve, for even though he eschews any practical implications that may flow from his analysis of the creation era, some contemporary Jewish religious spokesmen roundly condemned him for departing from long-established talmudic tradition. See ibid., 270f: "va-yalinu ʿalai lemor ki kol giluy maḥloq ve-sikhsukh ʿal shum davar mequbal me-rabboteinu . . . harei zu harisah ve-qiṣuṣ neṭiʿot ḥalilah."

24. Ibid., 276. Among the "respected individuals" was one of the leading contemporary qabbalists, Mordecai Dato, to whose work, *Migdal David,* on the imminent beginning of redemption in the year 5335 (1575), Azariah refers. David Tamar—dealing at length with the immense messianic ferment among sixteenth-century Italian Jews and notably with the anticipation of its fulfillment in 5335—has already noted the irony in Azariah's comment: "Amen ken yaʿas ha-Shem ʿimanu ke-divreihem ḥesed vi-yehi Migdal David ha-nizkar migdal ʿoz ve-taʿaṣumot lo migdal poreaḥ." See *M.E.* 2:369; and Tamar, *Meḥqarim be-Toledot ha-Yehudim be-Ereṣ Yisra'el uve-Iṭalyah* (Jerusalem: Reuven Maas, 1970), 17 n. 36. When Azariah indicates the contemporary conviction regarding the imminent coming of the Messiah, his phrase, "le-harim mikhshol mi-derekh ʿamenu," refers to himself, considering it "good and advantageous" to investigate the chronology "in order to remove the stumbling block," to disabuse his coreligionists of their error (*M.E.* 2:276) and thus to forestall delusion and disappointment (see *M.E.* 2:352). The living issue of Jewish messianic ferment—misguided in his view—perhaps initially aroused Azariah's interest in the question of chronology, but this was clearly accompanied by or at the very least furthered that profound interest in understanding the past for its own sake, which he displays throughout. In addressing even a far less pragmatic issue, like the many uncertainties regarding the ancient Jewish priestly vestments, Azariah's pursuit of truth per se is even more obvious. His reference to the pursuit of truth for its own sake, hardly limited to the context of chronological issues, is too emphatic, and in one form or another too periodic to be devoid of independent value for him (see, pp. 33f.). In chap. 29 of *M.E.* he *begins* his response to an anticipated challenge that the chronological investigation he plans to undertake is irrelevant ("mai de-hava' hava'") with emphasis on "truth itself," then follows his threefold justification by reiterating that for these *three* reasons especially ("asher taḥat shalosh eleh bi-ferat," p. 276) this study ought to be pursued. Cf. Robert Bonfil, "Some Reflections on the Place of Azariah de Rossi's *Meor Enayim* in the Cultural Milieu of Italian Renaissance Jewry," in *Jewish Thought in the Sixteenth Century,* ed. B. D. Cooperman (Cambridge:

Harvard University Press, 1983), 38f. Bonfil emphasizes "the defense of Judaism" as the main issue in Azariah's chronological investigations rather than the pursuit of "truth itself"; "apologetic tendency" and the honor of Judaism are seen as the main thrust of Azariah's studies. See below, chap. 5, n. 28.

25. E.g., *M.E.* 1:182, 189, 2:266.

26. Ibid. 2:275f. See below, pp. 74f., for further discussion of historical study as a pursuit of truth.

27. Ibid., 276; and see also, e.g., 1:189, 234. Cf. Salo W. Baron, "Azariah de' Rossi's Attitude to Life," in *History and Jewish Historians,* 195f. Baron views Azariah's emphasis on the pursuit of truth as essentially a way of apologizing for basically useless historical knowledge—a position that presumably results from his unalterably "legalistic . . . conception of Judaism," his conception of history being "theocratically medieval to an extreme" (p. 202). Baron does grant that much in the *Me'or 'Einayim* may have been intended "to conciliate popular opinion" (p. 196). Moreover, he writes elsewhere that Azariah "searchingly examined the records of the past in order to reconcile them with a modern point of view" and "contributed a series of searching studies into various aspects of ancient Jewish history which he analyzed with the critical methods of an advanced Renaissance historian." See Baron, *A Social and Religious History of the Jews* (New York: Columbia University Press, 1937), 2:207; idem, *Steeled by Adversity* (Philadelphia: Jewish Publication Society, 1971), 117, although the documentation for the latter statement continues to be Baron's original essays on Azariah (see *Steeled by Adversity,* 601 n. 19). Isaac Barzilay assumes as "rather plausible" that Moses Mendelssohn's "legalistic concept of Judaism" was directly influenced by Azariah's *Me'or 'Einayim;* see "The Italian and Berlin Haskalah," *Proceedings of the American Academy for Jewish Research* 29 (1960–1961):51, and n. 133. The actual model for Mendelssohn's view that Judaism was only law—the philosophical foundations and ramifications of which would not yet have been conceivable for Azariah—appears to have been Spinoza's *Tractatus Theologico-Politicus.* See Julius Guttmann, *Philosophies of Judaism,* trans. D. W. Silverman (London: Routledge and Kegan Paul, 1964), 299; and the more elaborate analysis in idem, "'Yerushalayim' le-Mendelssohn veha-'Masekhet ha-Te'ologit-ha-Medinit' le-Spinoza," in *Dat u-Mada',* trans. S. Esh (Jerusalem: Magnes Press, 1955), e.g., 195, 207.

28. *M.E.* 2:266.

29. See Spini, "Historiography," esp. 94–97; Cochrane, *Historians,* 486. The work of the Neapolitan statesman Pontano is discussed in some detail in Felix Gilbert, *Machiavelli and Guicciardini: Politics and History in Sixteenth-Century Florence* (Princeton: Princeton University Press, 1965), 205f., 208–211, 216.

30. Cochrane, *Historians,* 486ff.

31. Spini, "Historiography," 92–105. Although Spini notes certain inconsistencies in Patrizi's work (e.g., restoring "the concept of history as a source of salutary examples"; p. 103), he does view Patrizi's work as "a fundamental milestone . . . Methodology had taken the place of stylistics. . . . Although the solution was still only roughly sketched out . . . the problem of sources had already been

perceived in all its complexity" (pp. 104f). Cf. Cochrane, *Historians,* 482f.; and see also Bouwsma, *Venice,* 166f.

32. See Girolamo Cotroneo, *I trattatisti dell' ars historica"* (Naples: Gianini, 1971), who is much more reserved in his assessment of Patrizi. He notes that Patrizi lacked a criterion for evaluating historical sources, "a critical methodology of scientific character." He adds, however, that this lack of a certain criterion with which to refute skepticism is insufficient proof "to declare . . . Francesco Patrizi's firm adherence to the theory of historical Pyrrhonism" (p. 252).

33. Spini, "Historiography," 102; and see also the discussion in Cotroneo, *Ars historica,* citing Patrizi to the effect that "Two objectives are the principal ones for writing every history and every biography: *the apprehension of truth* and as a means to felicity" (p. 241, and n. 80; emphasis added).

34. In formulating this statement, I have found useful R. G. Collingwood's discussion of the transition from the pragmatic Renaissance conception of history to that of the seventeenth-century erudite scholar "activated by a sheer desire for truth" (*The Idea of History* [New York: Oxford University Press, 1957], 60f.). Bearing in mind the peculiarly Jewish considerations that lead Azariah to reject the didactic value of history and the fact that the search for truth does not exhaust his own historical preoccupation, I merely note an interesting parallel emphasis—apparently attendant to antiquarian scholarship—between him and the somewhat later European *érudits.*

35. *M.E.* 2:399, 400, 411f., 416, and generally chaps. 46–50.

36. Ibid., 266.

37. *Sefer Yuḥasin ha-Shalem,* ed. Zvi Filipowski, 2d ed. (Frankfurt am Main: Wahrmann Verlag, 1924). Freiman concludes in the introduction that the work was composed between 1479 and 1509 (p. x).

38. Ibid., 1, col. a: "ve-lo etgader lomar ki hi' ḥokhmah ʿamuqah."

39. Ibid., xif., and 216, col. b, where Zacuto refers to his extensive use of Ibn Daud's work. See too Abraham A. Neuman, "Abraham Zacuto: Historiographer," in *Harry Austryn Wolfson Jubilee Volume* (Jerusalem: American Academy for Jewish Research, 1965), 2:602f., 613f.

40. *Sefer Yuḥasin,* 2, col. a–3, col. a.

41. Zacuto insists, for example, that Jesus was born during the reign of the Hasmonean ruler Alexander Yannai (p. 15), almost ninety years before the generally accepted Christian date. Zacuto apparently relied here on Ibn Daud who in this matter emphasized that "we have it as an authentic tradition from the Mishna and the Talmud, which did not distort anything." See *The Book of Tradition by Abraham ibn Daud,* ed. Gerson D. Cohen (Philadelphia: Jewish Publication Society, 1967), 20ff., 114 nn. 100, 113–114, and 15f. of the Hebrew text.

42. *Sefer Yuḥasin,* 231; Neuman, "Abraham Zacuto," 604ff.

43. *Sefer Yuḥasin,* 231–250.

44. Ibid., 231. For the Josippon-Josephus problem in *Sefer Yuḥasin,* see Neuman, "Abraham Zacuto," 614–618. Zacuto adapts Ps. 144:8 in characterizing non-Jewish sources and also contrasts them with Jewish ones, like chaff and wheat

(*Sefer Yuḥasin,* 232, col. a; cf. Jer. 23:28). Baron, "Historical Method," 226f., finds "a more definitive formula" in Zacuto than in Azariah regarding non-Jewish sources. Lack of "formula," however, seems more than amply compensated for by Azariah's unparalleled variety and utilization of such sources, attested to by Baron himself. In the sixteenth century it was, after all, infinitely easier to enunciate a rather conventional position on the inferiority of non-Jewish sources than to argue forthrightly their admissibility into the universe of Jewish intellectual discourse. Azariah's position, therefore, is to be sought in the actual use to which he puts these materials, while his assertions or arguments about them are of greater value as a gauge of the contemporary Jewish cultural situation within which he had to function (see n. 21 above and below, pp. 51ff., 54–58).

45. See, for example, *Sefer Yuḥasin*, 232, col. a, regarding the function of this section, and ix, xxii, xxiv. In addition to the rather frequent anti-Christian polemic in the first five sections of the work (e.g., p. ix), the following illustrations from pt. 6 may be noted: 231, col. a, 232, col. a, 248, col. a, 249.

46. David Gans, *Ṣemaḥ David,* ed. H. Hominer (Jerusalem: Hominer Publications, 1966), 6, 7, for the usage "chronicle," and 92 for the discussion of the audience addressed and purposes served.

47. Ibid., 7. The two histories were intermingled by Gans at various points and there are some cross-references and double entries. Mordechai Breuer has observed that for Gans only the sources and documentation of universal history were secular while "universal history in itself, being the sphere of divine providence and . . . the stage of messianic enactment, was to him indistinguishable from Jewish history" ("Modernism and Traditionalism in Sixteenth-Century Jewish Historiography: A Study of David Gans' *Tzemaḥ David,*" in *Jewish Thought in the Sixteenth Century,* ed. Cooperman, 78). Yet while one might expect a religiously oriented sixteenth-century author to view all history in providential terms, Gans nevertheless viewed universal history as essentially the larger temporal framework within which one could discern God's special and continuing concern with his chosen Jewish "flock" (e.g., *Ṣemaḥ David,* 92). First among the ten "benefits" Jews will derive from the study of general history, Gans observes, is the heightened awareness that amidst all the conquests, violence, and Christian religious conflicts that have overtaken society, with consequent loss of innumerable lives, and even the disappearance of nations, the Jews have persevered. "In spite of all this, God . . . has delivered *us* under His wings . . . and His pledge to protect *us* has been continually fulfilled . . . and *we* dwell securely with the aid of Him who dwells on high who has acted in great kindness with *us,*" (ibid.; emphasis added). Gans, despite his modernism and desire to improve Jewish-Christian relations, appears no less committed to the qualitative distinction between general and Jewish history than to the distinction between their respective sources. Breuer (p. 77) may be right in assuming that Gans divided Jewish from general history in deference to his teacher, the Maharal of Prague, who had denounced Azariah's *Me'or 'Einayim* for having freely juxtaposed Jewish and non-Jewish sources. But his qualitative judgment of non-Jewish sources would logically seem to suggest a parallel judg-

ment regarding the status and historical experience of the non-Jewish society from which such sources emanate. Indeed, at times Gans's formulation seems almost to subsume both simultaneously (e.g., "And be aware that Christians . . . have added to the era of creation more than two hundred years beyond our reckoning. But *we, the holy congregation of Israel,* will place no trust in historical works authored by *those who are not of Jewish stock*" [*Ṣemaḥ David,* 102, col. b; emphasis added]). This passage leaves little doubt that Gans had serious reservations about the trustworthiness of non-Jewish sources, at least where they conflicted with Jewish ones, and also provides a striking contrast with Azariah de' Rossi for whom trustworthiness per se was never an issue, even where the materials clearly controverted Jewish ones.

48. E.g., *Ṣemaḥ David,* 102, col. 1.

49. E.g., ibid., 22, col. a; see also Breuer, "Modernism and Traditionalism," 64.

50. Gans, *Ṣemaḥ David*, 91. Prior to Gans, Azariah had expressed reservations about eyewitness evidence. See below, p. 134, and n. 1.

51. Breuer, "Modernism and Traditionalism," 50, 52–59, 61f., 64ff. Breuer notes Gans's broad erudition despite his inability to read Latin. He relied, in addition to Hebrew texts, on the many new German ones that had begun to appear during the Reformation era.

52. *Ṣemaḥ David*, 91, 92. Cf. Breuer, "Modernism and Traditionalism," 66, who maintains that "this ethico-pedagogical emphasis stands out much less in *Tzemaḥ David* (than in Melanchton's historical works) despite Gans's introductory declaration of intent." Nonetheless, Gans does provide moral lessons such as the caution to the successful man that he may fall from his fortune and, especially, the assertion that man is subject to retribution and that eventually the wicked have no peace in this world. For a sixteenth-century Jewish author and his readers, such maxims have "an unmistakable pedestrian, secular, and utilitarian touch" (Breuer, p. 66), but they simultaneously convey significant religious and ethical intent.

53. *Ṣemaḥ David*, 40, col. b; and see Breuer ("Modernism and Traditionalism," 64), who emphasizes Gans's "pursuit of truth" and presentation of "the maximum of impartiality of which he was capable." Breuer elsewhere emphasizes that Gans, particularly in his astronomical treatise *Neḥmad ve-Na'im,* sought to harmonize tradition and scientific knowledge. He sees such "harmonization" as exemplifying the sixteenth-century "coexistence" of the old and the new but also reflecting the "ideological confusion" of that age—whereas he views Azariah's position (e.g., in the matter of earthquakes) as "dualistic." See Breuer, "Qavim li-Demuto shel R. David Gans Ba'al Ṣemaḥ David," *Bar-Ilan Annual* 11 (1973): 102, and n. 28, 113. Baron, on the other hand ("Attitude to Life," 176), sees in Azariah's discussion of earthquakes "his harmonizing attitude toward Jewish and Greek thought."

54. *M.E.* 1:197.

55. *Ṣemaḥ David*, 39, col. b–40, col. b. Regarding Gans's "dialectic

and apologetic purpose" in utilizing the chronicle format, see Breuer, "Modernism and Traditionalism," 60 and n. 23.

56. Breuer, "Modernism and Traditionalism," 76.

57. *M.E.,* 2, chap. 43. The possible interest that Azariah may have had in messianism and apocalypse in his early youth, around 1531, is considered by Yosef Hayim Yerushalmi, "Messianic Impulses in Joseph ha-Kohen," in *Jewish Thought in the Sixteenth Century,* ed. Cooperman, 483, and n. 63.

CHAPTER 4

Sacred and Profane: Secular Knowledge and the Study of Classical Jewish Tradition

Azariah's relatively short, self-contained, critical essays in the *Me'or 'Einayim* cover subjects as diverse as the Hellenistic Jewish thinker Philo of Alexandria, the form and meter of biblical poetry, and the narratives in rabbinic literature with the manifold chronological, factual, and textual problems they present. These essays differ thematically from virtually every other Jewish historical work of the period. This novel departure is no doubt inspired as much by Azariah's intellectual curiosity as by his desire to create an awareness of the broadest possible spectrum of important Jewish historical issues, especially those that might perplex thoughtful coreligionists.

But Azariah obviously senses that the very novelty of the *Me'or 'Einayim*, even with respect to format, requires justification at the outset. He may, for example, liken his collected studies to "a little garden of differing plants" from which each reader will choose "according to his taste and the desire of his eyes." Nonetheless he proceeds on rather shaky talmudic grounds to uphold the diversity and the advantage of study that embraces a wide variety of topics, as compared with study that concentrates on one specific theme. He cites a number of talmudic passages that deal with the respective benefits of single and multiple sources of instruction and construes them to be addressing an analogous issue.[1] But given the difference in the mission of the early talmudic jurist-moralist and his disciples and in the intent of Azariah's critical essays written for the enlightenment of his sixteenth-century contemporaries, the analogy is irrelevant. Moreover, Azariah is really unable to derive a clearly compelling position from the Talmud in favor of variety of studies. And his use of another passage in which the Babylonian Talmud is itself referred to as an admixture of scripture, oral law, and the interpretive discussions of the sages is even wider of the mark. Azariah may insist that this variety is precisely what is attractive to a student of the Talmud, but as one who is entirely at home in the literature, he knows full well that neither the passage in question nor the context in which it occurs is complimentary. Rather, it reflects sharp criticism of the manner of study in the Babylonian academies, which, some sages held, lacked clarity and order—a point Azariah hardly allows to interfere with his argument.[2] The Talmud, for all of its compound nature, is essentially an organic whole and is Torah in the very traditional sense; its premises and categories of analysis, though arbitrarily appropriated here by Azariah, are inapplicable to the direction and contents of the *Me'or 'Einayim*.

If he seeks support for the format of his unconventional intellectual enterprise from traditional Jewish sources, Azariah in good humanist fashion invokes the classics as well. Cicero, who asserts that "histories that encompass much rise and fall and change will delight and attract their hearers," and Quintilian, who insists that "varied study will preserve us from weariness and strengthen the soul,"[3] seem in fact much more relevant than the Talmud at this juncture. But Azariah's juxtaposition of the two types of authorities almost immediately suggests to the reader the possibility that the qualitative distinction between them is relative. A primary question, however, is whether such non-Jewish sources are admissible at all, even for the kind of Jewish issues that Azariah investigates.

Azariah had already settled this question when he undertook to translate the *Letter of Aristeas* into Hebrew and to incorporate it as the second part of the *Me'or 'Einayim*. His devout sentiment that "God had touched my heart" to translate this work is no doubt genuine.[4] Azariah was certainly impressed with its positive portrayal of Judaism and of those ancient Jewish scholars so at home in both Jewish and Greek wisdom, although an increasingly pronounced sentiment among his Jewish contemporaries emphasized that the latter was a spiritual liability, not an asset.[5] As is also obvious from his preliminary observations in the introduction to the *Me'or 'Einayim*, Azariah places considerable, if not primary, emphasis on functional considerations. He is interested in the relevance of the *Letter* to the clarification of some problematic and cognate aspects of Jewish tradition that he intends to pursue in the main body of his work (*Imrei Binah*).[6] Azariah—moved to bring the *Letter* into the Jewish universe of discourse because of its inherently Jewish content and "for the honor of our God, His Law, and His people"[7]—in effect simultaneously legitimates the use of virtually any relevant outside sources to shed light on Jewish ones. Such legitimacy had yet to be dealt with formally in the *Me'or 'Einayim*,[8] but meanwhile Azariah prominently displays "this Aristeas from among the [gentile] nations of the earth"[9] as a fine example of the benefit to be had from such outsiders.

The *Letter of Aristeas* represented a challenge for Azariah from a purely historical point of view. He sought a fuller understanding of the classical Jewish condition in Ptolemaic Egypt and the "actual" circumstances relating to the Septuagint, especially since the Jewish record in the rabbinic literature appeared to be neither complete nor fully consistent. Azariah held in high regard this full-length, self-contained work of the third century B.C.E. written by an ostensibly gentile author. The *Letter* reported firsthand impressions of Judea, Jerusalem, and its Temple, conversations with the high priest Eleazar, King Ptolemy II's philosophical interchange with the gifted Jewish scholars sent to Egypt to do the translation, and more. It merited a place of its own in Azariah's treatise for the enlightenment of cultured Jewish readers.

Azariah is at home not only with the whole range of traditional Jewish literature and the much less conventional apocryphal scriptures and Hellenistic Jewish literature but with the classical, patristic, medieval, and Renaissance authors as well, and he draws freely on these various non-Jewish materials in his historical studies.[10] Most striking is his use of them where contemporary considerations of Jewish religious scruple would have dictated greater discretion. For example, in invoking God's name and support at the very beginning of his treatise, he quotes precedent from the Palestinian Talmud, the *Zohar,* Philo of Alexandria, and finally Plato's *Republic.* Since Azariah does not scruple to juxtapose the "divine" philosopher with the "divine" rabbi, Simeon bar Yohai,[11] supposed second-century author of the *Zohar,* he obviously considers the ethical precepts of the classical writers of value and relevance to the Jews.

His relationship to the classical and Christian sources reflects much of the humanist zeal for the idea of the unity of truth, expressed earlier by figures like Marsilio Ficino and Pico della Mirandola.[12] Such zeal naturally had its limits, since Jewish tradition served as a barrier against complete identification with and acceptance of Renaissance cultural trends.[13] Yet it is hardly unusual that one such as Azariah could function within the particularistic intellectual bounds conditioned by the continuing authority of Jewish religious law and doctrine; on the Christian side even a syncretist of the stature of Ficino remains entirely within the fold of his religion and its system of salvation.[14] And Pico's Christian posture is apparently such as to lead him and members of his circle to exploit qabbalistic materials for purposes of Jewish proselytism.[15]

But with Azariah, Jewish religious loyalty and cultural particularism are balanced by historical acumen. Both Jews and Christians, including Ficino, took quite seriously the apocryphal medieval Jewish story that the famous Greek thinker Aristotle had become a Jew toward the end of his life; indeed according to some he was originally of Jewish descent. Azariah has occasion to refer to the report in Don Isaac Abravanel's commentary to Mishnah Avot that Aristotle, together with his pupil Alexander the Great, had been in Jerusalem and had there conversed with the high priest Simeon the Just. Abravanel's source indicates that Aristotle was astounded by Simeon's profound theological wisdom. Azariah further notes that the late-fifteenth-century scholar Joseph ibn Shem Tov, in his commentary to Aristotle's *Ethics,* had exaggerated even more than Abravanel in saying that according to a work he had seen, Aristotle had acknowledged the truth of the entire Law of Moses and had become a righteous convert to Judaism. "If my memory does not deceive me," Azariah adds, "a similar account is to be found in the work *Magen Avraham,*" a treatise by the Jewish intellectual and communal leader in Italy, Abraham Farissol, completed in the early sixteenth century. Farissol seems to assume that Aristotle had been a Jew by origin. Among Azariah's immediate contemporaries, Gedaliah ibn Yahya repeats the Aristotle story in his well-known chronicle, *Shalshelet ha-Qabbalah,* first published in Venice in 1587. Gedaliah's discussion appears, in part, to be an unacknowledged adaptation of Azariah's, but obviously viewing the entire report as trustworthy, he deletes any suggestion of exaggeration, not to speak of error. Before Azariah's time even Solomon ibn Verga had taken the story seriously in his *Sheveṭ Yehudah,* and in the eighteenth-century chronological treatise *Seder ha-Dorot,* the Lithuanian talmudist and historian Yehiel Halperin still repeated it, elaborating some of its most apocryphal detail.

Azariah concludes, by contrast, that after considering certain relevant sources dealing with Aristotle, he finds no evidence that might confirm the story; nor does he find it tenable ("lo' shemi'ah li ve-lo' sevirah"). In short, Azariah does not propose to accommodate historical fact to long-accepted fiction or, as he elsewhere colorfully describes another historically problematic issue, "as the popular adage has it, to force the foot into the shoe." Not permitting his Jewish pride to get the better of his sense of scholarly integrity—even in an age when the inclusion of the great "authority" Aristotle in the ranks of Jewry might conceivably serve the honor of Judaism—Azariah indicates that the source of error is likely to be found in a misunderstanding of an account in Josephus's polemic against the Alexandrian anti-Jewish propagandist Apion and in the theological work *Praeparatio evangelica* by the fourth-century church father Eusebius.[16]

Azariah's familiarity with and utilization of the classics and other non-Jewish works is, of course, a phenomenon common to many Italian Jewish authors throughout the Renaissance era. His younger contemporary, friend, and respected critic, for example, the gifted Mantuan rabbi and preacher Judah Moscato, usually follows Cicero's outline of a properly constructed piece of oratory. He interweaves biblical and rabbinic citations with references to Greek mythology and a wide variety of classical authors in his sermons.[17] But Azariah is all the more remarkable in invoking sources of this kind for much more unconventional purposes and particularly with regard to religiously sensitive Jewish issues and subject matter. The Jewish spiritual climate at that time was increasingly inhospitable to such endeavors.

Opposition to secular learning in certain quarters of Italian Jewry long precedes the age of Azariah. In the fifteenth century, for example, the rabbi and humanist Judah Messer Leon in his important Hebrew rhetorical treatise *Nofet Ṣufim* disparagingly refers to those "wise in their own eyes among our coreligionists" (i.e., some religious spokesmen) who reject "truth" from gentile works—a passage Azariah approvingly cites.[18] A generation before Azariah, in the early sixteenth century Obadiah di Bertinoro, a well-known rabbi, addresses the issue in his popular commentary to the Mishnah. He defines the rabbinic category of prohibited "outside" reading as including "the works of Aristotle and his associates" and also gentile historical chronicles, which he considers devoid of wisdom and a sheer waste of time—time no doubt better spent in the study of the Law. Obadiah's correspondence of 1488 contains a similar observation and contrasts the spiritual situation in Palestine, to which he had journeyed, with his native Italy. He emphasizes how much greater than in Italy is piety in the Holy Land, where neither Jew nor Muslim holds heretical views, and no one is preoccupied with philosophy or drawn toward the opinions of Aristotle and his associates—upon whom Obadiah invokes ruin.[19]

The resistance to secular learning becomes more pronounced as the sixteenth century progresses, especially in the influential circles of the qabbalists, notable among whom is Immanuel Benevento. For him, writing at mid-century, the very juxtaposition of the profane with the sacred—especially the classics of qabbalah that he so actively helps to disseminate—is like "a pagan asherah planted alongside the altar of God."[20] Even Moscato must justify his efforts to synthesize humanism and Judaism. "Let it not vex you because I draw so much upon extraneous sources," for after all, as Jewish authors had been insisting for centuries, and as many Christian ones including Ficino and Pico agreed, "these foreign streams flow from our own Jewish wells. The nations of the earth derived their wisdom from our own sages. If I often make use of information gathered from secular books, it is only because I know the true origin of that information. Besides, I know what to reject as well as what to accept."[21] Moscato and other preachers of his intellectual disposition also find it necessary to exercise discretion in the allegorizing of aggadic materials, a tendency severely opposed by the traditionalists and qabbalists.[22]

The mood of the period is even more dramatically exhibited in the distinguished Mantuan physician and scholar Abraham Portaleone. He intends his encyclopedic work on Jewish antiquities, *Shilṭei ha-Gibborim,* written early in the seventeenth century toward the end of his life, as atonement for time and effort spent in secular learning and pursuits. "I failed to study God's Law as I was obliged to do," says Portaleone, who considers this to be his undoing and the reason for the paralysis that has overtaken him. He now seeks "to remove the magnitude of this iniquity which has been a burden upon me."[23] If Portaleone's *Shilṭei ha-Gibborim* reflects in many respects the Jewish cultural frame of mind of the Renaissance and its fascination with the classics, its main purpose is nevertheless penitential, and the work addresses itself extensively to the programmatic details of adult Torah study. With the upsurge of pietistic sentiment among Italian Jewry, Portaleone lends his own great talents to those of the religious leaders of the period who wish to intensify the study of the Law.[24] The deep pietistic-mystical strain is symptomatic of the age, and it is less surprising in Portaleone when one considers that, for all of his humanism, he is a leading disciple of "the grand master of all qabbalists of Western lands," Menahem Azariah da Fano.[25] In the 1570s, when the controversy erupted over Azariah de' Rossi's *Me'or 'Einayim,* some characteristically turned to da Fano for an authoritative opinion regarding the work.[26]

Outside of Italy in this period, interest in philosophy and other branches of secular knowledge and their possible bearing on traditional Jewish culture was generally far more limited. In contemporary Poland, which was fast becoming the main center of European Jewry, and in communities such as Prague, to which the intellectual and spiritual influence of Poland extended, there existed limited circles that displayed interest in secular studies. The fact that tendencies of this sort were limited in extent and in some notable cases were not even sustained throughout the lifetime of the individual is best illustrated by the example of the Polish talmudist Abraham Horowitz, whose views were among the most extreme. Around 1559, as a young man, he had been involved in a bitter controversy in Posen regarding the study of philosophy, notably that of Maimonides, and other branches of secular learning. These pursuits were opposed by the local rabbi, Aaron ben Gershon Land, his son-in-law Joseph Ashkenazi, and their followers. In a strongly worded pamphlet, Horowitz bitterly attacked Aaron's view that "no Jew need study anything other than the Talmud," that all other works were secular and forbidden, and that the study of scripture itself ought to be limited. Horowitz castigated Ashkenazi as the main source of inspiration for these views and especially condemned the opinion that "all the talmudic aggadot are to be taken literally"[27]—an opinion Ashkenazi developed with even greater intensity during a stay in Italy in the 1560s.[28] Ironically, Horowitz's own enthusiasm for the role of reason had waned with the years, and he eventually rewrote his earlier rationalistic commentary to Maimonides' *Shemonah Peraqim* to bring it into conformity with the spirit of mysticism and practical ethics to which he had later been drawn.[29]

An equally pronounced rationalistic approach can be seen in the work of the talmudist and biblical exegete Eliezer Ashkenazi, who had studied and lived for many years in the East, especially Egypt, but spent the last ten years of his life as a highly regarded rabbi in Poland. Azariah refers to him as "the greatest of the generation"[30] and reports Ashkenazi's views on biblical narratives, which he had apparently heard during one of the latter's stays in Italy. The high praise that Azariah confers on this contemporary is undoubtedly the result, not merely of Ashkenazi's talmudic erudition, but of his knowledge of general sciences and languages and his emphasis on freedom in the exegesis of scripture. In his 1583 exegetical treatise on the Pentateuchal narratives, *Ma'asei ha-Shem,* Ashkenazi insists that "we are all obliged to search out the hidden meaning of scripture . . . and to accept the truth from whomever has said it, after we have understood it. Let us not allow someone else's opinion, even if it is of a previous generation, to restrain us from inquiry." There is a clearly polemical intent in Ashkenazi's work, for he refers to the intellectual sloth or fear of many in his generation who seem to be overwhelmed by the reputation of great authorities. "Search out and choose, for this is the purpose of your having been created and endowed with reason. . . . For irrespective of whether your views are acceptable, the enlightened man will always benefit, and if the unenlightened is affected adversely, let it not concern you . . . since your intent has been for the sake of heaven."[31] Sentiments such as these, which Azariah no doubt also heard from or about Ashkenazi long before the latter's work appeared in print, surely won his enthusiastic approval.

Although for Ashkenazi, rabbinic aggadah is not a major area of investigation per se, his brief but pointed remarks on the subject in the introduction to the same treatise have a close affinity with the approach elaborated at great length a decade earlier by Azariah. Ashkenazi emphasizes the purely allegorical intent of talmudic narratives since, in his view, the majority of the sages' stories were invented only to convey parables—a device also used in the prophetic books. The element of hyperbole in such narratives was specifically intended to alert the student that the event described had never occurred and that some profound message lay hidden.[32] Ashkenazi also appears to have been the first of his type of eastern European Jewish scholars to express the view that as a matter of principle, Christians cannot be considered idolators like the pagan "gentiles" of antiquity, since they acknowledge the truth of the Mosaic law and the prophets. It seems that in this matter, Azariah and his associates in Italy were Ashkenazi's source of inspiration. But with respect to the messianic hope, Ashkenazi holds with the widespread spirit of the age rather than with Azariah; he calculates that its fulfillment will occur in 1594.[33]

But neither Ashkenazi nor Horowitz was, after all, typical of eastern European Jewish types.[34] And even for them, as for those native Polish talmudists who had been influenced by Spanish Jewish philosophical rationalism, the role of secular learning was becoming increasingly restricted. For it was to serve as the "maidservant" of traditional talmudic lore—which for Polish Jewry was significantly conditioned by its own roots in medieval German Jewish pietism—and especially of mystical doctrine, which was rapidly establishing its spiritual dominion,[35] just as it had in Italian Jewry.

Given this intellectual climate, the range of non-Jewish materials Azariah is prepared to admit is all the more extreme. Since the contemporary resistance to secular learning by Jewish spokesmen was directed primarily at Greek philosophy and the presumption of the human intellect, Azariah's citations must have been especially objectionable. In addition to the classics, he freely juxtaposes New Testament, patristic, and numerous other Christian sources with Hebrew scripture and rabbinic dicta. His practice may occasionally be motivated by apologetic considerations that lead him to call attention to Christian views paralleling those in the Jewish sources. But even here, it is his broad reading that first alerts him to such parallels and his historical sense that allows him to conjecture that some may derive from the Jewish background of the early founders of the church.[36] The extensive utilization of Christian exegetical, historical, and philosophical works is, however, as with all non-Jewish materials, intended in the first instance to shed light on Jewish antiquities. If the context and theological assumptions of these works are radically contrary to his own tradition, it nonetheless seems to him entirely appropriate to use them. Yet it is another matter to determine whether he is being candid or even realistic when he insists that he will cite no author who says anything "contrary to our Law" and who thus may dispose the reader to improper views.[37]

The manner in which Azariah sometimes cites patristic authorities was itself considered sufficiently offensive to warrant censorship of certain passages in the *Me'or 'Einayim.* The censored sections of the first printing (1573) contain, for example, a reference to Augustine as "a great Christian sage," in connection with the interpretation of a verse in Genesis. Azariah then notes that "the words of the aforementioned Christian in this matter *are [more] in keeping with the meaning of the Law and more authoritative*" (*u-mequbbalim yoter*) than the opinion of Maimonides that he cites. He adds that the view of Moses ben Nahman (Ramban or Nahmanides) in his commentary to Genesis is similar to that of Augustine. In the revised printing of the *Me'or 'Einayim* in the following year, Azariah was required by rabbinical authorities in Venice to modify various parts of his text. This section now describes Augustine as "the leading Christian sage," and the view of Ramban, which agrees with that of the church father, is immediately juxtaposed. Azariah then cites Maimonides, adding again that with all due respect to this towering authority, "the *other opinion* mentioned in this matter is [more] in keeping with the meaning of the Law and *is more acceptable*" (*u-mitqabbel yoter*).[38] What had no doubt appeared as an overly enthusiastic endorsement of Augustine is thus substantially toned down. The net effect of the rearrangement of the lines is to suggest that the "other opinion" refers more immediately to a Jewish authority (Ramban) rather than to an exclusively Christian one, and the change in Hebrew idiom is apparently intended to remove the original implication that Augustine could at times interpret Hebrew scripture in a more traditional manner than the leading medieval jurist and thinker (Maimonides)—although this is nonetheless exactly what Azariah means here.[39] The Jewish cultural anomalies of the period, or at least of Azariah, are such that in his *Maṣref la-Kesef* he even feels free to employ the term *rabbaneihem*—normally reserved in Jewish literature for rabbinic authorities—as the Hebrew equivalent of church fathers, among whom he designates Augustine as "the leading and most venerable."[40] And while there can be no doubt regarding Azariah's personal loyalty to Judaism, he does permit himself to undertake a scholarly exposition of certain passages from the Syriac text of the Gospels that would redound, from the Christian perspective of course, "to the glory and confirmation of the Christian faith."[41] Notably, this venture followed the controversial *Me'or 'Einayim* and its specifically Jewish scholarship by several years, close to the end of Azariah's life.

Not surprisingly Azariah explains early on in the *Me'or 'Einayim* that "in view of the work before me, I am compelled in some matters to seek clarification and elucidation with the aid of many gentile scholars."[42] Still, he refers to the Jewish ancestry of this "foreign wisdom" (in the fashion of Judah Moscato) only after first invoking many other arguments to justify his practice. Almost as an afterthought he adds: "Or it may be assumed, as Maimonides has said . . . that the essence of their [the gentiles] knowledge originated with our people."[43] The range of such material in the *Me'or 'Einayim* is far too extensive and the purposes for which it is utilized far too controversial for this argument to suffice.

Azariah himself may view the contemporary recovery of classical works that shed light on Jewish antiquities as virtually providential.[44] But he also realizes that he may be subject to the criticism of certain "pious, closeted" individuals on the basis of rabbinic prohibition against study of "outside books"—primarily seen as extracanonical, Jewish apocryphal and pseudepigraphical works such as Ecclesiasticus (Wisdom of Ben Sira), but more broadly construed by many as all non-Torah literature. He thus proceeds to marshal and analyze the relevant rabbinic sources in support of his case. Azariah's attempt to obviate certain apparent inconsistencies in the parallel talmudic and midrashic passages bearing on this point is very impressive, especially its conclusion that the original prohibition was perhaps less categorical than it appeared to be. But his subsequent claim that the casual reading of virtually all non-scriptural works had been permitted by the ancient rabbinic authorities is contrived to justify the wide variety of materials he himself utilizes.[45] No less problematic is Azariah's insistence that his use of "outside" sources conforms to the rabbinic sanction of cursory study or casual reading of such works, especially "if we may thus be alerted to the clarification of any matter in some way related to the interpretation of the Law." He observes that the rabbinic sages prohibited only the excessive preoccupation with outside materials, leading one to consider them of extraordinary value, to the neglect of the Torah. In fact, his own extensive recourse to such materials clearly transcends the bounds of cursory reading, and his utilization of them is hardly determined by considerations of the study of the Law in the conventional rabbinic sense.[46]

In order to strengthen his argument Azariah also invokes the fourteenth-century talmudist Yom Tov ben Abraham Ishbili (Ritba), whom he quotes as permitting the casual study of Ecclesiasticus, even though it is among the "outside books," as defined by the sages. But Azariah conveniently overlooks several critical qualifications with substantial relevance to his procedure in the *Me'or 'Einayim*: Ritba's permission extends specifically to Ecclesiasticus and then only for moralistic lessons to be derived from it, and he explicitly prohibits "actually heretical works" (*sifrei minim mamash*).[47]

Azariah further attempts to validate his practice by drawing an analogy with the rabbinic tradition, which states that although the prophetic books are considered holy writ, they do not carry equal weight with the Pentateuch; thus one may not derive any authoritative halakhic decisions from them, and a prophet cannot innovate in matters of religious law. And, Azariah adds, the non-Pentateuchal writ is considered as "foreign" and has no valid bearing on the understanding of the Law other than to provide some general clarification that does not affect the substance of any halakhic decision. By means of a facile (and questionable) analogy, Azariah exploits this position to draw his novel conclusion: acknowledging of course the distinction between the holy and the profane, he then argues that it should be permissible to utilize non-Jewish sources (as one would, for example, turn to the prophetic materials) for whatever guidance they may provide in elucidating a given issue.[48] In effect Azariah is arguing, at least for purposes of intellectual enlightenment, that non-Jewish works are no worse than the prophetic ones and are indeed equally respectable. This of course implicitly ignores the serious qualitative distinction from the traditional Jewish perspective between the rabbinic use of the prophetic books to shed light on halakhic matters and Azariah's use of secular materials to clarify basically historical questions, which are presumably inconsequential. It also glosses over the fact that in the rabbinic tradition the prophets formed an integral link in the chain of halakhic development in which they sometimes functioned, or were viewed, as sages, although qua prophets they generally had no role in the formulation of halakhic decisions. This very point is affirmed by Azariah in another context where it suits his purpose, just as he also strongly insists on the superior status of the prophet in comparison with the sage in the larger scheme of Jewish religious leadership.[49] Here, however, because the context requires as unauthoritative a characterization of the prophets as possible, he manipulates the hierarchy of religious authority inherent in the Jewish view of scripture in order to substantiate a rather artificial analogy.

Finally, there is the equally forced exposition of scripture itself to which Azariah resorts. For he proceeds to demonstrate that God himself has in numerous places in the Bible explicitly permitted, indeed—if one follows his arbitrary appropriation of words—virtually encouraged the use of "outside" works. He points to the following: "You have but to inquire about bygone ages" (Deut. 4:32); "Ask the generation past" (Job 8:8); "You must have consulted the wayfarers" (Job 21:29); "Stand by the roads and . . . inquire" (Jer. 6:16). In the last citation, Azariah even elides a word and runs two phrases together in order to elicit the necessary meaning from the text. Should one object that all these verses refer only to Jewish experience, Azariah's coup de grace is still another scriptural assertion (Jer. 18:13): "Thus said the Lord, inquire among the nations," which is as irrelevant as all the other scriptural proofs. Azariah is fully aware of the basic canons of sound biblical exegesis as understood at the time and does not generally engage in loose homiletical interpretation, or tongue in cheek reasoning. The arbitrary selection of scriptural verses is serious enough in Azariah's arsenal of arguments that he resorts to it again, in a subsequent historical investigation requiring the use of non-Jewish materials. Years later the chronicler David Gans found this particular argument sufficiently impressive to include in his own work, but without indicating its source.[50]

Ironically, Azariah even invokes the authority of his contemporary Joseph Caro, the leading sixteenth-century Sephardic rabbinic scholar and codifier, in support of the contention that occasional use of non-Jewish works is permitted, although he is aware of how different from his own intellectual and religious disposition is that of Caro and the circle in Safed. Caro, profound talmudic legist and qabbalist that he was, obviously saw the entire thrust of Azariah's *Me'or 'Einayim* in a radical light and is reported to have considered the work deserving of extirpation, expressing amazement that local rabbinic authorities had permitted its publication. Only his sudden death in 1575 prevented him from putting his name to the projected ban that he had already instructed his pupil and rabbinic colleague in Safed, Elisha Gallico, to prepare and disseminate and that was countersigned by the rabbi Moses Alshekh.[51]

Notes

1. *M.E.* 1:78ff. Azariah observes: "So then this manner of study in which the themes vary [*bilti shomer mino*], which . . . we will follow in our chapters, will not lack desirable advantage . . . and as we have suggested is, by its very nature [*hu' betiv'o*], also sweet to the soul" (ibid., 80; emphasis added). It is topical variety, by its "nature" appealing, that Azariah argues here.

2. *M.E.* 1:80. See the passage in B. Sanhedrin 24a; Tosafot takes it in a positive sense, but that this is quite contrary to the intent is already noted by Maharsha in his novellae (p. 7a) to Sanhedrin. The negative connotation of the passage is also clear from a response of Hai Gaon concerning the authority of the Babylonian Talmud relative to the Palestinian Talmud. See *Oṣar ha-Ge'onim le-Masekhet Sanhedrin,* ed. H. Z. Taubes (Jerusalem: Mosad ha-Rav Kook, 1966), 180. Azariah notes some negative opinion regarding Babylonian talmudic tradition but limits its meaning to the excessive casuistry of the Babylonian sages, and this, in any event, does not affect his understanding of the passage in question in Sanhedrin 24a.

3. *M.E.* 1:80; and see Cassel's nn. 2, 3. Azariah quotes Cicero's *Rhetorica ad Herennium* and his *Epistolae* and Quintilian's *Institutio oratoria.*

4. *M.E.* 1:4.

5. See below, pp. 51–54.

6. *M.E.* 1:3f.

7. Ibid., 1, 3f.

8. See below, pp. 54f., 56ff.

9. *M.E.* 2:400. Azariah's interest in the *Letter of Aristeas* as it relates to his study of the origins of the Septuagint translation is considered by Joanna Weinberg, "Azariah de' Rossi and Septuagint Traditions," *Italia* 5 (1985): 7–35.

10. See *M.E.* 3:161–176, for Cassel's annotated indexes of non-Jewish works cited; and see the discussion in Leopold Zunz, "Toledot Rabbi Azariah min ha-Adumim," *Kerem Ḥemed* 5 (1841): 7; Moses A. Shulvass, "Knowledge of Antiquity among Italian Jews," *Proceedings of the American Academy for Jewish Research* 18 (1948–1949): 297; Salo W. Baron, "Azariah de' Rossi's Historical Method," in *History and Jewish Historians* (Philadelphia: Jewish Publication Society, 1964), 226–230. Baron observes that Azariah "expressly states that he would never reject any ancient tradition because of conflicting non-Jewish sources" (p. 226 n. 129). Yet the relevant passage in the *Me'or 'Einayim*, far from being categorical, is conditional and virtually for purposes of rhetorical effect, for what Azariah appears to concede about the authority of ancient Jewish tradition—in the passage Baron cites from *M.E.*—he almost immediately qualifies and effectively

undoes in the second half of the passage. In a context that establishes the admissibility of non-Jewish evidence relative to problems in the creation era chronology and to the extent that such subject matter has no Sinaitic authority, Azariah declares: "Behold, although we agree as we appropriately ought to . . . that if all the gentile sages were in one scale of the balance and one of them [the Jewish sages] in the other, he would outweigh them all. . . . If there is some matter in the prophetic books that presents difficulties to the tradition received by them or received from them, we are then obliged to investigate and search for the solution of the issue in a straightforward manner and not [resort] to absurdity" (*M.E.* 2:278; i.e., as circumstances require, non-Jewish authorities should be given credence in this area of investigation). Moreover, Azariah's discussion here, like many others, revolves largely around historical and/or aggadic-exegetical material, material Azariah clearly views as open to critical assessment and at times subject to rejection. (See *M.E.* 2:277f., and, e.g., 1:156, 167, 196f.) Then too, Azariah's acceptance of foreign sources over an ancient Jewish opinion does not invariably, if at all, require that later Jewish authors had first "admitted" that such a particular opinion "had been controverted by dependable foreign sources" (Baron, p. 226, and n. 129, based on *M.E.* 2:410), for Azariah emphasizes that *in his own view* once post-talmudic commentators had opened the biblical verses or rabbinic dicta to judgment and speculation, relevant non-Jewish evidence needs to be considered as well. In his investigations, Azariah almost always assembles such evidence himself; much of it is rarely even familiar to the Jewish commentators in question, and many of them would have deemed it unworthy of use by Jews. Here, for example (*M.E.* 2:409), Azariah observes: "It happened that as I was personally conjecturing whether perhaps any of the Christian sages who had seen them [the Jewish priestly vestments] . . . or afterward, for whatever reason had recorded anything regarding their appearance . . . from whom we may take some suggestion—if not valid evidence—I attentively consulted their works and especially . . . Lipomanus, the ingatherer of the whole host of their commentators."

11. *M.E.* 1:1. For the epithets Azariah employs, see, e.g., *M.E.* 2:380, 1:113f. ("the divine philosopher Plato," "his divine words," "the righteous Plato"), 1:116 ("the divine Rabbi Simeon bar Yohai").

12. See Paul O. Kristeller, *Renaissance Concepts of Man and Other Essays* (New York: Harper and Row, 1972), 54–59; and see Salo W. Baron, "Azariah de' Rossi's Attitude to Life," in *History and Jewish Historians,* 201.

13. Moses A. Shulvass (*Ḥayyei ha-Yehudim be-Iṭalyah bi-Tequfat ha-Renesans* [New York: Ogen, 1955], 175f.) notes the "moderate" extent to which Italian Jews generally assimilated Renaissance culture, although he emphasizes that Jewish religious life and outlook were nonetheless influenced by it.

14. See Ernst Cassirer, *The Individual and the Cosmos in Renaissance Philosophy,* trans. M. Domandi (New York: Harper and Row, 1964). Ficino makes possible a philosophy of history "which, though bound to Christian dogma . . . succeeds in seeing the concept of religion embodied . . . in the *totality* of historical religious forms" (p. 71). But Cassirer further calls attention to the ascetic

features present from the very beginning in the outlook of the Florentine academy, which increasingly pervaded the thinking and moral persuasion of both Ficino and Pico. Following a serious illness, Ficino, concerned with guilt for pagan error, burns his commentary on Lucretius and directs his philosophical and literary talent entirely to the cause of Christianity. Pico ends his life "with renunciation, with a resigned return . . . to Christian-medieval forms of life" (pp. 62f.). See also Kenneth R. Stow, *Catholic Thought and Papal Jewry Policy, 1555–1593* (New York: Jewish Theological Seminary of America, 1977), 245f., regarding Ficino's discussion of Jews; and see Umberto Pirotti, "Aristotelian Philosophy and the Popularization of Learning: Benedetto Varchi and Renaissance Aristotelianism," in *The Late Italian Renaissance,* ed. and trans. E. Cochrane (London: MacMillan, 1970), 199: "The collapse of religious faith during the Renaissance is nothing but a myth." Cf. Baron, "Attitude to Life," 201f.

15. See the discussion in David B. Ruderman, *The World of a Renaissance Jew: The Life and Thought of Abraham ben Mordecai Farissol* (Cincinnati: Hebrew Union College Press, 1981), 43–52.

16. *M.E.* 1:246f.; and Azariah's use of the "popular adage," 2:296; *Shalshelet ha-Qabbalah* (Warsaw, 1881), 45f.; the Farissol passage is quoted in Ruderman, *World of a Renaissance Jew,* 192 n. 68, but Azariah and Gedaliah ibn Yahyah are juxtaposed without distinction in their reference to that passage (p. 193); *Shevet Yehudah,* 151, and see 224 n. 4; *Seder ha-Dorot* (Warsaw, 1882–1883), pt. 1, pp. 135f. The story regarding Aristotle's Jewish origin apparently originated with a fifteenth-century mistranslation of a passage in Eusebius's *Praeparatio evangelica* (see Ruderman, p. 49, who cites Chaim Wirszubski's edition of Mithridates' *Sermo de passione Domini* [Jerusalem, 1963] regarding this passage). Baron, "Attitude to Life," 415 n. 69, briefly notes Azariah's sharp rejection of the Aristotle story. See also Salo W. Baron, *A Social and Religious History of the Jews,* 2d ed. (New York and Philadelphia: Columbia University Press and Jewish Publication Society, 1952–1983), 8:63, regarding this legend, "widely believed all over Europe."

17. See discussion and references in Israel Zinberg, *Toledot Sifrut Yisra'el,* ed. and trans. S. Z. Ariel, D. Kenaani, G. Karu (Tel Aviv: Sifriyat Poalim, 1955), 2:287; and Israel Bettan, "The Sermons of Judah Moscato," *Hebrew Union College Annual* 6 (1929): 297–326.

18. *M.E.*, 1:89; and regarding such opposition, see also Baron, "Attitude to Life," 192; and Cecil Roth, *The Jews in the Renaissance* (Philadelphia: Jewish Publication Society, 1946) 43 n. 7. Alexander Altmann discusses Azariah's use of Messer Leon: "*Ars Rhetorica* as Reflected in Some Jewish Figures of the Italian Renaissance," in *Essays in Jewish Intellectual History* (Hanover: University Press of New England, 1981), 110ff.

19. Commentary to Mish. Sanhedrin 10:1; "Iggrot R. 'Ovadiah mi-Bertinoro," in *Sifrut ha-Historiah ha-Yisra'elit,* ed. A. Kahana (Warsaw, 1923), 2:47.

20. Isaiah Sonne, *Mi-Paulo ha-Revi'i 'ad Pius ha-Ḥamishi* (Jerusalem: Mosad Bialik, 1954), 127; and see chap. 3, n. 21 above. Benevento's particular choice of phrases is discussed by Isaiah Tishby in his study of the contemporary

controversy over the *Zohar*. Tishby has argued, contra Sonne and other moderns, that the efforts of Benevento and his compatriots to have the *Zohar* and related literature printed were not initially precipitated by the burning of the Talmud in 1553. Rather, such efforts preceded that event and grew out of the pervasive qabbalistic spiritual developments and considerations, inclusive of the wish to facilitate the messianic fulfillment. See Tishby, "Ha-Polmos ʿal Sefer ha-Zohar ba-Me'ah ha-shesh esreh be-Iṭalyah," *Peraqim* (1967–1968): esp. 171, n. 143, 157f., 173–182.

21. Bettan, "Judah Moscato," 305; Zinberg, *Toledot Sifrut Yisra'el,* 2:394–398, discusses the various authors, Jewish and non-Jewish, who from antiquity on took quite seriously the legend that Greek philosophy—indeed all wisdom—originated with the Jews. Whatever Azariah's view may have been in this matter (see above, p. 56., and below n. 43), he long precedes Leone Modena in rejecting the story of Aristotle's supposed conversion. Cf. Zinberg, p. 398; and see Modena, *Ari Nohem,* ed., N. S. Lebowitz (Reprint, Jerusalem: Maqor, 1970), 53, who merely describes as "divrei kesilut" (absurdity) such views as that Aristotle had conversed with and presumably been convinced by the high priest Simeon the Just.

22. Reuven Bonfil, *Ha-Rabbanut be-Iṭalyah bi-Tequfat ha-Renesans* (Jerusalem: Magnes Press, 1979), 198, 201. Concerning Moscato's influence on other preachers, see David Kaufmann, "The Dispute About the Sermons of David Del Bene of Mantua," *Jewish Quarterly Review,* o.s., 8 (1896): 513–524; and see below, n. 26.

23. See the long autobiographical citation from the end of *Shilṭei ha-Gibborim* in Mordecai Samuel Ghirondi and Hananel Neppi, *Toledot Gedolei Yisra'el u-Ge'onei Iṭalyah* (Trieste: Tipographia Marenigh, 1853; reprint, Israel, 1968), esp. 44. Roth, *Jews in the Renaissance,* 315–318, describes the general contents of Portaleone's work.

24. Shulvass, *Ha-Yehudim be-Iṭalyah,* 195f., 269f. In the generation after Azariah de' Rossi, the well-known qabbalist and pietist Aaron Berechiah da Modena—like Portaleone, a disciple of Menahem Azariah da Fano—urges avoidance of the "deceitful investigation" and "the prevarications, the falsified hypotheses fabricated by the ancient philosophers . . . which make the fundamentals of our Law dependent upon the putridness of their intellects and proofs derived from their lies" (*Ma'avar Yaboq* [Vilna: Romm, 1911], 234).

25. Isaac Barzilay, *Yoseph Shlomo Delmediqo, Yashar of Candia: His Life, Work, and Times* (Leiden: Brill, 1974), 228, and n. 2, quoting Delmedigo's *Maṣref la-Ḥokhmah.* Barzilay discusses the important role of Italian Jewry in the dissemination of qabbalistic doctrine from the mid-sixteenth century on.

26. See David Kaufmann, "Contributions à l'histoire des luttes d'Azaria de Rossi," *Revue des études juives* 33 (1896): 77–87. The appended documents include a 1574 letter of inquiry to da Fano from the rabbi in Cremona, Abraham Menahem Porto (pp. 85f.). About twenty-five years later, when the sermons of David del Bene elicited the scathing denunciation of some Italian Jewish spokesmen, it was again da Fano whom they expected to take the lead in con-

demning the offender. At issue was del Bene's use of classical mythology and his extreme allegorizing of rabbinic aggadah by reference to foreign works, which, as one leading rabbi (Nethanel Trabot of Modena) wrote, "it is forbidden to speak of and study." The young del Bene ultimately had a change of heart about the pursuit of foreign wisdom and turned to da Fano for instruction and guidance. See Kaufmann, "Sermons of David del Bene," 519–521 in the appended Hebrew sources.

27. P. Bloch, "Der Streit um den Moreh des Maimonides in der Gemeinde Posen um die Mitte des 16. Jahrh.," *Monatsschrift für Geschichte und Wissenschaft des Judentums* 47 (1903): 153–169, 263–279, 346–356. The citations are from the Hebrew manuscript pamphlet appended to Bloch's article (pp. 167, 271).

28. Gershom Scholem has demonstrated that Joseph Ashkenazi composed a treatise in the 1560s, during a stay in Italy and before his departure for Safed, that confirms the extreme views ascribed to him by his adversary in Posen. (See "Yedi'ot ḥadashot 'al R. Yosef Ashkenazi, ha-Tana' mi-Ṣefat," *Tarbiz* 28 [1958]: 59–89, 201–235). Ashkenazi's total rejection of allegorical interpretations of aggadah based on philosophical speculation may have become even more pronounced by his exposure to the peculiar Italian Jewish cultural situation in which philosophy and qabbalah still attempted to effect a kind of motley combination (Scholem, p. 74). If, however, as Scholem observes, Ashkenazi is one of the rare surviving expressions of "reactionary" protest against the continuing medieval effort to reinterpret problematic talmudic material (pp. 59f.), such views were more likely than ever before to find a receptive audience in the increasingly pietistic-qabbalistic climate of the sixteenth century. See too Bonfil, *Rabbanut,* 190 n. 115. It is in precisely this climate that Azariah's views concerning aggadah aroused significant opposition some years later.

29. Haim Hillel Ben-Sasson, *Hagut ve-Hanhagah* (Jerusalem: Mosad Bialik, 1959), 14, for a brief discussion of Horowitz. Cf. Mordechai Breuer, ("Qavim le-Demuto shel R. David Gans Ba'al Ṣemaḥ David," *Bar-Ilan Annual* 11 [1973]: 98), who refers to Horowitz's views and his role in the enlightened Jewish circle of Prague and in the Posen controversy.

30. *M.E.* 1:124, and Cassel's n. 1. Ashkenazi refers to the simultaneous validity of the literal and the metaphorical meaning of the Pentateuchal narratives. Cf. his *Ma'asei ha-Shem* (Warsaw, 1871), 4.

31. Quoted and discussed in Ben-Sasson, *Hagut ve-Hanhagah,* 36f. Ashkenazi's concern for the intellectually sophisticated class seems similar in tone to Azariah's (see below, pp. 69f., 71f., 78f., and *M.E.* 2:365).

32. *Ma'asei ha-Shem,* 4f.: "ha-ma'asiyot shehuv'u . . . rubam lo' hayu khen be-fo'al aval beduyim u-munaḥim le-mashal levad." See pt. 2, on Exodus, in Ashkenazi's commentary to the Haggadah of Passover (pp. 38f.).

33. Jacob Katz, *Masoret u-Mashber* (Jerusalem: Mosad Bialik, 1958), 53, and n. 12, with a reference to *M.E.*, chap. 45. In his *Exclusiveness and Tolerance* (New York: Schocken, 1962), 166, and n. 1, Katz, however, writes that Ashkenazi

was "influenced probably by the Italian scholar Solomon ibn Verga of the humanist era." But regarding Ibn Verga's relationship to Italy, see chap. 1, n. 2 above. Ashkenazi's messianic calculations are contained in a brief concluding paragraph following the end of *Ma'asei ha-Shem* (after part 2, p. 90). See also Moses A. Shulvass, *Roma' vi-Yerushalayim: Toledot ha-Yaḥas shel Yehudei Iṭalyah le-Ereṣ Yisra'el* (Jerusalem: Mosad ha-Rav Kook, 1944), 80f., regarding the continuing preoccupation in Italian Jewry with messianic anticipation and for a brief reference to Ashkenazi.

34. The point is made by Katz, *Masoret u-Mashber,* 53 n. 12, regarding Ashkenazi, but it would appear to be equally applicable to Horowitz in his earlier phase.

35. Ben-Sasson, *Hagut ve-Hanhagah*, 15f.

36. E.g., *M.E.* 2:449. See also Baron, "Historical Method," 228, on Azariah's use of Christian materials.

37. *M.E.* 1:85, and also 81. Azariah attempts to justify the use of informative citations from works, even those whose overall content may be objectionable, on the grounds of supposed talmudic sanction. See below, n. 45.

38. The censored 1573 material is assembled in Israel Mehlman, "Saviv Sefer *Me'or 'Einayim* le-R. Azariah Min ha-Adumim," in *Genuzot Sefarim: Ma'amarim Bibliographiyim* (Jerusalem: National and University Library Press, 1976), 25–39. Cf. p. 31 in Mehlman's essay with the Cassel edition of *M.E.* 1:221 (emphasis added). In chap. 20 of the *Me'or 'Einayim*, too, which was one of the most severely criticized and in which Azariah therefore was forced to make extensive textual changes (see below, pp. 116ff. and n. 6–9) explicit mention of Augustine by name was deleted in the second printing (see Mehlman, p. 34; and cf. *M.E.* 1:236). Elsewhere, the description of Augustine as "the great Christian sage" does occasionally appear (*M.E.* 1:124, 177), but in these instances the text was left unchanged since the entire context was apparently not offensive to the critics.

39. In replacing *mequbbalim* with *mitqabbel,* Azariah obviously intends a distinct difference in emphasis, the former connoting that which conforms to authoritative tradition. See, for example, his use of the phrase *mequbbalim ba-umah,* with reference to certain aggadot (*M.E.* 1:104); and see especially Moses Provençal's use of the same phrase to denote that which is accepted by Jews as authoritative tradition (p. 492, following the text of *M.E.*; and see below, chap. 5, n. 13).

40. *Maṣref la-Kesef* 75, 117. Azariah's deferential references to Augustine contrast sharply with the language Zacuto uses. See *Sefer Yuḥasin,* 234, col. a, regarding Augustine. Baron, "Historical Method," 227, has analyzed this contrast. Some earlier Jewish authors, at least in Italy, appear to have used the title "rav" to designate a high Christian clerical dignitary. See, for example, H. Vogelstein and P. Rieger, (*Geschichte der Juden in Rom* [Berlin: Mayer and Müller, 1896], 1:270), who note the thirteenth-century Moses ben Solomon of Salerno's reference to a bishop of his acquaintance as "shehu rav shelahem."

41. See Joanna Weinberg, "Azariah dei Rossi: Towards a Reap-

praisal of the Last Years of His Life," *Annale della Scuola Normale Superiore di Pisa,* 3d ser., 8 (1978): 495ff., and appended texts of two manuscript letters by Azariah and one by the inquisitor of Ferrara (pp. 509–511). Even before this last of his scholarly efforts, Azariah's contacts with certain churchmen in the years following the appearance of *M.E.* and his requests from them for financial aid in publishing his works precipitated not only interest in his scholarship but also efforts to convert him. From the inquisitor's letter of 1577 to the cardinal of Santa Severina, we learn of the failure to convert Azariah during 1575–1577 and now of Azariah's earnest request to inform the cardinal of his determination to remain a Jew although, it should be noted, not a fanatical one who would refrain from asserting the truth in behalf of every religion ("ma non pazzo hebreo, cio è che vogli cessar di dir la verita in favor d'ogni religione"; pp. 496, 511). In this appeal Azariah clearly hoped to elicit the cardinal's financial support toward publication of his treatise on the Gospels. Nonetheless, that he undertook to clarify certain problematic passages in the Vulgate, an effort that might serve "a gloria et conformaziöne della fede christiana," sheds considerable light on his intellectual posture.

42. *M.E.* 1:81.

43. Ibid., 87. Azariah cites Maimonides' *Guide of the Perplexed,* pt. 1, chap. 71, and *Derekh Emunah* by the fifteenth-century Abraham Bibago. See *Sefer Moreh ha-Nevukhim,* ed. Yehudah ibn Shmuel (Jerusalem: Mosad ha-Rav Kook, 1959), 2:389f.; and see n. 21 above. Azariah introduces Maimonides' and Bibago's position later too (*M.E.* 2:481), although more in possible support of a colleague's opinion on the subject of Hebrew poetry than as a spontaneous expression of his own view. Cf. Baron, "Historical Method," 222, and n. 93. After all, Azariah merely reports—he does not necessarily concede—Judah Provençal's view that certain admirable features of poetic style that appear to have been borrowed from non-Jews really originated with the Jewish ancients. Different in any event from his first, straightforward reference to the idea of the Jewish origin of all knowledge is Azariah's mention of King Solomon's proverbial wisdom, which presumably should have obviated any need for recourse to non-Jewish experience (*M.E.* 1:86f.). This latter point, however, is less an affirmation by Azariah than a part of the objection he anticipates one might raise against non-Jewish sources—an objection he then proceeds to demonstrate is untenable. Cf. Baron, "Attitude to Life," 185, and n. 69. It is also not at all obvious from another passage (*M.E.* 2:264) that "Azariah even supposes that all true knowledge of every age is included in the Bible" (Baron, "Attitude to Life," 415 n. 69). What Azariah deals with here is the self-sufficiency of scripture as a source of moral guidance and instruction as opposed to Livy's notion of the moral utility of history (see pp. 27ff. above).

44. *M.E.* 2:399f. Azariah refers to the *Letter of Aristeas* and the works of Philo and Josephus. That he mistakenly believes Aristeas to have been a gentile is irrelevant in this context; on the contrary, it reinforces his argument in favor of using non-Jewish materials. What he stresses here is that since *God* has granted contemporaries the good fortune of having recovered such works, gentile or Jew-

ish, "the spirit of both God and that of *rational-minded persons* will take delight" in their utilization to resolve certain doubtful historical issues (emphasis added). Azariah's adaptation of the mishnaic phrases "ruaḥ ha-beriyot" and "ruaḥ ha-maqom" (Mish. Avot 3:13) is noteworthy.

45. *M.E.* 1:81, 82f. Even Azariah must realize that the permission given in the Palestinian Talmud that "he who reads the books of Homer and all other books that were written beyond that [beyond scripture] is considered like one who is reading a secular document" (J. Sanhedrin 10:1) referred only to religiously innocuous works and could not possibly have included heretical or Christian ones. The *M.E.* is of course replete with references to all manner of the latter. See Saul Lieberman, "The Alleged Ban on Greek Wisdom," in *Hellenism in Jewish Palestine* (New York: Jewish Theological Seminary, 1950), 108ff., for the interpretation of the Yerushalmi passage. That Azariah does not take "sifrei Hamiros" to refer to the works of Homer (cf. *M.E.*, 1:83f.) does not affect the substance of the issue here. The opinion of Rabbi Akivah in Mish. Sanhedrin 10:1 that the reading of "outside books" causes one to forfeit his share in the world to come refers, according to an explanatory *baraita* in the Babylonian Talmud, to heretical or sectarian works ("sifrei ṣeduqim," B. Sanhedrin 100b; but cf. the variant "sifrei minim" in Raphael Rabbinovicz, *Diqduqei Soferim* [Munich: 1867–1886], 9:152; and cf. Hanokh Albeck, *Shishah Sidrei Mishnah,* Seder Neziqin [Jerusalem: Mosad Bialik, 1953], 202, and supplementary nn., 454). The medieval talmudic compendiums of Isaac Alfasi (p. 19b), and Rabbi Asher (p. 119b) elaborate this *baraita* as referring to works incorporating heretical elements that interpret scripture according to their own understanding rather than that of rabbinic tradition. In Alfasi's version even the initial proscription against Ecclesiasticus (Wisdom of Ben Sira) is because it too is comparable to heretical works ("nami ke-sifrei minim damei"). Various materials that Azariah utilizes, including Christian ones, which is what the phrase "sifrei minim" may originally have meant or included, certainly fall into this "heretical" category, despite his effort to dissociate at least his specific "outside" citations from the strictures of the *baraita* (*M.E.* 1:81. Azariah refers to the passage in B. Sanhedrin as Tosefta, but it is not in our text of that rabbinic work). Both Alfasi and R. Asher moreover forbid even the "commendable things" in such heretical works, whereas Azariah adopts the opposite opinion. And he quite arbitrarily subsumes this opinion under the talmudic concession that "the fine things" in Ecclesiasticus may be expounded, a concession made only with reference to that apocryphal work. The unlimited application given it by Azariah has no basis in the talmudic source (B. Sanhedrin 100b; and cf. *M.E.* 1:85).

46. *M.E.* 1:82f. There is, for example, no substance to Azariah's parallel between his "incidental" use of non-Jewish sources and the talmudic sages' recourse to heretical works on pagan worship in order to regulate Jewish religious behavior. To invoke Maimonides' use of such materials for purposes of clarifying Jewish philosophical outlook and religious opinion is perhaps a more relevant parallel (*M.E.* 1:85f.).

47. *M.E.* 1:83f.; and see the Ritba passage as given in Jacob ibn

Habib, *'Ein Ya'aqov,* B. Bava Batra 98b (Reprint. New York: Shulsinger Bros., 1944), which apparently was Azariah's source (see also Cassel, *M.E.* 1:83 n., regarding Ritba's novellae, and 3:152). Azariah's citations, especially from memory, were sometimes faulty (see Baron, "Azariah de' Rossi: A Biographical Sketch," in *History and Jewish Historians,* 170; idem, "Historical Method," 232; and Cassel, *M.E.* 1:xii, n. 1), but in this abbreviated quotation one wonders whether Azariah is likely to have forgotten Ritba's serious qualifications. Problematic too is Azariah's brief citation from a long responsum of the distinguished fourteenth-century Rivash (Isaac ben Sheshet Perfet) concerning the propriety of studying "Greek wisdom." Azariah uses Rivash to demonstrate that the only forbidden form of Greek wisdom consists of philosophical teachings contrary to the fundamental doctrines of Judaism, and Azariah himself presumably never invokes any doctrinally offensive authors (*M.E.* 1:84f.). The philosophical issues aside, however, Rivash specifically repeats Rabbi Akivah's prohibition (see n. 45 above) against the very reading of "outside books" not, Rivash adds, merely belief in them. Rivash moreover quotes in his own responsum an earlier one attributed to Hai Gaon, to which Azariah also briefly refers. One version of Hai's text concludes: "The fear of heaven and of sin, and zealousness, humility, purity, and holiness can only be found among those who engage in the study of Mishnah and Talmud *along with wisdom, not in matters of wisdom alone."* As recorded by Rivash and others, however, the italicized words are deleted, in effect representing a virtual rejection of Greek wisdom, a view that hardly strengthens Azariah's position. Rather, the shortened text reinforces the main thrust of Rivash's responsum, to emphasize the autonomous authority of Jewish tradition in doctrinal matters: "ve-khatvu be-sifreihem she-ein yedi'ah shelemah raq otah she-hi' mi-ṣad ha-ḥaqirah . . . va-anaḥnu meqabblei ha-emet da'atenu sheha-Torah shelanu shelemah . . . ve-khol ḥaqiratam efes va-tohu le-'erkah." It is virtually certain that Rivash would have found the *Me'or 'Einayim*—albeit a historical rather than philosophical inquiry—incompatible with his insistence on the integrity of the tradition. See *She'elot u-Teshuvot Rivash* (Vilna, 1805), 20, responsum 45; for the same text of Hai's responsum, see Ibn Habib, *Ha-Kotev,* in *'Ein Ya'aqov,* Ḥ agigah 14b; and see the fourteenth-century polemical letters collected by Abba Mari ben Moses Astruc, *Minḥat Qena'ot* (Reprint, Israel, 1967), 128f, 166f. Ibn Habib reports he copied Hai's responsum from a work in the possession of a "God-fearing scholar" from Catalonia. The fuller text is found in B. M. Lewin, ed., *Oṣar ha-Ge'onim,* Ḥagigah (Jerusalem: Hebrew University Press Assoc., 1931), 65f. Heinrich Graetz, (*Divrei Yemei Yisra'el*, trans. S. P. Rabinowitz [Warsaw, 1894], 4:9f., 424ff.) finds the entire responsum contrary to Hai's philosophical spirit and considers it inauthentic. However, Baron, (*Social and Religious History*, 8:27, 68, 311 n. 22) notes that Hai was "a moderate rationalist" and that the responsum in question, although not written by him, represents a widely held view "among the most influential and representative Jews" regarding the presumed danger of philosophical speculation. Azariah, in any event, was apparently unaware of the fuller text of the responsum, which would have served his purposes far better. He nevertheless tends to interpret Hai's position as much more rationalist than the facts warrant (see *Maṣref la-Kesef,* 101; cf. Baron, *Social and Religious History* 8:27, 68, 311, 6:176f.; and see below, p. 91.).

48. *M.E.* 1:88.

49. See Menahem Elon, *Ha-Mishpat ha-'Ivri* (Jerusalem: Magnes Press, 1973), 1:229f.; and Chaim Tchernowitz, *Toledot ha-Halakhah,* 2d ed. (New York: Jubilee Committee, 1945), 1:19–22, 2:101–106, for an analysis of the prophetic role in the formulation of halakhah. And see *Maṣref la-Kesef,* 102f., and *M.E.* 2:267f., regarding the status of prophets.

50. *M.E.* 1:88f., 216. Biblical citations here follow the new Jewish Publication Society translation. Gans (*Ṣemaḥ David,* ed. H. Hominer [Jerusalem: Hominer Publications, 1966], 91) utilizes Azariah's argument and some of his "proof" texts, but also adds Esther 10:2, which is perhaps more relevant than all the others in what it relates, but is not an "endorsement" of the kind that Azariah seeks in scripture.

51. *M.E.* 1:84. The text of the proposed ban, preserved by the eighteenth-century R. Hayyim David Azulai in his *Maḥziq Berakhah,* is quoted and discussed by Zunz, "Toledot Rabbi Azariah," 9. It is also cited by the seventeenth-century bibliophile Abraham Graziano of Modena who was perhaps Azulai's source, as suggested in the brief but informative discussion by David Tamar, *Meḥqarim be-Toledot ha-Yehudim be-Ereṣ Yisra'el uve-Iṭalyah* (Jerusalem: Reuven Maas, 1970), 109f. See too the Graziano manuscript material published earlier by S. J. Halberstam, "Sheloshah Ketavim 'al Devar Sefer *Me'or 'Einayim*," in *Festschrift zum achtzigsten Geburstage Moritz Steinschneider's* (Leipzig: Otto Harrassowitz, 1896), Hebrew section, 3f. Azariah himself once expresses concern that the scholars in Turkey and adjacent lands, especially those in Safed with their mystical preoccupation, might react negatively to his work, precisely because they were unaccustomed to acknowledge gentile intellectual achievement (*Maṣref la-Kesef*, 120, and his n. to 137, following the text of *Maṣref la-Kesef* and *Ṣedeq 'Olamim.* The pagination here is confused, as Cassel notes in his corrections, p. 178). Baron ("Historical Method," 213) suggests on the basis of the comment in *Maṣref la-Kesef* that "Azariah must have heard something about that hostile plan" to ban his book. The "hostile plan," to be sure, did not gain acceptance as such in Italian Jewish communities; nor does Zunz appear to have been correct in stating that the Mantuan rabbis disallowed the reading of *M.E.* before the age of twenty-five (see Halberstam, p. 2 n. 1). But as the documents published by Kaufmann make eminently clear, beginning in 1574 access to *M.E.* was restricted in a string of communities and required rabbinic authorization. This partial ban, in which Mantua did not participate, was in effect at least as late as 1635 (see Kaufmann, "Contributions," 78f., 80f., 83ff., 87; and idem, "La défense de lire le *Me'or Enayim* d'Azaria dei Rossi," *Revue des études juives* 38 [1899]: 280f.).

CHAPTER 5

On Behalf of the Enlightened Reader: Pursuit of Truth and Historical Refinement of Tradition

The supports that Azariah assembles from the Bible and from early and later medieval rabbinic tradition to justify certain of his scholarly procedures are contrived and uncompelling. Realizing that his work would be uncongenial to the many for whom the standard Jewish classics were the only legitimate source of authority and intellectual pursuit, he obviously deemed it necessary to use traditional or quasi-traditional points of departure to allay hostility. Furthermore, Azariah actually directed his efforts at a different, more open-minded audience. The intellectual priorities and purposes that are presupposed in the *Me'or 'Einayim* may be gauged from the fact that throughout the work he calls specifically upon the "enlightened" reader (*qore' maskil*) to consider his line of inquiry, distinguishing this reader from those whom he considers obscurantists or even intellectually deficient. He looked to a readership that included the "wise of heart," "the enlightened of upright heart," whose criticisms he welcomes, and "the discerning reader," "the intelligent" (as opposed to the fools), "those endowed with understanding," "those scholars too fastidious to swallow whatever is put before them," "the rational beings," "the enlightened alone and those who perceive the nature of this investigation." By contrast there are those whom he characterizes as unsophisticated, closeted men, as perverse fools, and in a most extreme expression of contempt, those who suffer from intellectual delusion and indolence.[1]

In both a rhymed preface and a conclusion, he describes the *Me'or 'Einayim* as a gift intended solely for *men of truth*, and he adjures all others, whom he describes as "fools, hypocrites, and those clothed in lies," not to touch this work, "for they would bite at it like the snakes." Azariah obviously knows the temper of the age and anticipates—indeed had already encountered—resistance and opposition to his scholarly endeavor. He would otherwise have no reason to introduce at the very outset the language of scathing prophetic satire in which, paraphrasing Isaiah, he repudiates "those who rave confusedly as they lie sprawling and delight in slumber" at least until they are capable of acknowledging the elements of truth in his work.[2] The poetic format of these introductory lines is not mere prefatory adornment in which Azariah tries his hand at Hebrew versification before getting down to the serious subject matter of his essays. Nor is his apprehension and antagonism toward prospective opponents without foundation. For within a few years he would have occasion to complain about the "persecution by ill-disposed hypocrites," coreligionists in fact, whose activity had jeopardized his ability to finance personally the publication of the *Me'or 'Einayim*.[3]

The divergence between Azariah and his more conventionally minded contemporaries is especially striking from the tone of his criticism in the preliminary discussion and defense of the use of non-Jewish sources: "Let not our approach seem strange to the man who has a brain in his head. . . . But as for the simpleton or hypocrite whose only interest is the exclusive study [of the talmudic law] of torts, in order that he may achieve fame or material gain, let him not lay his hands on this work of mine for I have not intended it for him . . . even though it may be assumed that the latter type are far more numerous than the former."[4] It is not that Azariah rejects talmudic learning; it is often central to his scholarship, and he is able to draw on it with great self-assurance. He refers to the rabbinic sages of antiquity with the deep respect normally accorded them by Jewish authors, frequently invokes their opinion, and is a loyal adherent of talmudic law and doctrine. He even attempts, as we have seen, to justify his own scholarly endeavor on quasi-traditional grounds although he knows full well that the *Me'or 'Einayim* is in no sense Torah, that indeed the study of Torah in its traditional sense is no longer for him the only or necessarily the primary area of intellectual concern. Yet the very chapter that uses talmudic and other halakhic sources to argue the primary case in favor of utilizing non-Jewish materials echoes in addition a type of critique of the exclusive study of talmudic law that had already been expressed by Jewish spokesmen such as Maimonides. But whereas they had been critical of the exclusion of philosophical study, which they viewed as vital to the proper understanding and realization of Judaism,[5] the Jewish intellectual concerns that Azariah addressed were different. They concerned primarily the refinement of historical perception, the general response to which, in Azariah's age, was at least as uncongenial as to philosophical rationalism.

Azariah's departure from the conventional Jewish intellectual posture and those who uphold it finds expression too in the debate over his analysis of the chronological system reckoned from creation. For when "certain of those cloaked in religious authority"—Azariah does not identify them—had become barely aware of this study, their ire was immediately aroused and opposition was signaled. Azariah notes caustically that, without bothering to familiarize themselves with the subject matter and his justification of it,

> they gave precedent to the mouth over the eye and complained and aroused protest against me. They declared that any exposure of conflicting opinion and dispute in whatsoever matter received from our sages—whether its source be Sinaitic or any other in time and origin, and all the more so where interpretation of some scriptural verses is involved contrary to that of the sages—constitutes undermining of the faith and heresy.

Azariah's response is that since the study in question involves no binding religious laws, his opponents are guilty of inflating the issue entirely out of proportion in the eyes of the multitude. In the context of this issue too, he refers disparagingly to those "*among the common herd of talmudists*" (emphasis added) who injudiciously vent their anger because they may imagine disagreement with the talmudic chronological tradition to be tantamount to heresy. So, too, several years later, in his supplementary treatise on the issue of the chronology, *Maṣref la-Kesef*, he distinguishes between the "reflective scholars," for whose reasoned judgment he respectfully expresses regard, and those, obviously his opponents, given to what he perceives as a perverse, destructive, and unbalanced way of thinking.[6]

This was a difficult time for Italian Jewry. The maintenance of Torah study was at best becoming more difficult,[7] and many perceived the preservation of the integrity of the tradition as dependent upon a closing of cultural ranks. But despite his strong personal Jewish loyalties, Azariah was not prepared to concede his avenues of investigation. Instead, he reproached the opposition for intellectual insensitivity to problematic issues in the rabbinic tradition, for hostility toward efforts such as his own to deal with them through unconventional methods and sources, and for hypocrisy. This appears to suggest that contemporary talmudists may have been aware of the thorny issues raised by Azariah, but they were not intellectually honest enough to admit them.

He was apparently faulted: (1) because of the disclosure of error in the traditional chronology and (2) because of the consequences for the masses. Such disclosure brought with it grave religious culpability, and the masses, in learning of such error, might consequently be disposed to take liberties in other matters. Undeterred, Azariah responded to this charge brought by an unidentified "friend," an "upright man from among the scholars of our generation." He argued that one may take exception only to disclosure of the matter in public discourse but not in book form intended for the enlightened. And should some among the masses and "those who sit at street corners devoid of knowledge and understanding" happen to learn something of the issues in question, it would be necessary to divert them with appropriate arguments. In other words Azariah, too, was sensitive to the unsettling effect that the critique of any long established aspect of the tradition could have for Jewish religious culture as a whole. His advice for allaying any doubts among the populace was to emphasize that Jewish religious practice was in conformity with the authoritative opinion of the ancient sages.[8]

The implication of this of course is that even when an examination of the documentary record reveals factual discrepancies concerning its origins and crystallization, the integrity of any customary usage is for practical purposes guaranteed by virtue of its enactment and endorsement by the rabbinic sages. However, regardless of the precautions necessary with respect to the general populace, Azariah insisted that the enlightened individual would not refrain from freely expressing views intended to benefit discerning persons simply out of concern that fools might be disposed to act rashly. He admonished the latter to "go the way of the wise and acquire wisdom,"[9] meaning in effect that they too must learn to compartmentalize their thinking as part of the process of religious and intellectual sophistication.

We have here a striking dichotomy between, on the one hand, the obligation to subscribe loyally to established and sanctioned religious usage such as the reckoning of the age of the universe and the calendrical system and, on the other hand, the conviction that the chronological foundations on which such usage rests are faulty. In this instance the foundations in question had been conditioned by the historical situation in the talmudic period, described by Azariah as combining existing "knowledge" of the old and widely accepted Seleucid chronology; a "selection" of established rabbinic chronological computations; and "necessity" imposed by various chronological uncertainties such as the duration of the Second Jewish Commonwealth under Persian rule.[10] Azariah categorically rules out the notion of a providentially inspired and prophetically transmitted chronological tradition. Although this suggestion had already been made by various earlier authorities and biblical commentators, he marshals and analyzes all the available evidence to develop it into a major thesis. Several times he underscores that existing calendrical calculations and usage had in fact not become known through a process proceeding "from the prior to the latter like a prophetic message, or all at once in the manner of 'the heavens being opened' [i.e., like the revelation in Ezek. 1:1], but rather [through investigation] beginning with the latter and going back to the prior as [is the method in examining] every branch of *human* knowledge" (emphasis added).[11]

This is like many assertions in the *Me'or 'Einayim* that underscore its historical perspective and consequently challenge traditions that the vast majority of Azariah's contemporaries still considered timeless, sacred, and not susceptible to historical analysis. Such assertions provide some insight into the implications of Azariah's thinking and the possible impact of his formulations on enlightened—or even popular—public opinion, at least as perceived by his opponents. Little wonder then that the text of the *Me'or 'Einayim* mirrors the crystallization of opposition to Azariah's views even before its publication[12] and the developing tensions between the author and those whom he rejects at the outset as being incapable in their present intellectual state of appreciating his efforts. For all the criticism, he always insisted, undoubtedly sincerely, on the binding nature of traditional usage and his personal loyalty to it.

The negative response of the "unsophisticated" is not surprising, especially when one considers that even the distinguished talmudist, scholar, and in some respects liberal-minded Moses Provençal of Mantua reacted with consternation to his friend's historically inspired line of reasoning in this matter of the chronology and sought to counter it with theological affirmation. In a formally prepared objection he vigorously argued the case for the certainty of the calendrical system "in that it had been handed down to Moses at Sinai or even prior to him to Adam and Noah, one shepherd having given it to all of them."[13] And even Provençal's highly cultured rabbinical colleague in Mantua, Judah Moscato, perhaps the Jewish scholar who most closely approximated the Renaissance ideal of the *uomo universale*,[14] expressed serious and, once again, fundamentally theological reservations in this matter. For all of Azariah's efforts to explain the problematic talmudic disposition of the chronological issue in the most reasonable and respectful manner, Moscato feared that the very fact of the investigation was more likely to serve the cause of doubt than of enlightenment. Maimonides had already observed, Moscato reminded his friend, that "if a man claims that he sets out to demonstrate a certain point by means of sophistical arguments, he does not, in my opinion, strengthen assent to the point he intends to prove, but rather weakens it and opens the way for attacks against it. For when it becomes clear that those proofs are not valid, the soul weakens in its assent to what is being proved." Moscato endorsed Maimonides' preference "that a point for which there is no demonstration remain a problem or that one of the two contradictory propositions simply be accepted."[15] Azariah might have been able to accept this position as a guide to practical religious usage or in a philosophical analysis of Judaism such as that of Maimonides. But it could not serve him in his search for historical truth. At the very least he did not agree that his own arguments were sophistical—his very high regard for Maimonides and Moscato notwithstanding.

For Azariah historical investigation had a dual function. On one important level he simply valued the encounter with and the clarification of historically problematic issues, texts, and traditions. He maintained the desirability of the continued accumulation of data and the clarification of subject matter even when it did not serve any practical purpose. Its value lay instead in increasing the power of discernment and analysis in all areas requiring rational perception.[16] Even where the conclusions reached in certain areas of historical investigation were in dispute, Azariah viewed the process itself as serving the commendable purpose of sharpening the intellectual powers of the audience.[17]

Historical study is a search for truth per se.[18] According to Azariah, the quest for truth has an inherent, independent value and is to be nurtured. Truth, after all, is the mark of the divine and the trait of the cultured individual as well. The latter, for whom tranquillity of mind consists of truth and justice, suffers incalculable perplexity from deceit, attributable for example to falsified texts. That the mind finds delight in truth is itself a reliable testimony to it.[19]

All this is not yet the modern ideal of the disinterested search for facts, but it begins to approximate the desire to understand the past for its own sake in a spirit akin to that of the seventeenth-century Christian *érudits*. Azariah, for example, might conclude after a detailed study of problematic rabbinic narratives that such investigation is of no consequence since it deals with matters long past and has no bearing on religious practice. Significantly, however, he adds here (as in a later analysis of well-known works that suffered textual corruption) that the cultured person seeks to ascertain truth irrespective of the area of study under consideration, even where the issues are personally irrelevant to him or the historical source being considered, like *Josippon*, is "nonessential" (i.e., in contrast to vital Jewish religious classics).[20] The theoretical inquiry attracts Azariah not only because it leads to abstract truth but also because it provides sheer intellectual pleasure and gratification.[21] Azariah sidesteps the issue of whether from the rabbinic point of view the Jewish scholar might allow himself such useless leisure to the implicit neglect of the study of the Law.

But for Azariah historical study clearly serves an additional function as well, one related to and as vital as the pursuit of truth but one that goes beyond it and is implicit in his reference to every matter requiring a rational outlook.[22] He deems it necessary to provide a historically precise and rationally acceptable formulation of those aspects of the Jewish tradition that he considers open to critical investigation. He rarely discusses what may be described as the historical foundations of the halakhic or juristic aspects of Jewish religious culture; but in one notable instance he deals with that category of talmudic traditions known as "law dating from Moses as delivered from Sinai." Several medieval commentators preceded Azariah in suggesting that talmudic laws for which there is no biblical warrant and that are described in the Talmud as "given to Moses at Sinai" are not necessarily all to be viewed as literally so. Azariah does not refer to these predecessors in his lengthy excursus on this matter, perhaps in order to allow himself greater freedom in his own more expansive analytical and explicit discussion. Aware that contemporary "Torah scholars" might not be receptive to his views, Azariah's analysis nonetheless reflects his historical sensitivity to the fact that at times the talmudic sages conferred Sinaitic status on certain usages (with the intention of indicating their great antiquity or some similar consideration) for which the evidence was dubious at best. He assumes that the use of the talmudic phrase in the case of subject matter that does not otherwise compel a literal meaning is purely metaphorical or may represent an effort by the ancient sages to strengthen and magnify the significance of their assertions—particularly in matters destined to spread among the masses.[23] Given the very sensitive doctrinal nature of this question, what undoubtedly spared Azariah exposure to attack and acrimony was the fact that these views appear in his *Maṣref la-Kesef*, which was destined to remain long unpublished.[24]

But as is to be expected in an age when both Jewish and Christian culture and society were still permeated by traditional authority, Azariah otherwise excludes the Mosaic and halakhic components of Judaism from historical investigation. This results from his belief in their Sinaitic authority. It needs to be emphasized that in matters perceived to be divinely mandated tradition or manifestations of the supernatural, Azariah is no more "medieval" than his non-Jewish Renaissance predecessors and contemporaries. For while stressing the human role within the historical process, they too have not yet dispensed with the belief in divinely revealed scripture, nor even fully with the notion of divine rule or intervention in profane history. Unless one makes a facile association between Renaissance and enlightenment and posits a narrow, no longer tenable Burckhardtian conception of the Renaissance, it is impossible to ignore the "medieval" character of much sixteenth-century thought. Divine intervention, prodigies, and the role of the inscrutable in human affairs, for example, become rarer but by no means disappear in the historiography of the Italian humanists. And in virtually all the works of the period, including at times those of the leading minds, one encounters signs of the most extreme credulity: monsters, apparitions, divine or diabolic omens, miraculous events, and foretelling of future ones.[25] For example, Azariah's French contemporary Jean Bodin authored both the *Heptaplomeres* with its attack on orthodox Christianity, and the *Démonomanie des sorciers* in which he sought to prove the existence of sorcery from the many laws made against it by God and man. And his celebrated *Methodus*, although the most thoughtful sixteenth-century book on history, nevertheless reflects a frame of mind characteristic of the entire period, which was midway between the medieval and the modern. In Bodin's perception, the role of the divine like that of the natural is constant in the course of man's history and he appears to have moved ultimately to the view that prediction or control of the course of history transcends human capacity.[26]

It is in the context of such intellectual incongruities of the age that for Azariah de' Rossi the "medieval" scheme of talmudic law and doctrine remains authoritative and certain folkloristic conceptions remain valid, even while he simultaneously develops a scholarly rationalism intended to open up significant dimensions of the Jewish tradition to investigation. In introducing the criterion of truth as a touchstone in examining Jewish literary sources such as the rabbinic aggadah, Azariah attempts to bring the past close enough so that its historical flaws and inconsistencies may be revealed, clarified, and rectified and even its conflicts with the realities of nature rationally analyzed and explained. He resolutely seeks acceptable accounts of particular events, existing versions of which are conflicting, or of widely accepted traditions that are historically indefensible. This determination derives from his conviction that the words of the rabbinic sages, especially in cases of well-known circumstances, should be free of contradiction and error and that accuracy ought to be the hallmark of the works Jews read. By the traditional criterion of relevance to law and commandments, such "trifling investigations" (as Azariah sometimes makes his studies out to be) are inconsequential. But insofar as a major objective of such studies is that "the works read by us contain nothing deceptive, but only true words honestly recorded,"[27] what is ostensibly trifling in fact constitutes the most serious and impressive scholarly undertaking. When Azariah adapts the prophetic expression that "a deceitful tongue shall not be in their mouths" (Zeph. 3:13) to the need for integrity in the sources, he implies that the erroneous and the credulous left unchallenged and perpetuated as fact constitutes deception and brings the rabbinic classics and the authorities for whom they speak into disrepute. Thus, the rabbinic sources need to be purged of their historically fallacious, even misleading, elements by discovering what these sources mean in spite of what they say.[28]

Azariah's formulation of these issues is integrally linked with his perception of history as a matter of "secular affairs," which, unlike scripture and the halakhah, gives expression to the human dimension of experience. He sees that for the talmudic sages the course of human events and the entire secular realm of experience, insofar as these have no implications for any Torah matter, were not deserving of thorough investigation either for the sages' own information or for the purpose of reporting such matters precisely for others.[29] To the extent that the sages devoted any time to theoretical affairs such as the narration of historical events or even to the interpretation of scripture unrelated to religious law, they did so, in Azariah's opinion, not in their capacity as expositors of authoritative religious tradition but merely as individuals engaged in purely human discourse, basing themselves on personal judgment or generally accepted knowledge. Consequently, one may entertain the possibility that there could be error in rabbinic narratives or that some narratives were simply invented for didactic purposes. Although Azariah views fallibility and incompleteness in the sages' accounts as something that should occasion no great surprise, he reiterates the point. For underlying his analysis is the belief that people are not accustomed to examine carefully the *modus operandi* of a matter in which they have no interest but simply pass it on as they themselves have received it.[30]

What further complicated the historical record in rabbinic literature was its encounter with aggadah, the creative religious imagination of the sages. The purpose of such "invention" and "magnificent wisdom," as Azariah calls it, adapted to historical events or out of which historical narrative was imaginatively constructed, was to implant the awareness of God's omnipotence among the populace. Azariah asserts that the sages often embellished their narratives with hyperbole intended to lead the multitude to a heightened sense of wonder and amazement. Sophisticated individuals were expected to perceive from the imagery that it was merely a device and simile.[31] It seemed unlikely to Azariah that the contemporary multitude might make the transition from what he implies is the uninformed state of astonishment to the realization that the sages, as he once puts it, "did not intend to force down our throats" as literal truth everything they said. After all, even some whom Azariah himself considers learned and from among the maskilim persisted in being literalists.[32]

In advancing these criteria Azariah proposes to confront the historically inaccurate, textually divergent, or rationally offensive elements in the tradition with the intention of exposing the fictitious and that which is unreliable.[33] Such exposure considerably unsettles some of his contemporaries, but since it does not, in his view, conflict with any Jewish doctrinal constraints, he sees its positive potential as including the opportunity to enhance the intellectual integrity of the ancient rabbis. There is an intimation of what Azariah has in mind from virtually the first page of the *Me'or 'Einayim*, which declares that it is far preferable to bring the explanation of a historically problematic issue into bold relief so that how it is to be resolved may be understood "rather than have the unattended 'symptom of leprosy' continue to plague the enlightened."[34] He is concerned above all with the intellectual and religious integrity of these enlightened, invariably a minority amidst the much larger number of "the most brutish people."[35] For this minority who cannot accept the impossible,[36] the positive and practical function served by his scholarship is the reconstructing, with varying degrees of success, of some basic aspects of Jewish experience and expression on sounder factual, chronological, and intellectual foundations.

Sixteenth-century Jewish historical literature is characterized at one end of the spectrum by the effort to perfect further the chronicle of rabbinic authority and at the other by the desire to popularize the annals of Jewish and general history for Jewish householders. But overall it is dominated by concern with contemporary political vicissitudes and speculation about future redemption—and this amidst a cultural climate of proliferating mystical, pietistic, and messianic tendencies often accompanied by a metahistorical approach to even those dimensions of Jewish experience conditioned by historical circumstances. Azariah's undertaking is an "antiquarian" pursuit of truth per se but one that is simultaneously addressed to the present need as he perceives it. The need is that of the coreligionist who "drinks thirstily" the words of the sages but who is also endowed with human reason.[37] For that individual the historical dimension must be brought into line with what the rational sense will bear and with what accuracy demands, even as a theoretical issue of intellectual integrity.

Notes

1. *M.E.* 1:77, 89, 100, 2:365, 368, 345, 399f.; *Maṣref la-Kesef*, 121; see also 108f. n. In *M.E.* 2:364, Azariah distinguishes between what may be written for "the maskilim" but not taken up in oral discourse for fear that the populace (*hamon*) will misunderstand it. For the contrasting types, see *M.E.* 1:81, 2:365, 345. Azariah adopts the phrase "hozim shokhvim ohavei lanum" (1:77, 2:345) from Isa. 56:10, where the somewhat difficult wording apparently refers to the hazy thinking and indolence of the people's spiritual leaders. In any event, his choice of biblical idiom is surely not fortuitous, and he appears to be criticizing a contemporary type of Jewish religious spokesmanship that he finds intellectually objectionable. In analyzing the problems associated with the talmudic chronological computations, for example, he refers to those scholars (*seridim, M.E.* 2:345; and cf. B. Sanhedrin 92a, for the use of the term) who, not being "min ha-hozim shokhvim ohavei lanum," seek trustworthy explanations and will not settle for farfetched ones.

2. *M.E.* 1:77, 2:485. Azariah occasionally uses the term maskilim to refer to some among the learned who find his views religiously objectionable, but at least once the maskil in question is also called a "*holekh tamim* me-ḥakhmei dorenu." (My italics are intended to suggest that Azariah may mean "unsophisticated" rather than "upright." See below, n. 8). See *M.E.* 1:219, 2:356, 358.

3. See L. Modona, "Une lettre d'Azaria de Rossi," *Revue des études juives* 30 (1895): 315. This letter of 1576 was addressed to the abbot of the Montecassino congregation. See also the discussion in Joanna Weinberg, "Azariah dei Rossi: Towards a Reappraisal of the Last Years of His Life," *Annali della Scuola Normale Superiore di Pisa*, 3d ser., 8 (1978): 501f.

4. *M.E.* 1:89f. Azariah's concluding line as quoted here is then reinforced by a passage from Maimonides' introduction to the *Guide*. See the English version by Shlomo Pines (Chicago: University of Chicago Press, 1963), 1:16.

5. Azariah's negative reference to preoccupation with Nezikin (Torts) is very reminiscent of, or perhaps even inspired by, Abraham ibn Ezra's

statement, "ve-yesh hogeh ba-Talmud le-hitpa'er, 'a"k kol 'asaqav be-seder Neziqin gam hu' meqabbel sakhar le-horot ha-peta'im." *Yesod Morah* (Prague, 1833), 15b. Azariah certainly has in mind some of Maimonides' sentiments in the *Guide*, like the following: (1) "It is not the purpose of this Treatise to make its totality understandable to the vulgar . . . nor to teach those who have not engaged in any study other than the science of the Law—I mean the legalistic study of the Law" (Pines, 1:5); (2) the reference to "an ignoramus among the multitude of Rabbanites" for whom difficult midrashim present no problem "inasmuch as a rash fool . . . does not find impossibilities hard to accept" (Pines, 1:10). The thirteenth-century translator Samuel ibn Tibbon renders the first phrase as "sakhal me-hamon ha-rabbanim"; and cf. *M.E.* 2:303: "ezeh sheyiheyeh me-hamon ha-lamdanim." In his glossary of unusual words Ibn Tibbon explains *hamon* as synonymous with ignoramuses and the most inferior of humans, so called because they are in the majority. See *Sefer Moreh Nevukhim* (Reprint, Jerusalem, 1960), 6b, and 4b, col. a of the appendixes following pt. 3 of the text; (3) concerning "jurists who believe true opinions on the basis of traditional authority and study the law . . . but do not engage in speculation concerning the fundamental principles of religion" (Pines, 2:619). Shem Tov ben Joseph, the fifteenth-century commentator to the *Guide*, refers to the many talmudists ("rabim meha-ḥakhamim ha-rabbanim") who reacted vehemently against this chapter, which, he asserts, they did not at all understand (*Moreh Nevukhim*, pt. 3, p. 64b). See also Marc Saperstein, *Decoding the Rabbis: A Thirteenth-Century Commentary on the Aggadah* (Cambridge: Harvard University Press, 1980), 174–177, for a discussion of Isaac ben Yedaiah and others who attacked the neglect of philosophical study among talmudists.

6. *M.E.* 2:271, 303; *Maṣref la-Kesef*, 121. For Azariah's interesting adaptation of biblical imagery, cf. *M.E.* 2:271, and Judg. 20:38, 40.

7. See Moses A. Shulvass, *Ha-Yehudim be-Italyah*, pp. 272ff.

8. The title of *M.E.* 2, chap. 42 refers to this exchange between "the author and his friend regarding one who raises doubt in the matter of the years since creation according to our reckoning" (p. 356, and pp. 362, 364f., for the details of Azariah's argument; cf. *Maṣref la-Kesef*, 123). Toward the end of the chapter (pp. 366ff.), Azariah refers as well to "a great Italian [rabbinical] authority," again unidentified, before whom he had set forth his views on the chronology (Cassel [3:156] suggests that this may have been Moses Provençal of Mantua). Azariah reports that this individual, on the basis of only cursory familiarity with the outline of his thesis, asserted that all doubt in this matter—*and all the more so doubt based on the popular report of some chronicler or other*—was undeserving of consideration in the face of established talmudic opinion. One was always obliged to accept all the ancient sages' words as recorded and to believe in their superior wisdom as a matter of certainty—a position virtually identical with that of Provençal (emphasis added; see below, p. 122f.). This, as we shall later note more fully, is not Azariah's position on the matter of the "ancients" and the "moderns." Even here he is merely prepared to grant that the view of his antagonist may be appropriate for those who are truly "upright" (or does he mean naïve or

unsophisticated? "hineh *kol ha-tamin be-libo* . . . yehi me-eloheinu barukh uve-emunato yiḥyeh"; and cf. p. 356, "holekh tamim," and p. 295, "ki-devar qeṣat ha-temimim"), and who, without "hypocrisy and flattery," are prepared to accept the dicta of the ancient sages implicitly. Another contemporary, Abraham Menahem ha-Kohen Porto of Cremona (see Chap. 4, n. 26 above) reports of Azariah that "he whispered this evil thing [i.e., the critique of the traditional chronology] in my ear while I was in Mantua."

9. *M.E.* 2:365.

10. Ibid., 344.

11. Ibid., 2, chap. 35, esp. p. 305, for "min ha-me'uḥar el ha-qodem ke-khol mada' enoshi," and p. 309, for the same formulation, in part. See also p. 339, where Azariah reacts with irony to the suggestion in Isaac Israeli's fourteenth-century treatise on calendar calculation, *Yesod 'Olam*, that the chronological computations may have been prophetically inspired. He endorses Israeli's alternative view that the computations were "revealed" to the ancients in the course of "their investigation," but for Azariah this of course entirely precludes revelation in any conventional sense, "human investigation" being, as he explains it, a process that traces back from the established situation of the latter moment in time to what were conceivably its origins at a prior moment in time. For further critique of what Azariah deems the confusion and error in Israeli's views of the origins of the calendrical tradition, cf. *Maṣref la-Kesef*, 87ff.

12. Baron has noted Azariah's anticipation of his opponents' criticism but emphasizes Azariah's "pervasive sense of insecurity" ("Azariah de' Rossi's Historical Method," in *History and Jewish Historians* [Philadelphia: Jewish Publication Society, 1964], 232f., and n. 161). If Azariah was quite so insecure, and so "timid" in his love for truth (Baron, "Azariah de' Rossi's Attitude to Life," in *History and Jewish Historians*, 174) the *Me'or 'Einayim* is the least likely kind of work he would have undertaken given the Jewish cultural climate of the later sixteenth century. He was obviously keenly aware of the cultural and dogmatic constraints with which he had to function. But the cautious posture that this awareness sometimes, even often, led him to assume is virtually offset by the conviction, even by the tiring repetitiveness itself, with which he argued some of his most unconventional and criticized views. For example, that "he allotted so much space to his chronological studies because he anticipated violent opposition on this score" (Baron, "Historical Method," 234) is at the same time a significant testimony to his determination to demonstrate their validity. Indeed, in his supplementary treatise on the traditional chronology and calendrical system, *Maṣref la-Kesef*, and the separate detailed response, *Ṣedeq 'Olamim*, to the sharp critique of Isaac Finzi of Pesaro, Azariah is undaunted in reiterating and reinforcing some of the most vigorously disputed opinions previously asserted in the *Me'or 'Einayim*. That *Maṣref la-Kesef* and *Ṣedeq 'Olamim*, although completed in 1575 (see *Maṣref la-Kesef*, 122), remained in manuscript until the nineteenth century was, even as Baron observes, "not part of his design" ("Historical Method," 237). The tone and language here clearly suggest that Azariah intended to publish this material too. Financial diffi-

culties and poor health would appear to explain best why it was not. (See *Maṣref la-Kesef*, 121, for his reference to his precarious physical condition; and cf. Weinberg, "Azariah dei Rossi," 496f., 510f.).

13. See Provençal's *Hasagah* (dated 1573), 492, following the text of *M.E.*, where he also argues the validity of the calendrical system on the grounds that various other Jewish traditions have authoritative status although no seer or prophet makes reference to them either. Cf. Azariah's long response to the *Hasagah*, 2:496–506. The Geonim Saadya and Hai had already affirmed the Mosaic antiquity of the calendrical system. See Baron, *Social and Religious History*, VIII, 205f., and 378, n. 72.

14. Isaac Barzilay, *Between Reason and Faith: Anti-Rationalism in Italian Jewish Thought, 1250–1650* (The Hague: Mouton, 1967), 167.

15. See David Kaufmann, "Contributions à l'histoire des luttes d'Azaria de Rossi," *Revue des études juives* 33 (1896): 77f., and 82 of the appended text of Moscato's response to Azariah, regarding chap. 35 of the *M.E.* For the Maimonides passage, see Pines, *Guide* 2:293.

16. *M.E.* 1:80.

17. Ibid. 2:367, where Azariah uses the talmudic idiom "le-ḥaded et ha-talmidim." See too the title page of *Maṣref la-Kesef.*

18. See pp. 31f. above.

19. *M.E.* 2:275f., 1:239, 244. Azariah's affirmation of study as an endeavor to track down truth is several times simultaneously described as an endeavor "for the sake of heaven," although in his formulation "truth," characteristically perhaps, precedes "heaven" (*M.E.* 1:197, 2:496, in his response to Moses Provençal's *Hasagah*).

20. *M.E.* 1:189, 234.

21. Ibid., 79ff., where this attention to intellectual gratification—sometimes analogically with physical gratification derived from nourishment—is several times repeated. Note the terms *'oneg, 'arvut, matoq la-nefesh, davar ṭov ve-neḥmad el ha-nefesh, ve-hit'aneg qeṣat 'oneg.*

22. Ibid. 1:80.

23. *Maṣref la-Kesef*, 105–109 n. In their respective commentaries to Mish. Yadayim 4:3, Asher ben Jehiel and Samson of Sens refer to the particular use of "halakhah le-Mosheh mi-Sinai" as "lav davka," although Samson adds that it is only *like* a law given to Moses at Sinai. However, the wording of the parallel passage in the Tosefta that Samson quotes leads him to observe that as a logical conclusion from that text, the law in question should be understood as literally (*mamash*) of Sinaitic origin. Asher's view is briefly amplified in his *Hilkhot Mikva'ot*, following his commentary to B. Niddah ("davar barur ka-halakhah le-Mosheh mi-Sinai"); and cf. Chaim Tchernowitz, *Toledot ha-Halakhah*, 2d ed. (New York: Jubilee Committee, 1945), 1:29–32.

24. Two points are noteworthy. First is the concluding caution to the maskil regarding the limits within which this entire analysis applies. Second, since at least for some of the supposedly Mosaic traditions of Sinaitic origin that

he questions Azariah asserts that he can find no other confirmation of his views, he considers the issue still subject to resolution by future authorities (*Maṣref la-Kesef*, 109 n.). How sensitive was the issue that Azariah had in all this touched upon can be judged from the vigorous controversy engendered even in the nineteenth century and among central and western European Jewish spokesmen, by Zacharias Frankel's "positive-historical" approach to "halakhah le-Mosheh mi-Sinai." See his *Darkhei ha-Mishnah* (reprint; Warsaw, 1923), 20, 386; see also *Encyclopaedia Judaica* (1972), s.v. "Frankel, Zacharias"; Tchernowitz, *Toledot ha-Halakhah* 1:32f. Had they been seen in print by his contemporaries, Azariah's remarks would have been no less perceived as "a declaration of war against traditional Judaism" than were Frankel's. And even with Frankel, after all, there was still an "unclearness of thought and indefiniteness of expression concerning the term 'Sinaitic Tradition.'" See Louis Ginzberg, *Students, Scholars, and Saints* (Philadelphia: Jewish Publication Society, 1928), 207f.

25. See, for example, Myron P. Gilmore, *Humanists and Jurists*, (Cambridge: Harvard University Press, 1963), 46–53; Bernard Guénée, *Histoire et culture historique dans l'occident mediéval* (Paris: Aubier Montaigne, 1980), 209f.; Lucien Febvre, *Life in Renaissance France*, ed. and trans. Marian Rothstein (Cambridge: Harvard University Press, 1977), 38f.; and idem, *Le problème de l'incroyance au XVIe siècle: La religion de Rabelais* (Paris: Albin Michel, 1968), 414, and, on 392, his observations regarding even the most advanced thinkers of the age, those of the Italian school—Pomponazzi, Machiavelli, Cardan, Campanella. Febvre's *Problème de l'incroyance*, though published in 1942, remains indispensable for an understanding of the sixteenth-century *mentalité*, even if more recent work in the "popular culture" of early modern Europe makes some modifications of Febvre's study necessary. See, e.g., the critique (nonetheless acknowledging the legitimacy of Febvre's type of research) in Carlo Ginzburg, *The Cheese and the Worms: The Cosmos of a Sixteenth-Century Miller*, trans. J. and A. Tedeschi (New York: Penguin Books, 1982), xxiiif., 133f., 156, 160.

26. Jean Bodin, *Method for the Easy Comprehension of History*, trans. Beatrice Reynolds (Reprint, New York: Octagon Books, 1966), xi; Gilmore, *Humanists and Jurists*, 56f. Relative to the *Démonomanie*, see also Baron's description of Bodin ("Attitude to Life," 409 n. 29), the emphasis on the typically geocentric and anthropocentric outlook of the period, reflected in Azariah too (Baron, p. 179), the characterization of even the great humanists' reverence for ancient sources, since they viewed them as "authentic beyond doubt" (Baron, p. 410 n. 34). Yet Baron displays a pronounced emphasis regarding Azariah to the effect that "in all essentials he still belongs to the Middle Ages" (pp. 201f.). That in some matters of science Azariah is prepared to grant that there is some erroneous opinion in the Talmud, even Baron sees as "certainly . . . in Azariah's time, although less in Italy than elsewhere, a rather daring point of view which required no little courage" (p. 180). Yet, in Italy too, even someone like Moses Provençal adamantly rejects naturalists' views when in conflict with those of the ancient rabbinic sages. See, e.g., below pp. 122f., and n. 35. And it required no less courage

for Azariah to bring into question a good deal of historical information in the rabbinic sources. We should have to conclude from all this either that the "medievalism" of Azariah on many basic issues was much like that of the "great humanists" and that they, by the criteria set forth here, were equally "theocratically medieval" or that the "spirit of the Renaissance" itself was so saturated with "medievalism" that Azariah does not differ from the rest in many fundamental attitudes.

27. *M.E.* 1:182: "lo be'ad gufa' de'uvda' demai dehavah havah raq lemai deikhpat lan . . . shelo' yimaṣe'u divrei ḥakhameinu be-sippurim shel me'ora'ot mefursamot soterim zeh et zeh"; p. 189; and see *M.E.* 1:2 n. 1.

28. In discussing affirmations of Jewish distinctiveness in Renaissance Italy, Reuven Bonfil gives Azariah de' Rossi as a case in point and asserts that this concern is at the very heart of his historiographical effort. Azariah undoubtedly shared the sentiment regarding Jewish distinctiveness, but there is no indication that his study of the past was motivated by the desire to discover every possible suggestion of gentile acknowledgment of the preeminence of Jewish religious tradition. (See "Bituyim le-Yiḥud 'Am Yisra'el bi-Tekufat ha-Renesans," *Sinai* 76 [1974]: 39.) In support of his view, Bonfil cites a passage in which he presumes that Azariah "*attests that he had only labored out of the desire to find among* 'the ancient works . . . any observation whatsoever that relates to some matter in our Torah'": "*hu' he'id 'al 'aṣmo shelo' pa'al ela' mitokh ta'avah li-mṣo' betokh* 'hasefarim ha-qadmonim . . . eizo he'arah mityaḥeset le-shum davar mi-Toratenu.'" (I italicize Bonfil's formulation, which is followed by the quotation from *M.E.* 1:101. See also Bonfil, "Some Reflections on the Place of Azariah de Rossi's *Meor Enayim* in the Cultural Milieu of Italian Renaissance Jewry," in *Jewish Thought in the Sixteenth Century*, ed. B. D. Cooperman [Cambridge: Harvard University Press, 1983], 39, referring to the same passage.) But the context of the passage is in connection with the works attributed to Hermes Trismegistos, which Azariah, like Ficino, Patrizi, and others, believed to be authentic sources of ancient pagan wisdom (see, e.g., Cochrane, *Historians*, 441f.). In these Azariah finds affinities with and favorable disposition toward Hebrew scripture. Because of his "great desire for those ancient works" that have any bearing on Jewish religious tradition, Azariah hopes at a future date to translate Hermes' works into Hebrew, indeed for the glory of God's name. There is no suggestion in this statement concerning the motivating force in Azariah's historiographical studies, however it may address the issue of Jewish distinctiveness. In fact, Azariah indicates that he will undertake this translation after he has seen some sign of success with this present treatise (i.e., *Me'or 'Einayim*) so that the studies in *Me'or 'Einayim* are independent of whatever praiseworthy things one may conceivably find in these gentile works. Moreover, whatever in ancient works "relates to any matter in our Torah" is neither invariably complimentary nor a confirmation of Jewish spiritual superiority. Azariah's phrase, "eizo he'arah mityaḥeset le-shum davar mi-Toratenu," is neutral and does not per se imply that which is supportive of or that which places Jewish tradition in a superior light. Cf. a similar formulation in *M.E.* 1:83. Much of what Azariah found in the many ancient works he consulted was either in the nature of clarification of prob-

lematic or historically inaccurate traditions in the Jewish sources or more intellectually plausible criteria for assessing those sources (e.g., *M.E.* 1:3f., regarding the *Letter of Aristeas*, which Azariah at least believed had been written by a gentile author; 1:214, as he prepares to analyze the story of Titus' death; and 2:409f.).

29. *M.E.* 2:265.

30. See, e.g., *M.E.* 1:196f., 2:270f., and the reference to "milei de-alma'." Azariah reiterates: "ve-hu' ha-davar asher pe'amim rabot debbarti ki ba-sippurim shel milei de-alma' lo' yaḥushu he-ḥakhamim 'al shemirat pirteihem ya'an le-lamed 'al ha-klal belvad yaṣe'u" (1:246 n.). And see 2:266: "ki milta delo ramya' 'al benei adam ein darkan le-hitbonen bi-derakheha." (For the phrase "milta delo ramya 'alei de'inash," see, e.g., B. Shevu'ot 34b.)

31. *M.E.* 1:203, 212, 218f.; *Maṣref la-Kesef*, 108 n. Azariah's term, *hamṣa'ah*, to describe the "invention" or rhetorical device employed by the rabbinic sages in their aggadic narratives is apparently borrowed from Messer Leon's *Nofet Ṣufim*. See Alexander Altmann, "*Ars rhetorica* as Reflected in Some Jewish Figures of the Italian Renaissance," in *Essays in Jewish Intellectual History* (Hanover: University Press of New England, 1981) 107, on Leon's rendering of *inventio*, in Cicero for example, as *hamṣa'ah*, and p. 110, regarding Azariah's novel, if limited, reference to the classical rules of rhetorical art in analyzing aggadah: "In so doing he consciously followed in Leon's footsteps."

32. *Maṣref la-Kesef*, 108 n.; *M.E.* 1:217, 219.

33. He is persistent in scrutinizing various problematic historical traditions, in the course of which the reader is made most fully cognizant of the difficulties posed. There is, for example, the confused rabbinic reckoning of the line of high priests and of Persian rulers during the early Second Temple period. See, e.g., *M.E.* 2:312ff., 318f., 321: "tameha aḥi 'al 'aṣmekha hafle' va-fele' . . . ule-khol ha-panim . . . mi-peshaṭ ha-ketuvim nir'eh eikh maṣ'ah l"d ha-shanim shel Rabbi Yose qaṣar hu' me-histare'a bam kol malkhei Paras."

34. *M.E.* 1:2 n. 1. The thrust of Azariah's concluding comment to *M.E.*, chap. 14, p. 201, is rather similar: "*ve-tir'eni marḥiv ha-dibbur* . . . ka'asher le-dimyon ha-rofe' ha-ṭov hirḥavti maḥaṣ makato el qabbalat ha-refu'ot ve-hata'alah ha-nidreshet" (emphasis added).

35. *M.E.* 1:109.

36. See, e.g., ibid., 217.

37. Beyond the pursuit of truth for its own sake, Azariah's historical studies are a response to the intellectual dilemmas of enlightened coreligionists, dilemmas generated by a contemporary Jewish mood increasingly ill-disposed to concede any aspect of the ancient tradition to critical inquiry. In the chapter devoted to the rabbinic account of Titus's death, for example, he tells us that he does not intend a display of wisdom when he calls attention to talmudic narratives, such as those of Rabba bar Bar Ḥana, which are incomprehensible if taken literally. Their allegorical nature is well known to all but fools. "However since I have heard in this respect [of those], especially from among individuals whom I too consider learned in the Torah, who have affirmed their belief in these matters

exactly as recorded and have been vehement in their slander of those who do not believe it, I have argued the case for the benefit of the individual who drinks thirstily the words of our sages but is simultaneously drawn by human reason, as Maimonides has put it . . . for there is reason to be concerned that when he learns of the curse of Titus [i.e., the rabbinic account of his supposed affliction and death], or every similar acount, he will be appalled and astonished, unable to make himself believe it" (*M.E.* 1:216f.). Obviously concerned about the religious integrity of such individuals when confronted with an insistence upon a monolithic perception of the tradition, Azariah takes it upon himself to demonstrate that even classical Jewish authorities and sources cannot induce belief in the impossible or in what can be shown to be erroneous or inadequately documented.

PART TWO

CHAPTER 6

Azariah's Uses of the Past: Post-Talmudic Perceptions of Aggadah in the Me'or ʿEinayim

Azariah finds rabbinic aggadah especially in need of explication, since it often embodies historically or rationally problematic material. He reexamines the important issue of the religious authority of this nonlegal material and the question of whether it was invariably intended to be taken literally. He begins with the views of predecessors, notably from the geonic period and from among medieval Spanish and certain Italian Jewish spokesmen. These predecessors had tended to narrow the aggadah's scope of authority and to play down its literal meaning wherever this seemed doctrinally or rationally unacceptable. The underlying principle, already found in the Talmud and reasserted by such leading geonim as Sherira and Hai, was that aggadah did not constitute authoritative tradition from which one could derive normative rulings; one therefore did not rely on it. Sherira, for example, described aggadah as supposition or guesswork (*umdanah*), only acceptable when supported by reason and scripture.[1] His son Hai further refined the issue. He reaffirmed the general principle that "one does not rely on aggadah" but emphasized the special status of talmudic aggadic material as distinguished from aggadah in other rabbinic sources. If the former was found to be erroneous, one was obliged to resolve its difficulties wherever possible. Hai's argument was based on the premise that this aggadic material would not have been included in the Talmud in the first place if it did not embody some significant midrashic interpretation.[2] This suggests how highly Hai assessed talmudic authority despite his efforts to set limits on the status of its aggadic component.

In considering the seemingly contradictory attitude toward aggadah in the rabbinic sources themselves—highly praised but at times virtually damned—Azariah declares, "In truth what will get us out of this impasse is the true gaon Rav Sherira . . . and also his son who follows in his path, the gaon Rav Hai." He concludes from their opinions, the essence of which he reproduces, that "beyond any doubt the aggadot are not certain, authoritative norm but merely the supposition [*umdanah*] of *whoever invented it.*"[3] This reasonably approximates the words of the two geonim, although when Azariah then refers to "*every aggadah*" as mere supposition "in conformity with Rav Sherira's aforementioned statement,"[4] he tends to overstate the geonic position. One also senses here a far greater emphasis on fabrication regarding the nature of aggadah than in the formulations of the geonim.

With respect to the content of aggadah, Sherira, despite his general assumption that aggadah is mere supposition, sometimes displayed an innocence generally characteristic of his age. In his famous *Epistle* for example—which Azariah informs us he had the pleasure of consulting[5]—Sherira reported, apparently as fact, the talmudic account regarding the most unusual circumstances surrounding Rabbah bar Nahamani's death. Albeit in abbreviated form, it includes the aggadic reference to the "missive that fell from heaven" announcing that the sage Rabbah had been summoned to the heavenly academy. Without any qualification Sherira went on to refer his reader to "the story in its entirety, as explained in the gemara."[6] Even more striking is Sherira's description of "what we have heard from the early authorities and seen written in their chronicles" regarding the fifth-century Persian king Yazdegerd II. At the end of the talmudic period this ruler had forbidden the practice of the Jewish religion and was, according to Sherira's report, miraculously punished by a monstrous snake that swallowed him up as he lay on his bed.[7] These examples demonstrate that Sherira still lent credence to aggadah, even when it mixed history with legend. Azariah ignores these accounts and merely avails himself of the gaon's general principle, which he finds in sources other than Sherira's *Epistle*. He then appeals to this principle in confronting specific aggadot that he is not prepared to view either as bona fide tradition reaching back beyond talmudic times to "the sages of antiquity" or as "prophetic tradition."[8]

Hai had occasion to clarify the status of aggadah further when he took exception to the view of his father-in-law, the gaon Samuel ben Hophni, "and others like him who have extensively studied the works of the gentiles" and who consequently denied those rabbinic accounts that tell of pious scholars to whom visions are revealed and who perform miracles. Although not prepared to confer normative status on every tannaitic opinion, Hai urged the need to be aware that all the early authorities affirmed that God indeed performs miracles and wonders through the righteous as He had done through the prophets and that He reveals visions to them as He had to the prophets. For Hai, some miracles may have been projected, as it were, through a vision in the mind's eye. But when he referred to the firm belief of the early authorities in the miraculous events associated, for example, with the sage Hanina ben Dosa and others,[9] there can be hardly any doubt that Hai himself subscribed to such belief. Azariah therefore provides us with fuller insight into his own rather than Hai's perspective on the aggadah in suggesting that Hai's position was an expression of his pious concern for the religious sensitivities of the multitude but that he himself, as one of the "exceptional individuals," did not personally subscribe to those beliefs.[10]

Among later medieval Jewish authorities as well, there are those who leave some room for individual disposition but also insist on the validity of aggadah in even more inclusive terms than those specified by Hai. Jehiel of Paris, for example, in his version of the famous debate with the apostate Nicholas Donin in 1240, indicated that the aggadic element in the Talmud was less authoritative than the halakhic but went on to observe that in the aggadah there are extraordinary things

> [difficult] . . . for the impious, skeptic, and sectarian to believe and I have no need to respond to you concerning them. If you wish, believe them, and if you do not wish to, do not believe them, for they are not the basis of deciding any matter of law. Truly [however] I know that the sages of the Talmud wrote only those matters that are truthful and certain. And [if they seem] extraordinary to those that hear them, there are also many like them in scripture, such as the mouth of Balaam's donkey, the wife of Lot, who became a pillar of salt . . . the gourd of Jonah, which appeared overnight and perished overnight . . . and many more like them.[11]

Since there is no reason to suppose that Jehiel took biblical miracles figuratively, his analogy suggests the same for the aggadic ones: he took both equally literally. To be sure, there are aggadot that he considered hyperbole (*guzma'*) noting, as the Talmud had already observed, that scripture itself often used hyperbolic language.[12] But he explained further that others should or, at least he meant, could be taken literally in spite of Donin's derisive comments about them; these included the aggadah that Adam had been responsible for the birth of certain demons as a result of a liaison—unbeknown to him—with Lilith. Since the Bible did not account for the creation of these demons their existence could only be explained with reference to Adam, in accordance with the relevant aggadic exegesis of scripture.[13]

In the Barcelona disputation of 1263, Nahmanides used language similar to that of Jehiel in his response to the main Christian spokesman, Pablo Christiani. He defined the nature of midrash and its aggadic content, as distinguished from scripture and Talmud, and noted, "whoever believes in it, fine, and whoever does not believe in it, no harm is done."[14] But Nahmanides did not qualify his statement as Jehiel had done and thus seems entirely sincere in his declaration that the status of aggadah was nonobligatory. At the very least he was disposed to view the range of aggadic materials susceptible to nonliteral interpretation far more broadly than someone like Jehiel; there is no reason to think that he was masking his own sentiments in the interest of weakening Pablo Christiani's christological manipulation of aggadah.[15] Nahmanides' only apparent deviation from this position is encountered in one of his halakhic works, with respect to those aggadot that had implications for religious law and practice and that were therefore "not to be assigned to the category of metaphor and riddle."[16] Azariah does not mention Jehiel of Paris anywhere in the *Me'or 'Einayim*; he does refer with approval to Nahmanides' latitude of thought in the matter of aggadah, noting also the Spanish rabbi's reservation regarding those aggadic traditions in the Talmud itself that bear upon matters of religious law.[17]

Beyond the Babylonian geonim Sherira and Hai, Azariah enlists other authorities in support of a nonliteral approach to aggadah: Spanish scholars, notably Judah Halevi and the talmudists Solomon ibn Adret and Yom Tov ben Abraham Ishbili, and the North African talmudist Nissim Gaon, who maintained close relations with both Babylonia and Spain.[18] Such "men of understanding," Azariah tells us, confronted difficult rabbinic aggadot and stories from the point of view of reason "and sought to give it fitting meaning, 'like golden apples in silver showpieces.' "[19] The imagery from Proverbs 25:11 is undoubtedly intended to allude to Maimonides' use of this biblical verse in his exposition of the nature of prophetic parables. Maimonides writes in his *Guide* that when the sage declared that "a word fitly spoken is like apples of gold in settings of silver," he presumably was referring to the external and internal meaning of a saying. "When looked at from a distance or with imperfect attention, it is deemed to be an apple of silver; but when a keen-sighted observer looks at it with full attention, its interior becomes clear to him and he knows that it is of gold. The parables of the prophets . . . are similar."[20] Azariah is then suggesting that, both prior and subsequent to Maimonides, authorities like Nissim Gaon and Solomon ibn Adret also most appropriately treated rationally or doctrinally problematic aggadot as parables.

Indeed, Maimonides himself had even promised to write a work that would "explain all the difficult passages in the midrashim where the external sense manifestly contradicts the truth and departs from the intelligible. They are all parables." He concluded, however, after beginning this undertaking, that such a work did not commend itself since it was especially intended for "the vulgar"; and "if . . . we explained what ought to be explained it would be unsuitable for the vulgar among the people."[21] For Azariah the essence of Maimonides' unwritten work is nonetheless contained in his brief description of the difficult midrashim as "all parables." This description together with several other important discussions in the *Guide* and in the commentary to *Pereq Ḥeleq* constitute Maimonides' effort, as Azariah puts it, "to scorn those who believe in the *derashot* according to their literal meaning."[22] Although Maimonides gave relatively limited treatment to the subject—and despite what Azariah views as a not wholly harmonious relationship between Maimonides the sagacious author of the *Guide* and Maimonides the talmudic authority[23]—Azariah obviously looks upon him as a central figure in the postulation of a sophisticated and intellectually refined approach to aggadah.

To Azariah, Nissim Gaon, Solomon ibn Adret, and certain other talmudists whom he cites reflect a basically Maimonidean position, with the emphasis on aggadah as parable.[24] They too wished, from their respective intellectual positions, to emphasize the internal or moralistic intent of aggadot and midrashim, the external format of which often staggered both imagination and reason or worse yet might be doctrinally misleading. Their emphasis may not quite accord with the philosophical import that Maimonides might find in the *derashot* of the rabbis. Nevertheless there is in the aggadic commentary of Ibn Adret, for example, enough in the way of allegorical exegesis and spiritualizing of aggadic material into "matter and form" to make it clear that he was no stranger to Jewish speculative thought, both philosophical and mystical.[25]

If this distinguished Spanish rabbi was one of those "men

of understanding" who perceived the symbolic nature of aggadah, this did not prevent him, however, from attempting to sustain the literal meaning of some rather extraordinary passages. For example, the saintly talmudic sage Phinehas ben Jair is reported to have commanded a certain river to divide itself for him and some fellow travelers because he was on his way to perform a very worthy religious deed, and the river acquiesced. Ibn Adret understands this as one of those instances in which the very pious, in time of special need and by virtue of their elevated spiritual condition, are able to effect something miraculous, that is, a change in the natural order.[26] Azariah never informs his reader of such aspects of Ibn Adret's exegesis; no doubt he wishes to minimize the issue of the miraculous in the aggadic material and the hostile criticism that would likely ensue from any attempt to qualify Ibn Adret's approach.

To support his argument regarding aggadah Azariah also invokes another post-Maimonidean authority, his countryman Isaiah di Trani the Younger. This late-thirteenth-century talmudist, with his extremely negative attitudes toward secular learning, would have taken little comfort in Azariah's use of his views. Nor would he have approved of Azariah's handling of aggadah or of much else in the *Me'or 'Einayim*. To be sure, Isaiah directed his criticism in particular at "the works authored by Aristotle and his associates which are heresy, and it is forbidden to learn from heretics even whatever good they may have to teach. . . . And whoever ponders these matters will come to the realization that man's greatest benefit consists in being occupied with the Torah and the commandments."[27] He observed that even Maimonides, for all of his ability to maintain a balanced perspective, became suspect in the opinion of the leading Jewish sages because he devoted himself to the speculative sciences and was caught up in their ways. Those who occupy themselves with these sciences always judge everything on the basis of the normal course of events and "only believe what they perceive with the eyes."[28]

The particulars of Isaiah di Trani's critique and his explicit mention of those who allegorize biblical texts should be seen against the background of the contemporary controversy over Maimonides' works and of the restrictions placed on the study of philosophy[29] (Ibn Adret was a primary figure in the controversy). But the overall emphasis on "sacred" learning and the arguments for the exclusion of other sciences drawn from both scripture and rabbinic sources[30]—a far more extreme position than that of the geonic and Spanish authorities—is at complete variance with Azariah's brand of scholarly endeavor. Isaiah di Trani would undoubtedly have viewed Azariah's historical orientation as it was viewed by similarly disposed minds in the sixteenth century—as fraught with danger for the integrity of Jewish tradition.

Azariah nonetheless finds it useful to quote Isaiah's expansive, if not wholly novel, threefold categorization of midrashim. These include (1) midrashim intended as hyperbole (*derekh guzma'*) for, as the Talmud had already said, both scripture and the sages sometimes resort to "exaggeration in rhetorical speech," and "there are many instances of this as in the sayings of Rabbah bar Bar Ḥana"; (2) midrashim that are in the nature of miraculous occurrences intended to demonstrate God's power through awesome and astonishing events. Just as the prophets have experienced these (e.g., Daniel and Jonah, who was swallowed and then ejected by the whale, as well as others), so too "there are many to be found in the words of the sages as stated . . . concerning R. Bena'ah who used to point out the burial places, and the entire matter related there [i.e., B. Bava Batra 58a]. . . . And all those matters were miraculous like the ones performed and revealed to the prophets, which other individuals do not experience. And of this kind there are many, like the occurrences of Rabba bar Bar Ḥana, which are wondrous things that He would show to His pious ones who believe in Him wholeheartedly"; (3) midrashim intended to interpret scripture in whatever manner the subject matter permits, the rabbinic view being that although a verse can never lose its literal meaning the sense of a biblical verse may be varied. There are therefore midrashic interpretations that intimate something other than the literal intent of scripture. Thus the assertion that the patriarch Jacob never died obviously refers to the continuing spiritual influence of the righteous even after their demise. Isaiah concludes his discussion of this category with a reference to the Palestinian Talmud to the effect that the rabbinic homilies do not constitute matters of mandatory religious belief. They are merely intended, he explains, to elicit whatever may be hinted at in the particular passage, and the interpreter, the Talmud suggests, merits the reward of having engaged in the worthy act of expositing scripture.[31]

Although Azariah claims that Isaiah di Trani's words "agree more than any others with my view,"[32] the two positions are not compatible. Especially problematic is Isaiah's second category regarding the report of miracles in aggadic sources; he plainly insisted on their reality. He did not suggest that the phenomena in question were divinely induced visions in the minds of the pious or that they were the consequence of their lofty thinking.[33] It is clear from his formulation of category (2) that he subscribed, like Jehiel of Paris earlier, to the literal truth of biblical miracles (he objected vigorously to the allegorization of scripture) which he used to draw analogies with aggadic miracles.[34] His choice of illustrative aggadic narratives is no less striking in its accentuation of the marvelous—notably the talmudic legend concerning R. Bena'ah, of whom it is reported that having come upon the burial place of Abraham in the cave of Machpelah, he was informed by Eliezer, the patriarch's servant, that Abraham was resting in Sarah's lap.[35]

Azariah omits all the supportive argumentation and cites Isaiah di Trani only briefly: "And there are midrashim that are accounts of miracles like the stories of R. Bena'ah."[36] Azariah's terse reference to these "stories"—the word is his not Isaiah's—is suggestive of his stance. He undoubtedly finds aggadah of this kind as incredible as the famous one regarding the affliction and death of Titus, which he subjects to critical and detailed analysis. At the most he might grant, as with the Titus story, that the events concerning R. Bena'ah were "undoubtedly possible within divine decree"—but they were impossible within the natural scheme of things.[37] Indeed, since Azariah is not prepared to accede to the position of Hai Gaon that God performed miracles through pious scholars as He had done through the prophets, there is no reason to suppose that he feels obliged to concede the point to Isaiah di Trani, a much later authority. We must assume that Azariah considers the exoteric meaning of the aggadah concerning R. Bena'ah as impossible from a rational and logical standpoint.[38] We may also assume, judging from Azariah's more elaborate presentation of Isaiah's other two categories (especially the third with its emphasis on the purely homiletic character of many midrashim, which Isaiah asserted are not doctrinally binding) that these are the points Azariah seeks to impress on the reader. But Azariah must attenuate even the formulation of the third category in order to adapt Isaiah's views to his own needs. Since Isaiah believed that the "words of wisdom" embodied in that category had been "uttered under prophetic inspiration," Azariah omits this section of the passage.[39]

In subsequent discussions of aggadah, Azariah invokes only those aspects of Isaiah di Trani's categorization that reinforce his own efforts to establish the nonliteralist position;[40] he notably omits any further reference to Isaiah's suggestion regarding aggadah as an expression of the miraculous. Whatever Azariah's attitude toward the miraculous in general may be—and given the sixteenth-century cultural climate one must avoid categorical assumptions—he views the strange features in rabbinic homilies and stories as "only a great and glorious wisdom on their part, commensurate with the magnitude of the extraordinary as it appears to us"; and it remains for the man of spirit to employ his intellect to search out and reveal the lore it embodies.[41] This statement reveals little sympathy with Isaiah's notion of God effecting "awesome and astounding" events, which he believes have their own reality.[42]

The tendency toward literalism with respect to aggadah persisted, then, at least as one dimension in Isaiah di Trani and also even among some of those "men of understanding" to whom Azariah previously refers. For Azariah, all these authorities are in effect merely a point of departure. He is not fully of one mind with them, for in his view the aggadot

> are in some part similar to the angels created from the [fictitious] Fire River mentioned in several places by the sages. After these angels render their song they depart, never to return. Similarly, there are [imaginative] aggadot. Once the expositor has achieved his desired purpose through them, as indicated, they should neither be referred to nor cited as evidence that the events described therein actually occurred or as substantiation of matters far removed from the rational sense.[43]

With the exception of Maimonides and Judah Halevi,[44] Azariah invokes primarily talmudists as authorities in favor of a nonliteral approach to aggadah. Among these authorities of distinction—the geonim Sherira, Hai, and Nissim and the rabbis Solomon ibn Adret, Yom Tov ben Abraham Ishbili, Isaiah di Trani—even those who were at home in philosophical learning acknowledged only a limited legitimacy for the role of secular knowledge and reason relative to religious tradition, and Isaiah di Trani entirely opposed such secular distractions. Even Maimonides, whose views regarding aggadah and midrash were pivotal for Azariah, after all commanded tremendous respect for his halakhic achievements. Although there had been bitter controversy over his philosophical works, his views in matters of talmudic law and doctrine, while often debated and challenged, nonetheless figured prominently in even the most intellectually closeted circles, generation after generation. Indeed, precisely because of that controversy Azariah may have concluded that while the view on aggadah adumbrated by Maimonides in some of his works, notably the *Guide*, constituted weighty support for his own point of view, it had to be supplemented by talmudic authorities who were less controversial.

This consideration probably explains the striking absence in the *Me'or 'Einayim* of certain significant post-Maimonidean opinion concerning aggadah expressed by those who—whatever their stature as talmudists may have been—were known primarily for their attainments as rationalists or exponents of the philosophical tradition in Judaism. Not mentioned in *Me'or 'Einayim* are the fourteenth-century authors Jedaiah Bedersi, Joseph ibn Kaspi, and Shem Tov ibn Shaprut—this despite the fact that their formulations regarding aggadah would have reinforced his own position substantially. And there is every reason to believe that Azariah was familiar with all these predecessors. Ibn Kaspi, for example, definitively declares in his testament *Guide to Knowledge* that

> there are many haggadot the literal wording of which posits ideas inadmissible rationally, or attributes to God corporeality, change, or any other affection. Perchance thou mayest eat to satiety from these *evil viands, these deadly poisons—I refer to the before-mentioned haggadot as literally interpreted*, God deliver thee! Therefore my son, understand that most of the haggadot found in the Talmud and other rabbinic books, which on the surface seem to imply the ideas I have named, are figures of speech, with an inner meaning, which we can sometimes discern, sometimes not.

Ibn Kaspi urges that talmudic teachers who explain such haggadot literally be rejected.[45] Equally incisive is his severe criticism of those who are preoccupied exclusively with "talmudic argumentation" and treat the study of the sciences with contempt; he regards "the faculty of expounding the existence and unity of God" as being as important as a knowledge of the details of ritual law. Given these sentiments and his emphasis throughout the testament on the importance of philosophical knowledge, it is not surprising that at a later date he should have been attacked as having ridiculed talmudic studies and for unsettling the masses in their "simple faith."[46]

Ibn Kaspi's observations are a brief but significant expression of fourteenth-century Jewish rationalist concern with the nature of rabbinic lore. This concern is far more elaborately addressed by Jedaiah Bedersi and Ibn Shaprut. In his epistle to Ibn Adret defending his Provençal coreligionists against charges of religious improprieties, Jedaiah categorized aggadot and utilized, as a point of departure, the philosophers' distinction between two classes of the impossible—that which man cannot alter but which God can and the purely absurd.[47] His detailed categorization, which included several varieties of the impossible in the first class, is very different from the categorization of his older contemporary Isaiah di Trani. In addition, Jedaiah prepared a lengthy commentary on aggadah, apparently widely known and cited until the sixteenth century. In it he gave free rein to his philosophical disposition and resorted to allegorization, not merely of difficult and farfetched aggadot, but even of those rabbinic passages that were best interpreted literally and where the use of allegory was forced. Jedaiah apparently intended to interpret all aggadic material philosophically and to apply rationalistic categories as a means of demonstrating the philosophical truths contained in the classical rabbinic literature. One of his principal aims was to refine the popular mind and raise its consciousness to a more spiritual perception of Jewish religion.[48]

Perhaps even more striking than Azariah's total silence regarding Jedaiah's work on aggadah (which he would at the very least have known from authors close to his own time such as Isaac Abravanel)[49] is his failure to mention Ibn Shaprut's *Pardes Rimonim*.[50] This commentary on talmudic aggadah, published in Italy only twenty years before *Me'or 'Einayim*, should have been particularly attractive to Azariah because of the author's firm assertion that the rabbinic sages used "riddle and metaphor" in the aggadah as a means of conveying ideas otherwise too profound for the masses to grasp and liable to be distorted by them. Consequently, "the more bizarre the riddle the more impossible its literal meaning." Whatever esoteric meaning conceivably inhered in the aggadah was of no concern to Ibn Shaprut. He viewed himself like one who sought to "interpret the Torah according to its plain meaning . . . leaving secret things behind."[51] In his opinion, the sages would attribute certain actions to God in order to establish His authority and providence in man's heart. "And understand this very well and pay attention to it, for it is a great principle in interpreting the aggadot."[52]

Ibn Shaprut's *Pardes Rimonim*, its title inspired by the suggestive imagery of the outer and implicitly dispensable pomegranate husk protecting the attractive and tasty fruit within,[53] exemplifies this "great principle." As the author moves from one talmudic tractate to the next, excerpting and interpreting strange passages or those that stagger the imagination, he reiterates his position: It will be apparent to the enlightened person that such and such statements are not to be taken literally; no person is able to declare that the circumstances described really occurred; while no one can contradict miracles, indeed, if the matter can be explained rationally that is preferable; there are those who look for an esoteric meaning where there is none, and I see no need for such meaning here; we ought not to delve into the matter of miracles, yet . . . be aware that this matter pertains to a dream; the difficulties in this aggadah are such that no person with "seeing eyes" can accept its statements literally.[54]

By the mid-sixteenth century it was precisely Ibn Shaprut's metaphorical approach, informed and inspired by earlier Jewish philosophical tradition,[55] that encountered extreme criticism in some quarters. Symptomatic of the increasingly spiritualistic and mystically charged cultural climate in Italy were the sentiments of the prominent Italian rabbi and qabbalist Moses Basola, especially known for his support of the effort to publish the *Zohar*. It was a pity, he sardonically declared, that *Pardes Rimonim*, this commentary to the aggadah and certain other recently printed rationalistic type works, had survived. These were "vanities that deserve to be burned and that it is forbidden to read."[56] In the same vein was the view of the German talmudist Joseph Ashkenazi, who became familiar with *Pardes Rimonim* during his stay in Italy in the 1560s. He went even further, to denounce what he perceived as Ibn Shaprut's calculated effort to undermine aggadic miracles without openly declaring that miracles per se were impossible. He heaped opprobrium on "this wicked heretic (*min*), author of *Pardes ha-Minim* (!) . . . May his name and memory be obliterated."[57] That contemporary halakhic authorities and those of a qabbalistic bent in Italy such as Basola viewed this work as particularly dangerous[58] suggests that Ashkenazi was not alone in his "reactionary" opinion even if his literalist attitude toward aggadah was most extreme.[59] Indeed, Ashkenazi's views struck a responsive chord in Italian Jewish qabbalistic circles that had totally rejected philosophical rationalism.[60]

Azariah also makes no reference to the late-fifteenth-century philosopher Elijah Delmedigo of Crete, who resided in Italy from 1480 to 1490. The most well-known work of this Averroist scholar—whose many Christian disciples included Pico della Mirandola—was his *Beḥinat ha-Dat*. This treatise, written at the request of his student Saul ha-Kohen Ashkenazi, deals primarily with the relationship between philosophy and Judaism but includes a significant critique of the qabbalah, the authority of which Delmedigo denied.[61] It also includes a discussion of rabbinic aggadah. Although the latter is brief and essentially follows the views of Maimonides, Delmedigo's formulation is noteworthy. He draws a sharp distinction between the halakhic rulings of the rabbinic sages, which are not to be challenged, and the aggadic material with which "it is possible that we sometimes disagree and this does not constitute a transgression." Underlying this distinction is Delmedigo's conviction that the Torah requires that the authority of the sages be accepted in matters of religious law that involve some act or with respect to doctrines of faith agreed upon by them. But in those matters where they spoke not as teachers of the Torah but rather from the standpoint of conjecture, "we are undoubtedly not obliged to put our faith in them when it is apparent that they are in disagreement with the truth."[62] This distinction is perhaps implicit in Maimonides' reference, for example, to those "ignoramuses" who think "that the *Midrashim* have the same status as the traditional legal decisions."[63] Delmedigo's formulation, however, much more directly suggests that *whenever* the sages addressed matters other than halakhic and doctrinally binding ones, they did so not wearing the mantle of rabbinic authority but rather from an ordinary human perspective. Their views in such matters were therefore susceptible to all the possible limitations—or errors—implicit in subjective personal opinion and experience or in the contemporary range of knowledge on which they may have drawn.[64]

We find in the *Me'or 'Einayim* that Azariah bases his approach to aggadah on a similar distinction, although he develops it far more elaborately and frequently uses a historical frame of reference. It is inconceivable that Azariah was unfamiliar with the well-known and relatively recent work of Delmedigo.[65] His silence with respect to the *Beḥinat ha-Dat* can best be explained in the light of the hostility that Delmedigo had already encountered among the growing number of qabbalistically oriented German Jews in northern Italy, notably Padua, who took exception to philosophical studies and their bearing on Jewish religion and whom he in turn had criticized as intellectually deficient. His departure from Italy and return to Crete apparently resulted from the negative reaction engendered by this controversy. The departure was perhaps even precipitated by the conflict between him and the rabbinic authorities in Padua.[66] By Azariah's time the overall Jewish climate in Italy had become far less favorably disposed toward the philosophical exposition of Judaism. Among Azariah's influential contemporaries and countrymen, for example, the renowned qabbalist Menahem Azariah da Fano characteristically viewed the philosophical work of Maimonides with hostility. He explained that it was not, heaven forbid, to diminish the honor of Maimonides that his twelfth-century contemporary Abraham ben David of Posquières had leveled his strictures but in order that "everyone not adhere to him in the study and teaching of the opinions expressed in the *Guide* and similar works."[67]

It is thus hardly surprising that Azariah is purposely selective in invoking earlier authorities to justify a nonliteralist approach to aggadah before proceeding to develop the subject further from his own vantage point. He seeks support among the most highly respected and widely recognized *rabbinic* spokesmen of the post-talmudic centuries, including of course the towering Maimonides; he does not look to those authors whose views are unequivocal, even extreme, and who had been challenged, even though these are much closer to his own emphasis on the metaphorical and doctrinally nonbinding character of rabbinic lore. The pervasive religious attitudes among his contemporaries with respect to an increasingly sensitive area of the tradition no doubt led him to realize that he would best serve the interests of his endeavor by being discreet. Overt reliance on Jewish works whose orthodoxy had been recently impugned in Italian Jewish circles and whose authors did not have the many great and saving graces of Maimonides could only serve to raise even more extreme doubts regarding the legitimacy of his handling of rabbinic tradition. Since there was a long-established tradition of response to the problems inherent in or charges leveled against the aggadah, Azariah could best attempt to confer respectability on his own investigation of the subject by establishing continuity with the geonic and leading rabbinic authorities of the previous centuries. This element of continuity might, in other words, serve to temper criticism of the conspicuous element of novelty that permeates his discussions.

Notes

1. See *Oṣar ha-Ge'onim Masekhet Yom Tov, Ḥagigah u-Mashqin,* ed. B. M. Lewin (Jerusalem: Hebrew University Press Assoc., 1931), Ḥagigah (ha-Perushim), 59f. The source of this information is Sherira's *Megillat Setarim* as cited in Isaac Aboab's *Menorat ha-Ma'or*, which is quoted by Azariah (see below, n. 3). In somewhat more qualified, and fuller form, it also occurs in Abraham ben Isaac of Narbonne's *Sefer ha-Eshkol*, ed. B. H. Auerbach (Halberstadt, 1869), 2:47: "Amar Rav Sherira hanei milei denafkei mi-pesukei u-mikrei midrash ve-aggadah *harbei umdanah ninhu, ve-yesh meihem shehu kakh* [i.e., reliable] . . . *ve-yesh she-eino khein* . . . lakhein ein somkhin 'al aggadah . . . veha-nakhon meihem mah she-mitḥazek min ha-seikhel umin ha-mikrah nekabel meihem, ve-ein sof ve-tikhlah la-aggadot" (emphasis added). B. M. Lewin reads: "harbei [meihen] umdanah." See his *Mi-Tekufat ha-Geonim*, vol. 1, *Rav Sherira Gaon*, an appendix to his *Iggeret Rav Sherira Gaon* (reprint, Jerusalem, 1971), 26 n. 3. See too the entry *guzmah*, in Nathan ben Yehiel of Rome's *Arukh*, ed. A. Kohut (reprint, New York: Pardes, 1955), 2:266f., where the rabbinic use of hyperbole is explained according to a responsum of Sherira and Hai.

2. Ibid., 60; see also *M.E.* 1:210; and *Maṣref la-Kesef*, 42, for Azariah's occasional use of the distinction Hai had drawn. Regarding Hai's interpretation of aggadic anthropomorphism concerning God, see *Oṣar ha-Ge'onim,* Berakhot, ed. B. M. Lewin (Haifa, 1928), 131.

3. *M.E.* 1:210 (emphasis added). Azariah's source for these geonic statements, as he indicates, is Isaac Aboab's *Menorat ha-Ma'or* (see below, n. 10) and in one instance the supercommentary to Abraham ibn Ezra's commentary to the Pentateuch, *Ṣofenat Pa'aneiaḥ* (see *Maṣref la-Kesef*, 44). However, his summation, and notably the phrase I have italicized ("ha-mamṣi otah"), is Azariah's and does not occur in the geonic sources cited.

4. *M.E.* 1:211. Nevertheless, Azariah's own formulation in this regard is not without some caution. For he too at times refers to "some aggadot"

(*M.E.* 1:212) that were devised in order to convey various lessons. He even cautions his reader (1:219) not to apply the type of critical analysis he used in dealing with the rabbinic account of Titus's death indiscriminately, "for not all of their sayings are to be explained in one way." The context of this remark, however, primarily indicates concern with adverse criticism of his approach and in any event does not preclude a nonliteral or metaphorical interpretation of most problematic aggadot even if in a manner different from that used with the Titus story. Moreover, the caution to the reader is almost immediately qualified and virtually undone when Azariah juxtaposes Maimonides' assertion regarding a special work he had intended to write explaining the difficult passages in the *derashot*, and noting that "they are all parables" (*The Guide of the Perplexed*, trans. Shlomo Pines [Chicago: University of Chicago Press, 1963], 1:9). In effect, Azariah observes, Maimonides "wrote the entire work for us through these two words in which he declared that they are '*all parables.*' " Why Azariah feels compelled to pursue the matter further since Maimonides has reduced it to its essence is an issue that will be addressed.

5. *M.E.* 1:254. Azariah apparently saw the *Epistle* in manuscript and later in print. Cf. *Maṣref la-Kesef*, 8; and *M.E.*, 3:157.

6. *Iggeret Rav Sherira' Ga'on*, ed. B. M. Lewin (reprint, Jerusalem, 1971), 86f. The talmudic passage is in B. Bava Meṣi'a 86a. In one instance Azariah has occasion to note talmudic references to the supposed appearance of the prophet Elijah among the sages, adding that "according to the words of Rav Sherira Gaon in his *Epistle*" the same phenomenon transpired in the days of Rav Joseph Gaon (*M.E.* 2:267). Sherira refers to this predecessor's great piety and reports that on the day of Rav Joseph's demise "there was a great stormwind and the earth shook" (*Iggeret*, 109f.).

7. *Iggeret*, 96; and cf. 94f. In the thirteenth-century *Shibbolei ha-Leqeṭ*, ed. S. Buber (Vilna: Romm, 1886; reprint, New York, 1958), 38, Zedekiah ben Abraham Anav reports a similar story, giving as his source "teshuvot ha-ge'onim." Simhah Assaf, *Tequfat ha-Ge'onim ve-Sifrutah*, ed. M. Margaliot (Jerusalem: Mosad ha-Rav Kook, 1954), 150, notes that when Sherira relied on talmudic aggadot that are historically problematic he was careful in his reference to them (e.g., "the former generations have said." Sherira, however, makes no qualifications in reporting the story concerning Rabbah bar Nahamani). Describing the long-preserved records that served as sources for the *Iggeret*, Assaf even gives as one example of Sherira's precision in citation the reference to "the early authorities . . . and their chronicles," from which he reported the Yazdegerd story. Lewin, too (*Iggeret*, xvii) does not consider Sherira as having been excessive in his reliance on aggadah, but neither he nor Assaf appears to deal with the problematic substance of what Sherira sometimes documented so carefully. See also Salo W. Baron, *A Social and Religious History of the Jews*, 2d ed. (New York and Philadelphia: Columbia University Press and Jewish Publication Society, 1952–1983), 6:427 n. 66.

8. See, e.g., *M.E.* 1:191f., 2:345.

9. See Hai's responsum in *Oṣar ha-Ge'onim*, Ḥagigah (ha-Teshu-

vot), 15, and with some variations in Jacob ibn Habib's *Ha-Kotev* to *'Ein Ya'aqov*, Ḥagigah 14b. Hai clearly distinguishes between miracles and visions: "ha-Kadosh Barukh Hu' 'oseh otot ve-nora'ot 'al yedei ha-ṣaddiqim . . . u-mar'eh et ha-ṣaddiqim mar'ot nora'ot." Several lines down in the same responsum he observes: "ve-anu sovrim ki ha-Kadosh Barukh hu' 'oseh nissim la-ṣaddiqim ve-nifla'ot *gedolot ve-lo' raḥoq mimenu she-hu' mar'eh otan befi nimiyot mar'ot heikhalav u-ma 'amad mal'akhav*" (emphasis added). Ibn Habib's text omits all of the italicized words and merely adds "u-mar'eh lahem *heikhalav*," thus suggesting a much more definitive association between Hai's position and that of the early authorities. The tone of Ibn Habib's version is in keeping with his quotation of another of Hai's responsa, which follows the first. See Chap. 4, n. 47 above, inclusive of the reference there to Ibn Habib. Regarding Hanina ben Dosa, see B. Yevamot 121b, where this sage in fact disclaims any prophetic powers. Baron (*Social and Religious History*, 6:176f.) has referred to the "ambivalence" among the medieval Jewish scholars toward aggadah, "most clearly noticeable in the attitude of Hai Gaon. . . . In this very responsum, however, the gaon insisted, in contrast to Samuel ben Ḥofni, that God performed miracles through the mediation of rabbinic scholars, as well as of prophets. . . . Even Samuel ben Ḥofni merely preached discrimination in the use of ancient homilies and tales, not their outright repudiation." Cf. S. P. Rabinowitz's earlier formulation of this issue, which reduces the different approach of the two geonim to "lo' be-eṣem ve-'iqar he-de'ah, ki im be-ṣurat ha-devarim" (in his Hebrew edition of Heinrich Graetz, *Divrei Yemei Yisra'el* [Warsaw, 1890–1899], 4:14 n. 4). See too Jacob Mann (*Texts and Studies in Jewish History and Literature* [New York: Ktav, 1972], 1:312), who notes that the gaon of Palestine, the eleventh-century Solomon ben Judah, reveals "the same rationalistic tendency as maintained by the Babylonian Geonim like Sherira and Hai and also Samuel b. Ḥofni." He points out however that the strong Karaite presence in Jerusalem at the time had a bearing on the tendency to steer away from the aggadic type of scriptural interpretation. For the Hebrew text of Solomon's comments, see Mann, p. 322, and for Mann's discussion of what he terms "ha-raṣiyonalismos ha-memuṣah" of Hai, as of his father Sherira, as opposed to "ha-raṣiyonalismos ha-kiṣoni" of those like Samuel ben Ḥofni, see pp. 579f.

10. *Maṣref la-Kesef*, 101. Azariah gives as his source for Hai's opinion the *assufot* of Aboab. Cassel's view (*M.E.* 3:153) that this refers to the work *Nehar Pishon* presupposes that the author in question is the fifteenth-century Isaac Aboab II, who presumably, then, was also the author of *Menorat ha-Ma'or*. Cf. *Encyclopaedia Judaica* (1972), s. v. "Aboab, Isaac I," where the authorship of *Menorat ha-Ma'or* is ascribed to the late-fourteenth-century Isaac Aboab I, whose existence, however, first proposed by Zunz, is rejected by H. G. Enelow. See the latter's edition of Israel ibn Al-Nakawa, *Menorat ha-Ma'or* (New York: Bloch, 1929), 1:17–22.

11. *Vikuaḥ Rabbenu Yeḥi'el mi-Pariz*, ed. R. Margaliot (Lwow, n.d.), 13.

12. Ibid., 25; and see B. Ḥullin 90b, for some of the biblical illustrations Jehiel invokes.

13. *Vikuaḥ Yehi'el*, 26. Regarding the aggadah in question, taken from B. Eruvin 18b, the Talmud refers to a situation not of Adam's own volition; but there is no mention here of Adam's presumed cohabitation with Lilith. See also Bereshit Rabbah 20, 24, for a variant version. The only other reference I find suggestive of Jehiel's account is with respect to a brief conjugal relationship between Adam and Lilith, cited by Louis Ginzberg from the *Alphabet of Ben Sira*. See Ginzberg, *The Legends of the Jews* (Philadelphia: Jewish Publication Society, 1954), 1:65f., 5:87 n. 40.: cf. also Pines, *Guide* 1:32f. According to another aggadic account, Adam had sexual relations with every species of animal but found no satisfaction until his relationship with Eve. This too was biblically well founded according to Jehiel and is described by him as a proper conclusion from the text of scripture ("din hi' lomar kakh"; *Vikuaḥ*, 26); and see B. Yevamot 63a, although his biblical support is more elaborate and explicit than that given in the Talmud. Although this particular aggadic passage "was, at an early period, explained figuratively" (Ginzberg, *Legends* 5:87 n. 39), Jehiel obviously takes its literal meaning quite seriously, even adding that through such sexual liaisons Adam was guilty of no transgression since no prohibition against them was yet in force. See too Hyam Maccoby, *Judaism on Trial: Jewish-Christian Disputations in the Middle Ages* (Rutherford: Fairleigh Dickinson University Press, 1982), 37. He describes Jehiel's position as saying "that the Aggadic stories *need* not be believed literally, but in many cases, they *can* be believed literally." This may be a reasonable description but it nonetheless reinforces the impression of Jehiel's greater proclivity for literalism than was true with geonim like Sherira and Hai, literalism itself implicitly conferring on aggadah a substantial authority—even if different from or lesser than the authority of halakhah. That Azariah, in his treatment of aggadah, never refers to the views of Jehiel may be because he lacked familiarity with the details of the 1240 disputation, although he surely was generally aware of those thirteenth-century events. He also probably found Jehiel's position quite incompatible with the one he himself was attempting to develop.

14. *Vikuaḥ ha-Ramban*, in *Kitvei Rabbenu Mosheh ben Naḥman*, ed. H. D. Chavel (Jerusalem: Mosad ha-Rav Kook, 1963), 1:308. In discussing Nahmanides' view, Chavel (p. 309 n.) cites among others the nineteenth-century Joseph Saul Nathanson, but the latter's critique and qualification of the geonic position on aggadah—i.e., Hai—is based on an inaccurate wording of that geonic tradition. It does not correspond to the text in *Menorat ha-Ma'or* (see n. 3 above), to which Nathanson refers. Nathanson does of course draw the important distinction already made earlier by Nahmanides between the status of the aggadot that have implications for Jewish religious law and those that do not (see p. 92 above, and below, nn. 16–17).

15. See too the relevant comments of Baron (*Social and Religious History* 9:79–85, 279 n. 32) regarding the different circumstances surrounding the two disputations and the respective position on aggadah of the Franco-Jewish and Spanish Jewish spokesmen. Cf. Robert Chazan, "A Medieval Hebrew Polemical Mélange," *Hebrew Union College Annual* 51 (1980): 110 n. 68. Regarding the

position of Nahmanides, Yitzhak Baer considers it erroneous to assume that he did not believe in aggadot ("Le-Biqoret ha-Vikuḥim shel R. Yeḥi'el mi-Pariz ve-shel ha-Ramban," *Tarbiz* 2[1931]: 184). This view, however, is convincingly challenged by Saul Lieberman, *Sheqi'in* (Jerusalem: Bamberger, 1939), 81f. Lieberman also calls attention to explicit talmudic sources upholding the view that aggadah was not deemed a matter of religious belief. Chaim Tchernowitz (*Toledot ha-Posqim* [New York: Jubilee Committee, 1947], 2:109, and n. 2) emphasizes Nahmanides' effort, even in his halakhic work, to explain aggadah in a rational sense or as hyperbole where the context clearly demanded this. The tenor of the age and the circumstances that he had to confront, even if less menacing than those in Paris of 1240, certainly did not permit Nahmanides to be nonchalant in this matter. In a noteworthy analysis of the Barcelona disputation Maccoby (*Judaism on Trial*, esp. 44–47, 62) points to the multidimensional nature of aggadah, which particularly in the context of disputation with Christians required other than a monolithic handling of it by Jewish spokesmen. In his article "Nahmanides on the Status of Aggadot: Perspectives on the Disputation at Barcelona, 1263," *Journal of Jewish Studies* 40, no. 1 (Spring 1989), Professor Marvin Fox of Brandeis University provides extensive evidence from Nahmanides' commentary to the Pentateuch to demonstrate compellingly that this distinguished medieval spokesman was not dissembling when he asserted that one was not obliged to believe in all rabbinic aggadot.

16. The quotation is from his *Torat ha-Adam*, as cited by Lieberman, *Sheqi'in* 82; and see Chavel, *Kitvei Rabbenu Mosheh ben Naḥman* 2:285.

17. *M.E.* 1:211.

18. Ibid. 1:13, 202, 205–207, 211, 2:336, etc. Azariah's citations from Nissim Gaon, Solomon ibn Adret, and Yom Tov ben Abraham are apparently all taken from Jacob ibn Habib's *Ha-Kotev* to the *'Ein Ya'aqov* (see Cassel, *M.E.*, index 1 for the respective entries) and in part from Isaac Aboab (*M.E.* 1:13, 206). As noted above, Azariah could not have found an Ashkenazic view such as that of Jehiel compatible with his own. Most extreme perhaps in this regard, at least among the authorities before Azariah's own age, was the astonishment expressed by Samson of Sens that it should even occur to anyone to declare "that we ought not to take the words of the aggadah literally. . . . All their words [i.e., the sages] are as goads and like nails well fastened and may our Rock enlighten our eyes in His Law that the eyes of the blind may be made to see" (from the correspondence collected by the thirteenth-century Meir Abulafia, *Kitāb 'al-Rasā'il*, ed. Y. Brill [Paris, 1871], 136). Noteworthy too is Abraham ibn Ezra's comment on Exodus 33:23 ("and you will see My back; but My face must not be seen"): "and our sages declared that He showed him the knot in the band of the tefillin (resting on the back of the head), and their words are correct, *although not in the literal sense as explained by the scholars of our generation* (emphasis added), for it is a profound mystery." And see also Jacob N. Epstein, "R. Mosheh Taku ben Ḥasdai ve-sifro 'Ketav Tamim,' " in *Meḥqarim be-Sifrut ha-Talmud uvi-Leshonot shemiyot*, ed. E. Z. Melamed (Jerusalem: Magnes Press, 1983), 298f. Commenting on Taku's extreme literalism with respect to aggadah, Epstein notes that "he was not singular in this regard."

19. *M.E.*, 1:205.

20. Pines, *Guide* 1:11f.

21. Ibid., 9.

22. *M.E.* 1:219, 211. Azariah notes especially *Guide*, pt. 2, Chap. 6, e.g., "In all these texts [i.e., regarding angels] the intention is not, as is thought by the ignorant, to assert that there is speech on the part of [God] . . . or deliberation or . . . recourse for help to the opinion of someone else. For how could the Creator seek help from that which He has created? . . . How great is the blindness of ignorance and how harmful! . . . *Midrash Qohelet* has the following text: *When a man sleeps, his soul speaks to the angel and the angel to the cherub.* Thereby they have stated plainly to him who understands and cognizes intellectually that the imaginative faculty is likewise called an *angel* and that the intellect is called a *cherub*. How beautiful must this appear to him who knows, and how distasteful to the ignorant!" (Pines, pp. 263–265).

23. *Maṣref la-Kesef*, 72; and see below, p. 119, n. 18. Regarding the question of bifurcation, or unity, in Maimonides' work and with brief reference to Azariah, see Isadore Twersky, "Some Non-Halakic Aspects of the *Mishneh Torah*," in *Jewish Medieval and Renaissance Studies*, ed. A. Altmann (Cambridge: Harvard University Press, 1967), 97, and n. 8; and idem, *Introduction to the Code of Maimonides* (New Haven: Yale University Press, 1980), 432, and n. 190.

24. Nissim Gaon in the eleventh century, for example, comments on some extremely anthropomorphic statements concerning God. He begins almost predictably with the rabbinic dictum: "We do not rely on the words of the aggadah." But he goes on to note that such passages (e.g., God's tears, as it were, because of the exile of Israel, create a sound from one end of the world to the other) were intended in the manner of parable, "just as the Torah uses language adapted to human understanding. For the prophets in this manner speak metaphorically and say 'Behold the eye of the Lord, . . .' which [is] not meant literally but rather in the manner of parable and human speech." And in the thirteenth century Solomon ibn Adret, commenting on the same passage, refers to Hai and Nissim, and observes—using a phrase virtually identical with that of Maimonides (as rendered in Ibn Tibbon's Hebrew translation of the *Guide*)—that "they are all parables, . . . which we explain as we do the scriptural verses cited in the aggadah [itself] . . . for all these are parables and metaphors [intended] to assist a person's perception." See *Ha-Kotev* to *'Ein Ya'aqov*, Berakhot 59a. Azariah gives these citations in abbreviated form (*M.E.* 1:13, 211). While he sometimes refers to "what I have seen in the Rashba's [i.e., Ibn Adret's] *Commentary to the Aggadot*" (*M.E.* 1:13 n. 1; and see 2:336), I am unaware of any evidence to suggest that he had access to it other than through the citations in *Ha-Kotev*. Parts of this commentary on various talmudic tractates have been published. See, e.g., Leon A. Feldman, ed., "Perush ha-Aggadot la-Rashba' le-Masekhet Bava Batra," *Bar-Ilan Annual* 7–8 (1970): 138–161, and the bibliographical references to the other published portions.

25. See, e.g., Feldman, "Perush la-Rashba'," regarding Ibn Adret's

discussion of the Leviathan in B. Bava Batra 74b: "*ve-im heyotenu loqḥim ha-devarim bi-fshutan* (p. 143); da' ki be-haggadah zo . . . be-'inyan livyatan . . . ramzu lanu 'inyan ha-nefesh veha-sekhel, ve-gam 'inyan ha ḥomer veha-ṣurah" (p. 146); "ve-'atah gilu lanu meqom 'iqar aṣilut ha-nefesh . . . ki nefesh he-adam hi' aṣilut ne'eṣal mi-meqom ṣeror ha-ḥayyim u-mishtalshel me-aṣilut le-aṣilut" (p. 151; emphasis added).

26. See *Ha-Kotev, 'Ein Ya'aqov*, B. Ḥullin 7a. Cf. the version in J. Demai 1:3. Elsewhere in his commentary, Ibn Adret urges against rejection of another problematic aggadah: "*'Al tarḥiq lihyot la-ṣaddiqim le-'olam ha-ba' se'udah ki-feshatei ha-devarim* shebah lahem za"l be-miqṣat ha-haggadot ba-Talmud uva-midrashot" (emphasis added). In the long analysis that follows he attempts to establish the credibility of the aggadah regarding the Leviathan and the feast prepared for the righteous in the world to come as a prior physical stage facilitating the spiritual fulfillment of the soul. Having been prepared for the purpose of this feast from the very period of creation, Leviathan was especially suited to increase the intellectual powers of the soul. See Feldman, "Perush la-Rashba'," 140–142; and *Ha-Kotev, 'Ein Ya'aqov*, B. Bava Batra 74b. The sixteenth-century talmudist Joseph Ashkenazi (see p. 53 and n. 28 above) is explicitly critical of Ibn Adret's attempt to subscribe to both a literal understanding of aggadah and a philosophical one: "Ve-hineh mah temihah nifla'ah hi' *meha-Rashba' ha-ma'amin be-feshutei rov divrei haza"l* mah ra'ah lirkov atrei rikhashei le-ha'amin ba-Torah ve-lelekh aḥarei darkhei ha-pilosofim ha-'arurim . . . ve-hineh kol ha-ba'im aḥarav . . . mosifim 'al devarav *ki he'emin be-feshuto shel davar* af 'al pi she-'asah lo ṣurah 'aval hem maṣe'u mi-devarav 'ilah shelo le-ha' amin bekhol ha-Torah kulah" (from the manuscript edited by Scholem, "Yedi'ot ḥadashot 'al R. Yosef Ashkenazi, ha-Tana' mi-Ṣefat," *Tarbiz* 28 [1958]: 233 [emphasis added]). Regarding the story of Phinehas ben Jair there is a rather different treatment than that of Rashba in an anonymous eleventh- or twelfth-century manuscript published by Georges Vajda, which represents a rationalistic though "not heretical" approach to miracles that run counter to the established order of nature. See "Hesber raṣiyonalisti bilti yadua' me-Yemei ha-Beinayim 'al ha-Nissim," in *Hagut 'ivrit be-eiropah*, ed. M. Zohori and A. Tartakover (Tel Aviv: Brit Ivrit Olamit, 1969), 71–74. The late Professor Alexander Altmann kindly provided the Vajda reference.

27. These remarks from Isaiah di Trani's talmudic novellae are found in the sixteenth-century marginalia *Shilṭei ha-Gibborim* (1554/1555) of Joshua Boaz to Alfasi, B. Avodah Zarah 5b. Isaiah di Trani notes that he has dealt with this matter at greater length in his *Kuntres ha-Re'ayot*.

28. From the manuscript of *Kuntres ha-Re'ayot* quoted in Simhah Assaf, *Meqorot le-Toledot ha-Ḥinukh be-Yisra'el* (Tel Aviv: Dvir, 1930), 2:96–98.

29. Ibid. 98, and 96 n. 8.

30. *Shilṭei ha-Gibborim*; Assaf, *Meqorot*.

31. *Shilṭei ha-Gibborim* 6a, which apparently was Azariah's source, although he also refers directly to Isaiah di Trani's novellae (*M.E.* 1:205). There is a somewhat fuller version of Isaiah's discussion in David Sasson, *Me'aṭ Devash*

(Oxford, 1928), 42f. Isaiah's concluding point appears to be specifically with respect to category (3) of midrashim or other such loosely construed midrashic interpretations. In any event it would not affect his apparent conviction regarding the category (2) stories, which report miraculous events. The talmudic passage is in J. Nazir 7:1, although Isaiah's wording of it elicits Azariah's passing comment regarding a variant reading of the quotation. In this instance, one of the many where Azariah calls attention to textual discrepancies and deals with the problem of establishing a correct text, he decides in favor of the standard version of the Palestinian Talmud and attempts to interpret it accordingly, although losing some of the force of Isaiah's point (*M.E.* 1:206). Cf., however, Lieberman (*Sheqi'in*, 82), who establishes the accuracy of Isaiah's text, and Azariah himself later uses the quotation exactly as Isaiah has it (*M.E.* 1:211). Chavel's commentary to *Vikuaḥ ha-Ramban* (pp. 308f.) merely notes the discrepancy between Isaiah's text of the passage in J. Nazir and the standard printed version. With respect to the most unusual talmudic account concerning R. Benaah, Sherira Gaon had earlier declared that it was not a visual experience but that of a dream: "ve-amar hai ma'aseh de'itmar be-ḥalom ra'ah oto ve-lo' be-marit 'ayin" (quoted in I. H. Weiss, *Dor Dor ve-Dorshav* [Vilna: Romm, 1904], 4:153 n. 18).

32. *M.E.* 1:205.

33. There is no reference to allegory (*mashal*) in Isaiah di Trani's discussion of the miraculous in aggadot. And his discussion lacks the greater refinement of analysis that one finds for example in Judah Halevi's discussion (*Kuzari*, pt. 3, par. 73) and obviously in Maimonides, but even among the talmudists whom Azariah introduces into his discussion. In this respect, and in his general outlook, Isaiah seems closer in spirit to certain of the medieval Ashkenazic spokesmen.

34. As with Jehiel of Paris (see pp. 91f., and n. 11 above) Isaiah's choice of scriptural illustrations appears to have been calculated to emphasize accounts in which the miraculous and the element of supernatural causation is of the most unusual sort.

35. If, as seems very likely, Isaiah di Trani's general intellectual attitude was in part conditioned by the contemporary conflict regarding the study of philosophy, it is interesting that precisely the talmudic legend he viewed as a matter of the miraculous was viewed by some in the rationalist camp as requiring allegorical interpretation. In response to the charge that Jews in Provence were treating the Torah as allegory and claiming that Abraham and Sarah represented "form and matter," Jedaiah Bedersi, in his defense of Provence addressed to Ibn Adret after the ban of 1305, argued that the talmudic legend (B. Bava Batra 58a) had been allegorized, not the biblical account. That this view had been presented publicly, Jedaiah said, was the only point on which the individual responsible could be faulted. See A. S. Halkin, "Yedaiah Bedershi's *Apology*," in *Jewish Medieval and Renaissance Studies*, ed. A. Altmann, 166f. At an earlier date Rashbam in his commentary to B. Bava Batra 58a casually notes the rabbinic tradition that Eliezer, Abraham's servant, was one of the pious ancients who had never died (cf. *Derekh Ereṣ Zuta'*, chap. 1).

36. *M.E.* 1:205.

37. Ibid., 215.

38. This was the position of one of Isaiah di Trani's Provençal contemporaries. See Abba Mari ben Moses Astruc, *Minḥat Qena'ot* (Pressburg, 1833), 69; and see n. 35 above.

39. Cf. *Shilṭei ha-Gibborim* 6a with *M.E.* 1:205. Azariah's quotation of Isaiah di Trani is not quite word for word, but the implications of this section are much too serious and the omission much too glaring to be viewed as mere abbreviation. Azariah also omits Isaiah's opening and concluding censure of those who mock the words of the sages. He was by no means guilty of that offense, but he may have deemed it wiser to omit anything that might be suggestive of criticism of his own position. After all, aside from the serious substantive criticisms of the *Me'or 'Einayim*, the rumor had at least been bandied about that Azariah had treated the sages' words derisively (see the letter of Menahem ha-Kohen Porto in David Kaufmann, "Contributions à l'histoire des luttes d'Azaria de Rossi," *Revue des études juives* 33 [1896]: 86). In at least one context, Azariah himself refers to some contemporaries who vociferously accused him of discrediting the sacred dicta of the sages (*M.E.* 1:219). Later in the century, Judah Loew of Prague specifically referred to Azariah's "words of mockery" and derision in dealing with aggadah (see below, pp. 136f. and n. 16). Regarding the circumstances leading Porto to retract his original criticism of the *Me'or 'Einayim*, see his responsum in S. J. Halberstam "Sheloshah Ketavim 'al Devar Sefer Me'or 'Einayim u-Mikhtav eḥad el R. Azariah Min ha-Adumim ve-'od Mikhtav 'Odotav," in *Festschrift Zum Achtzigsten Geburstage Moritz Steinschreider's* (Leipzig: Otto Harrassowitz, 1896), 1ff.

40. *M.E.* 1:211, 234. It is surely no oversight on Azariah's part that in citing the view of the Palestinian Talmud that the rabbinic homilies are not doctrinally binding (p. 211), he uses precisely Isaiah's version of that text, far clearer and direct in intent than the printed, somewhat garbled version that just several pages earlier he had attempted to sustain and adequately interpret (see n. 31 above).

41. Ibid. 1:203. The phrase "glorious wisdom" (*ḥokhmah mefo'arah*) is used in the Talmud with respect to Torah wisdom per se (see, e.g., B Ta'anit 7a). Here, however, it is intended to underscore purely human (rather than divine) wisdom as the source of rabbinic lore. He uses it too to characterize the sages' tendency to explain disastrous events in Jewish history by pointing to religious offenses, which Azariah himself clearly does not believe are commensurate with the consequences (see *M.E.* 1:187). Sometimes the phrase is used by Azariah even with respect to an area of rabbinic discourse that has significant halakhic implications. Thus in defending his argument concerning the relatively late origin of the traditional system of calendrical calculations and the various practices deriving from it, he refers to "consensuses of *splendid wisdom* that are not from Sinai" (*Maṣref la-Kesef*, 72; and see *M.E.* 2:275: "ha-derekh sheheḥeziqu . . . be-minyan ha-shanim haytah ḥokhmah mefo'arah").

42. Even the philosopher and defender of Maimonides Hillel of

Verona, Isaiah di Trani's contemporary in Italy, was not so different in his assessment of aggadah. In his categorization he included of course the many puzzling aggadot or those involving farfetched interpretation of scripture. These he considered to be purely allegorical in nature. Many others, which utilized extreme language and imagery, either frightening or promising, he viewed as intended wholly for the religious and moral edification of the masses. Still other accounts, which in fact involved the undoing of the natural order, were in his opinion serious prophetic visions granted to certain sages and whose content instructed them concerning future events and hidden things. Finally, there was the category pertaining to literal truth, those "miracles and wondrous acts (e.g., reviving the dead, bringing down rain, etc.) that God was wont to perform through the pious sages. . . . And all those stories . . . which are very great in number . . . performed through God's power . . . we are obliged to believe all of them according to their plain meaning and as recorded . . . and whoever denies these matters and mocks them is a heretic"—the only condition being, he adds, that every such miracle had to have served a pressing religious or moral need. It was not mandatory to believe aggadic marvels where they were merely rhetorical exaggeration without meaningful purpose and need. To do so would in fact be foolishness. (See *Tagmulei ha-Nefesh*, ed. S. J. Halberstam [Lyck: Mekiẓe Nirdamim, 1874], 25a–b, 26a.) This is a more elaborate and analytical treatment of the subject, and in certain respects more explicit, than Isaiah's, but it clearly has many affinities with it. The talmudist and antagonist of philosophy Isaiah was undoubtedly as committed to the view of literal truth as an important component in aggadah as was the far more philosophically oriented Hillel of Verona. The view that Hillel of Verona himself moved toward an increasingly modified form of philosophical rationalism is set forth by Isaac Barzilay, *Betweeen Reason and Faith: Anti-Rationalism in Italian Jewish Thought, 1250–1650* (The Hague: Mouton, 1967), 42–57.

43. *M.E.* 1:212. Jacob Elbaum ("Rabbi Judah Loew of Prague and His Attitude to the Aggadah," *Scripta Hierosolymitana* 22 [1971]: 28–47) discusses Loew's criticism of Azariah's views, but he inadvertently describes this passage in the *M.E.* as "de Rossi's quotation from the Letter of R. Sherira Gaon" (p. 35). These are Azariah's own words, as is clear from the language, and the entire passage is independent of Azariah's earlier reference to Sherira. There is no such formulation in the *Letter*, nor indeed any discussion in it of the status of aggadah, and Sherira is hardly likely to have made such a statement. Azariah's brief citations from Sherira regarding aggadah are from the gaon's *Megillat Setarim* as quoted in Isaac Aboab's *Menorat ha-Ma'or* (see n. 3 above).

44. See *M.E.* 1:204f, where Azariah briefly cites Halevi's *Kuzari* (pt. 3) relative to his discussion of aggadic midrash.

45. *Guide to Knowledge*, in *Hebrew Ethical Wills*, ed. Israel Abrahams (Philadelphia: Jewish Publication Society, 1948), 1:155f. (emphasis added). The Hebrew phrase that Abrahams renders "figures of speech" is, again, "ve-hem kulam meshalim" and corresponds to Maimonides' formulation in the *Guide*. See above p. 93, and n. 24, regarding Ibn Adret. Ibn Kaspi refers to Maimonides' philosophical classic as the "holy *Guide*" (Abrahams, p. 158).

46. Abrahams, *Hebrew Ethical Wills*, 148, 152. For a brief discussion of criticism of Ibn Kaspi by the fifteenth-century anti-rationalist and opponent of secular learning Joseph Jabez and others, see Abrahams, pp. 128f; and see *Encyclopaedia Judaica* (1972), s.v. "Kaspi, Joseph ben Abba Mari ibn." Abrahams considers Ibn Kaspi's attitude toward the Talmud as undeserving of criticism and judges that "Jabez can hardly have had the full text of the Testament before him." He argues that what Ibn Kaspi "really contended for was the duty to seek a philosophical justification of religion." Isadore Twersky, referring to the "halakocentric" character of Judaism, describes Ibn Kaspi's approach as revolutionary in that he wished to displace Talmud study in favor of philosophy. In Ibn Kaspi's "universalist-rationalist position" he finds "in sum, a definite *odium Talmudicum* which was detected and detested by R. Joseph Jabez in his *Or ha-Ḥayyim*." See "Joseph ibn Kaspi: Portrait of a Medieval Jewish Intellectual," in *Studies in Medieval Jewish History and Literature*, ed. Isadore Twersky (Cambridge: Harvard University Press, 1979), 243–244, 246, 256 n. 52.

47. See Halkin, "Yedaiah Bedershi's *Apology*," 168, and n. 24, where Jedaiah's application of the distinction is discussed and the fuller details of his division of aggadot into four groups are spelled out. Halkin distinguishes between Jedaiah's attitude toward biblically recorded miracles, the literal truth of which was possible in the light of the philosopher's distinction, and the "greater liberty with Rabbinic aggadic lore" that he took.

48. For this characterization of the commentary see Isadore Twersky, "R. Yeda 'ayah ha-Penini u-Perusho le-Aggadah," in *Studies in Jewish Religious and Intellectual History Presented to Alexander Altmann*, ed. S. Stein and R. Loewe (University, Ala.: University of Alabama Press, 1979), 63, 65, 69f.

49. Ibid., 75 nn. 2–4, for references to the works of Abravanel, who held Jedaiah's work on aggadah in high regard, and to Isaac Arama, who was critical of it, observing that it had no basis either in scripture or logical argument. Both authors are cited in the *Me'or 'Einayim*, Abravanel with notable frequency.

50. The *Pardes Rimonim* was published in Sabionetta in 1554. A modern edition was done by Eliezer Zweifel (Zhitomir, 1866), and a photo-offset of the original printing was issued in Jerusalem in 1968. Citations here are from the 1866 edition.

51. *Pardes Rimonim*, 1f.

52. Ibid., 106.

53. Ibid., 2.

54. Ibid., 5, 7, 51, 58, 82, 92. The rationalist position is exemplified with such frequency in Ibn Shaprut's commentary that the work serves as a useful source of illustrative contrast with the earlier, far less definitive, even ambivalent attitudes of the geonim. Thus, in his purely metaphorical interpretation of the aggadah regarding Rabbah bar Nahamani's demise, for example, the "heavenly academy" is explained as the leading talmudical academy of the time, the "Holy One, blessed be He" refers to the head of the academy (!), the "missile that fell from heaven" refers to information disseminated by the leading sage or, possibly,

God's instruction to one of the sages in a dream, and so on (*Pardes Rimonim*, 10). Sherira apparently took the same aggadah at face value, for he after all included it and others without comment in an important responsum intended to be historically as well as halakhically authoritative (see p. 90f. above).

55. Ibid., 1f. His intention was to explain the aggadot "in accordance with religious opinions well known to us" from Maimonides and Abraham ibn Ezra "since these are logical assumptions close to philosophy." Although Ibn Shaprut claimed to have found Ibn Adret's approach to aggadah unsatisfactory because it combined philosophy and qabbalah, which "are in truth two opposites" (p. 1), he apparently adopted some interpretations from Ibn Adret without identifying their source. Indeed, some are presented as his own (e.g., "Amar Shem Tov ha-meva'er"). Cf., e.g., *Pardes Rimonim*, 106–110, with Ibn Adret's commentary as cited in *Ha-Kotev, 'Ein Ya'aqov*, Ḥullin 7a, 60a. Only as he presents an additional commentary to these passages in Ḥullin (see *Pardes Rimonim*, 113–116) does he mention in passing that Ibn Adret has explained some of them. He does not however indicate that those explanations are incorporated into his own treatise.

56. Meir Benayahu, *Haskamah u-Reshut be-Defusei Veneṣiyah* (Jerusalem: Ben-Zvi Institute, 1971), 86, and see 88. In 1586, when R. Jehiel Trabot initiated the renewal in Ferrara of an earlier restriction on the printing of Hebrew books, he even went so far as to refer to certain works that had been written and published but that ought instead to have been hidden "or thrown into the fire along with their authors." It seems possible that he had Azariah in mind (Benayahu, pp. 94, 96). Trabot had after all signed the 1574 declaration restricting the possession and reading of the *Me'or 'Einayim*.

57. Ibid., 88, and n. 3. The quotation is from the manuscript treatise published by Gershom Scholem. See chap. 4, n. 28 above.

58. Benayahu, *Haskamah*, 88. Benayahu calls attention to the special concern with Ibn Shaprut's treatise following the burning of the Talmud in 1553 and the fear that philosophy and secular learning would take the place of talmudic studies.

59. See chap. 4, n. 28 above, for a brief discussion of Gershom Scholem's assessment of Ashkenazi.

60. Reuven Bonfil, *Ha-Rabbanut be-Iṭalyah bi-Tequfat ha-Renesans* (Jerusalem: Magnes Press, 1979), 180 n. 115.

61. See David Geffen, "Insights into the Life and Thought of Elijah del Medigo Based on His Published and Unpublished Works," *Proceedings of the American Academy for Jewish Research* 41–42 (1973–1974): 69–96. This otherwise informative article does not deal with Delmedigo's views on aggadah.

62. *Beḥinat ha-Dat*, ed. I. S. Reggio (Vienna, 1833), 55ff.

63. Pines, *Guide*, 2:573.

64. See too, Reggio's commentary to p. 57 of *Beḥinat ha-Dat*.

65. Geffen, "Life and Thought of Elijah del Medigo," 79, notes the relatively late date at which *Beḥinat ha-Dat* was published (1629); it was nonetheless "well known in Crete and Italy" prior to its publication. See too Barzilay, *Reason and Faith*, 144 n. 58.

66. Geffen, "Life and Thought of Elijah del Medigo," 76ff. See Mosheh David Cassuto, *Ha-Yehudim be-Firenze bi-Tequfat ha-Renesans* trans. M. Hartom (Jerusalem: Kiryat Sefer, 1967), 229. Cassuto finds no certain evidence for any of the reasons usually suggested for Delmedigo's departure from Italy.

67. Da Fano, *She'elot u-Teshuvot* (Duhrenfurt, 1788), 67b (responsum 108). Even serious native Italian Jewish thinkers like Jehiel Nissim da Pisa were already rejecting the possibility of a meaningful role for philosophical rationalism with respect to Judaism. (See Bonfil, *Rabbanut*, 183f., and n. 78). Relevant too are Jehiel Nissim's views concerning aggadah. See below pp. 122.

CHAPTER 7

Defining the Limits of Aggadic Authority: Old Affirmations, New Departures, and Contemporary Responses

Azariah's novelty resides in his broadly formulated principle that the religiously binding authority of the talmudic sages is limited to the foundations of the Oral Torah; beyond that, according to him, the sages did not seek to prevent later generations, using "good sense," from challenging their views. These foundations include everything transmitted as a tradition received from Moses and therefore directly endowed with Sinaitic authority. They include as well that which the sages derived through the application of the traditional hermeneutic principles to scripture and the preventive measures enacted by them to safeguard the Law. "But from this point on 'there is neither law nor judge,' and no one standing in the breach"[1]—no one, Azariah obviously means, either capable of or obliged to uphold consistently the validity of their views. Azariah turns to Maimonides' *Guide* for support, although the passage to which he refers and whose sense he transfuses does not definitively confirm his position. In a discussion specifically dealing with astronomical matters Maimonides had asserted that he did not intend to defend everything the sages had said. "For at that time mathematics were imperfect. They did not speak about this as transmitters of dicta of the prophets, but rather because in those times they were men of knowledge in these fields or because they had heard these dicta from the men of knowledge who lived in those times."[2] Azariah's version of this is that "it is unnecessary to be particular where the sages' words do not conform to known truth since they had not spoken on the issue [i.e., any non-halakhic matter] in the manner of a prophetic tradition but only as scholars of the time with respect to that matter, or because they heard it from scholars of those times." This being the case according to Azariah, rabbinic opinion is not binding in "matters that by their very nature could not conceivably have been uttered at Sinai, as for example some historical story . . . or matters that you clearly know were stated as one's own opinion, uncompelled by holy scripture."[3]

It is uncertain whether Maimonides would have agreed to this broad reformulation of his specific assertion with respect to astronomical matters and its application to the entire range of non-halakhic rabbinic dicta.[4] For in spite of his emphasis in the *Guide* on the metaphorical nature of midrashim, he did not in various of his ethical and juristic formulations[5] relegate midrashim and aggadic material to the realm of parable or poetic figure, except where he found it philosophically or theologically necessary to do so. In the *Mishneh Torah* he sometimes conferred the authority of "tradition" on talmudic opinion regarding the rewards assured for the performance of certain religious obligations, or he sanctioned the extreme censure and condemnation assigned for the violation of certain prohibitions. Azariah deems these nothing more than characteristic rabbinic hyperbole, utilized to underscore in the strongest possible terms the gravity of the matters under discussion. For example, on the strength of the talmudic passage that "whoever celebrates the Sabbath pleasurably is given boundless possession," Maimonides included assurance of such earthly reward in his concluding summation of the Sabbath laws, for it had been "already made explicit in the tradition," supported by rabbinic exegesis of relevant scripture. Azariah views this statement as intended merely to encourage the zealous performance of the religious act. Further, Maimonides gave official status to the mishnaic statement that "he who puts his fellow-man to shame in public . . . has no share in the world to come," whereas Azariah places it in the category of rabbinic exaggeration.[6]

It is of considerable importance to note that Azariah's position precisely with respect to such talmudic assurances or condemnations in matters of religious practice and ethical behavior led to his condemnation by some contemporary rabbinical authorities in Italy who deemed his views contemptuous of the tradition and its teachers ("milei de'afqaruta"). This, together with the displeasure expressed in his native Mantua by learned spokesmen whom he held in high regard, forced Azariah to make revisions in the *Me'or 'Einayim* after the work had appeared in print. He also deleted a number of passages that questioned the moralistic explanations of catastrophic historical events in Jewish experience (e.g., that Jerusalem was destroyed because there was no sense of modesty or because the great and the small were placed on an equal standard; Betar was destroyed because of the violation of the Sabbath). Azariah deems such reasons insufficient to account for the momentous events in question. He obviously still subscribes to the idea of God's providential role in history, but his refusal to take literally the explanations given in the aggadah suggests that he also sees the need for dealing with the problem of historical causation in more temporal terms as well. Even if Azariah's handling of such aggadic passages did not quite scandalize his rabbinic opponents as did the others referred to, he nonetheless deleted them in revising the chapter that had come under attack, an indication that his position here too was religiously offensive.[7]

The opposition to Azariah's views makes it clear that the definition and limits he sought to impose on authoritative classical rabbinic opinion were not acceptable to his opponents and other contemporaries. Despite his efforts to extrapolate a definitive view supportive of his own position from certain of Maimonides' assertions, opinion had hardened sufficiently by the later sixteenth century so that to question the literal meaning of religiously sensitive rabbinic statements would be controversial irrespective of what Maimonides might have intended. Azariah surely complicated his predicament even further with his suggestion that certain passages from the Zohar that reinforced the very severe talmudic threats against "the effusion of seed in vain" were not really to be taken literally. The authority vested in this qabbalistic classic was by then such that his denial of the literal intent of some of its statements could only be construed as irreverence. It obviously made no difference to his critics that, with respect to these particular rabbinic dicta (i.e., that the perpetrator is viewed as one who has committed murder and idolatry, and thus merits the death penalty), Azariah attempted to strengthen his argument on the basis of a passage from Maimonides' *Commentary on the Mishnah* to the effect that the strong language used by the sages had been intended "to intimidate and frighten" would-be violators of this prohibited act.[8] Azariah's opponents might, after all, point to Maimonides' *Mishneh Torah*, in which he clearly reflected the talmudic view in describing it not merely as "a great prohibition" but added that the perpetrator was under excommunication and it was as if he had committed murder.[9]

In historical matters with religious implications, Maimonides relied extensively on aggadot; he adopted highly imaginative and even chronologically impossible traditions, some of which include rationally problematic assumptions. In the *Epistle to Yemen* he recorded that "our sages of blessed memory, tell us that God . . . charged a prophet before the time of Moses to go to the Romans and another to go to the Arabs with the purpose of presenting them the Torah, but each of them in turn spurned it."[10] Maimonides' concern to eliminate anthropomorphism is obvious; it is a prophet who is charged with the mission and not God himself, as the aggadah has it. That the midrash itself makes no mention of the prophet despite the importance of his mission (leaving one hard pressed to identify this prophet) seems irrelevant for Maimonides. In his discussion of Abraham's religious development in the *Mishneh Torah*, Maimonides described the patriarch as having begun to speculate extensively about the nature of the universe from the moment he was weaned from the breast. This led him to conclude the necessity of a supreme divine power. By the time he was a mature adult he had perfected his understanding of monotheism and was driven to remonstrate with his contemporaries in Ur about their fallacious polytheistic beliefs and to destroy their idols. And when the ruler attempted to kill him, Abraham was miraculously saved.[11]

Such aggadic reconstructions of biblical events and personalities, as well as some of the problematic data Maimonides included in his introduction to the *Mishneh Torah*, represent an order of historical perception that differs from that of Azariah. In tracing the transmission of the tradition in his introduction, Maimonides followed a talmudic account according to which the prophet Ahijah of Shiloh presumably spanned the generations from the time of Moses to that of King David.[12] In considering the phenomenal life-spans attributed by the sages to various biblical figures, Azariah evaluates the accounts on the basis of relevant biblical evidence. He also reviews the efforts of medieval authorities such as Rashi and the tosafists (even if he does not find their explanations wholly satisfactory) to explain one or another such rabbinic passages more reasonably than what the plain meaning appears to be. He suggestively reminds the reader how difficult it would be for the rational mind to believe the scriptural accounts describing the length of the generations from Adam to Noah "were it not for the fact that Moses wrote them as they were dictated from the mouth of the Divine Majesty." Azariah is therefore confident that the reader "will not run and stumble"[13] into literal belief of what the sages intended for purely didactic purposes.

Among the historically problematic issues that Azariah extensively investigates is the telescoped and confused rabbinic chronology of the Second Temple period. In this regard he examines Maimonides' statement, again in the introduction to the *Mishneh Torah*, that Simeon the Just was among the members, albeit the youngest, of Ezra the Scribe's court (the men of the Great Assembly) and that he served as high priest following Ezra.[14] In the process of calling into question the thirty-four-year span between the rebuilding of the Temple in Jerusalem and the Persian defeat by Alexander the Great, which this chronology presupposed, and in demonstrating the many substantive problems it entailed, Azariah makes it clear that one is dealing not with a Sinaitic or prophetic tradition but with nothing more than an unauthoritative and uncompelling historical account.[15] Maimonides, working with the same data, believed them to be factually reliable and apparently vital to the integrity of the chain of religious tradition. Here Azariah finds it necessary to call attention to the errors in his great predecessor's statement of the facts.[16] Nonetheless, in concluding this very analysis of historical inaccuracies, Azariah not only attributes them, again, to the purely homiletical element in the rabbinic literature, but also seeks support for his departure from classical rabbinic tradition in Maimonides' *Guide*. Azariah is aware of the apparent problem that in the *Guide* Maimonides gave preference to his own view of certain biblical matters over that of the talmudic sages, whereas in his *Mishneh Torah*, "where all his words follow the opinion of the talmudic sages, [he] did not depart from their method" in this matter.[17] But Azariah does little more than occasionally mention such seeming incongruence, usually limiting his comments to what bears immediately on his own line of investigation.[18] For insofar as he relies on Maimonides to justify his own greater latitude with respect to midrashic interpretations and aggadic materials, he draws basically on certain relevant statements in the *Guide*, which—as his own occasional allusions suggest—do not exhaust the Maimonidean formulation.

The attempt of various medieval Jewish spokesmen to delimit the authority of aggadic material, whether in response to Jewish or non-Jewish critics, was an effort fraught with risk. For if indeed the Oral Torah was an organic whole, integrally related to scripture and therefore endowed with divinely sanctioned religious truth, then the attempt to draw distinctions between the status of its halakhic and aggadic components might seriously compromise the authoritativeness of both—regardless of what some talmudic sages themselves may have said about aggadah. The tendency to draw such limits, which after the geonim was largely the work of Spanish Jewish authorities, shows considerable signs of waning in the late middle ages and by Azariah's time, even among Sephardic scholars.[19] Isaac Aboab, one of Azariah's sources for Sherira Gaon's characterization of aggadah as mere guesswork, himself restricted the application of the gaon's pronouncement and viewed the vast majority of aggadot as exalted wisdom and moral doctrine, part of authoritatively transmitted rabbinic tradition—a consequential point that Azariah conveniently glosses over. According to Aboab, one was obliged to believe in the midrashic and aggadic assertions of the sages just as in the Law of Moses. If something appeared to be exaggeration or beyond the natural course of events this was a deficiency to be attributed not to their dicta but to limitations of our intellect.[20] Abraham Zacuto, as noted earlier, considered virtually every rabbinic account and statement, even the most imaginary, as historical truth.[21] David ibn Abi Zimra (Radbaz), one of the outstanding rabbinic authorities of the sixteenth century, affirmed his belief "in all the words of the sages even their casual talk." He had no doubt that the aggadah was as "true and fundamental and revealed from heaven as the rest of the Oral Law" and that it contained both an apparent and a hidden meaning, the latter being intended only for "those adept in mystical lore [*yod'im ḥen*]." He sharply criticized David Kimhi, the biblical commentator who had referred to some aspects of the aggadah as being far from reason. Abi Zimra observed that Kimhi was *far* from giving the plain meaning of the matter, whereas the words of the sages were indeed *near* to truth and reason.[22]

A consideration of the contrast between Abi Zimra and his younger contemporary Azariah is instructive. Abi Zimra, for example, attempted in one of his responsa to harmonize the apparently contradictory sentiments of the talmudic sage Joshua ben Levi regarding the value and desirability of pursuing aggadic study; he suggested that this sage's negative statements were only intended to preclude the public preaching of aggadot and committing them to writing. Aggadah, in other words, was to be transmitted only orally from one person to the next in order to avoid misinterpretation either by the ignorant or by the scoffers.[23] Azariah makes some effort to obviate the same apparent contradiction. He first offers the stock solution of the tosafists that the sources refer to two different sages by the same name, as well as the possibility that Joshua ben Levi changed his opinion, as the Talmud itself reports in various other instances. But he concludes that "however you look at it, the fundamental difficulty remains, for aside from R. Joshua b. Levi we have encountered the very aforementioned contradiction in the ranks of the sages so that, truthfully, whosoever considers this contradiction will in his amazement declare: 'What is this all about?' " The only resolution of the problem then is to view aggadot not as certain and authoritative halakhah but as the expression of the particular expositor's fancy, with the result that some are fitly spoken and are charming and others not. For not everyone who presumes to undertake this art succeeds, "as occurs too in the other areas of intellectual endeavor."[24] Although both Abi Zimra and Azariah describe the function of aggadah as "drawing the heart"[25] of the listener, that is, to some moral lesson or religious awareness, Abi Zimra attaches that function to the level of "apparent" meaning only, whereas Azariah draws no distinction between the "apparent" and the "hidden." His emphasis is on the symbolic or metaphorical meaning achieved through rational understanding rather than on any additional mystical meaning that presumably inheres in aggadah[26] and is ascertained only by means of special spiritual insight.

Azariah then has not only ruled out a divinely revealed status for aggadah, which Abi Zimra so categorically insisted upon, but in reducing it to "a manner of teaching through literary devices that . . . was very common among the gentile sages of antiquity," he simultaneously divests it of the esoteric dimension that Abi Zimra and others attached to it. The gentile sages based their lessons on stories involving animals and worldly affairs, and in dealing with matters of wisdom they would make allusions through the accounts they invented about gods and men—whether to hide these matters from the masses or in order that the listener take pleasure in the presumed story and remember it. "Our sages, who assumed that everything is contained in the Torah, derived their lessons from biblical narratives, although they knew clearly that their remarks did not convey the plain sense of the words." Every people, Azariah declares, has used literary devices in the service of religious edification. He even demonstrates that in order to impress some point on the audience the Jewish sages sometimes adopted material from non-Jewish authors such as the Greek fabulist Aesop.[27]

Such analysis and comparison had the virtue on the one hand of providing a historical perspective on ancient forms of Jewish religious expression and of placing them in a broader literary and intellectual context, thus making them more meaningful and comprehensible for Azariah's enlightened contemporaries. But on the other hand it could not leave unaffected the distinction between the "sacred" and the "profane," between the words of the talmudic sages and the Greco-Roman parallels Azariah had in mind. Wittingly or unwittingly, such comparison was suggestive of a relativism toward the aggadic dimension of the Oral Torah that could prove dangerous to the Jewish public.[28] His criteria and the comparative materials he utilizes for assessing aggadah, a central aspect of the Jewish tradition, is, after all, no longer firmly Judeocentric. The implications of this were perhaps not fully grasped even by Azariah himself. Azariah certainly emphasizes the significant Jewish ethical ideals and spiritual truths rabbinic homilies are intended to teach and reinforce, as well as, in his opinion, the intellectual refinement they also seek to inculcate: "Either to acknowledge the ways of His goodness and the mighty acts of our Lord, or else to praise a virtue and condemn a vice, or to teach something apprehended by the intellect and distance one from some foolishness."[29] But in the process of insisting on the purely human authority of aggadah and in stressing its similarity to the non-Jewish literary forms of "metaphor, symbol, and allegory"[30]—views that Abi Zimra, for example, would never have entertained[31]—Azariah significantly attenuates the sanctity normally attached to this rabbinic material.

That there was by Azariah's time an increasingly pronounced tendency to view the religious authority of aggadah as virtually on a par with that of halakhah is clear from his leading Italian Jewish contemporaries. In his *Minḥat Qena'ot*, intended to demonstrate the unshakable superiority of religion over philosophy,[32] Jehiel Nissim da Pisa, for example, granted that most midrashim are not to be taken literally but rather according to their secret meaning. However, Jehiel Nissim asserted that the efforts of earlier spokesmen to give aggadah rationalistic interpretations compromised this lore, which had been uniquely intended for Israel. Consequently the aggadic dicta of the sages "would not be contained in the well-known secrets of the Law that had only been handed down to Moses our master at Sinai from whom they were received by the prophets generation after generation."[33] It is noteworthy that in his capacity as a member of the Ferrara rabbinate, Jehiel Nissim, himself a highly cultured and accomplished student of philosophy, qabbalah, and rabbinic literature and in the forefront of Jewish intellectual and religious life, was among those who signed the 1574 declaration subscribed to in a number of Italian Jewish communities. This declaration forbade the possession and reading of the *Me'or 'Einayim* except by prior written approval of the local rabbinical authorities. His participation in this ban demonstrates his commitment to the principles set forth in his treatise[34] and reveals that he was no doubt offended by Azariah's handling of aggadah.

In the sixteenth century even the scholastic Moses Provençal, who continued in the tradition of medieval Jewish rationalism, did not treat the subject matter of aggadah allegorically. He insisted on the literal meaning of rabbinic aggadah even where it seemed to run counter to empirical knowledge and logical argument. In response to a question from one of his students regarding a rabbinic statement that upheld a view contrary to the opinion of physicians and naturalists, Provençal responded as a matter of theological principle that one could bring no proof from such opinion against the sages: "We have only the words of ben Amram [i.e., Moses] and his [Sinaitic] tradition, passed on from mouth to mouth to the sages, on whose authority we rely."[35] Provençal, unlike Jehiel Nissim da Pisa, did not sign the 1574 declaration, but other evidence indicates that this distinguished rabbi "utterly poured out his wrath" on Azariah "regarding every principal point," in particular the one concerning Azariah's view that in magnifying the punishment to be incurred for many transgressions, the sages were merely resorting to hyperbole. "And R. Moses Provençal took issue with him and wrote concerning him, 'Woe unto him who holds this view, seeking to permit forbidden things.' And so too he was furious with what he had written regarding the calculations of the time of redemption and rebuked him in language as distasteful as wormwood."[36]

Notes

1. *M.E.* 2:269f. For his brief summation of these foundations, Azariah refers to Maimonides' *Mishneh Torah* (*Hilkhot Mamrim* 1), but the context there otherwise has no bearing at all on Azariah's line of argument. Azariah's formulation, moreover, of the first of these foundations departs from Maimonides' wording (*Hilkhot Mamrim* 1:2: "Eḥad devarim shelimdu otan mi-pi ha-shemuʿah ve-hem Torah she-beʿal peh"). Azariah writes: "she-kol ha-davar ka-qatan ka-gadol ha-nimsar lanu mehem be-omram she-kakh nitqabbel mi-Mosheh rabbenu . . . ha-qabbalah mi-Sinai." Whether Azariah's greater specificity than Maimonides' and his reference to that which is Mosaically and Sinaitically mandated in the rabbinic tradition is intended to suggest a more restrictive meaning is a matter for some consideration.

2. *The Guide of the Perplexed*, trans. Shlomo Pines (Chicago: University of Chicago Press, 1963), 2:459.

3. *M.E.* 2:270. It is clear that Azariah was not simply paraphrasing the *Guide* loosely or quoting imprecisely from memory but in fact making the passage conform to his own needs. For in an earlier chapter in which he considers rabbinic views on astronomy and geography, he quotes the same passage rather precisely (*M.E.* 1:156). In the course of that chapter Azariah tends to imply that in all "speculative and non-Toraitic matters" the rabbis reflected the contemporary level of knowledge and thus its limitations (1:164; and see the introductory paragraph, p. 154). But he only formalizes and generalizes this position later on and then, as indicated, bases it on his own adaptation of Maimonides' statement.

4. Elijah Delmedigo, as we have noted, did clearly generalize with respect to the nonbinding status of aggadic material (see p. 100f. above), although there is no indication in the *Beḥinat ha-Dat* that he did so on the basis of this particular passage in the *Guide*.

5. See the discussion in Salo W. Baron, *A Social and Religious History of the Jews*, 2d ed. (New York and Philadelphia: Columbia University Press and Jewish Publication Society, 1952–1983), 6:177ff., 412f. n. 32.

6. *Mishneh Torah*, *Hilkhot Shabbat* 30:15, *Hilkhot Teshuvah* 3:14, *Hilkhot De'ot* 6:8, on the basis of Mish. Avot 3:15. I have chosen these passages from Maimonides' code in order to illustrate specific contrast with Azariah's position. Azariah's pertinent views are in the original version of *Me'or 'Einayim*, chap. 20, as reproduced by Israel Mehlman, in *Genuzot Sefarim*: *Ma'amarim Bibliografiyim* (Jerusalem: National and University Library Press, 1976), 33f.; and see p. 36, for the concluding paragraph, in which Azariah refers to "segulat maskilim" who urged him in the strongest terms to remove several rabbinic passages, and also one from the *Zohar* that they insisted had to be understood exactly as stated—advice that he was not yet prepared to follow. See Azariah's elaboration of his own position in his apologia (p. 38); and cf. Cassel, *M.E.* 1:ivff.

7. See Azariah's description of the situation as viewed by the rabbis in Venice who had taken strong objection to his approach, his reference to "kamah maskilei Mantua ve-zulatam," and the terms in which he formulates his concession (Mehlman, *Genuzot Sefarim*, 38f.). Although, according to Azariah's account, his view of the dictum concerning the public shaming of a fellow human being was not among those specifically challenged by the rabbis in Venice, it is nonetheless deleted in his revised version of chap. 20 of *M.E.* Regarding the historical aggadot, I find no reference to Betar in the source Azariah cites. He appears to have had in mind the aggadah in J. Ta'anit 4, and Ekhah Rabbati 2:5, regarding Tur-Simeon. See too *M.E.* 1:186f., also referring to Jerusalem and Betar and the "splendid wisdom" of the sages in explaining the events. As to how Azariah understood such "wisdom," see p. 96. and n. 41 above.

8. Mehlman, *Genuzot Sefarim*, 33f. The passage from Maimonides' *Commentary* is to Mish. Sanhedrin 7:4. Azariah views these talmudic threats (in B. Niddah 13a) and the related ones in the *Zohar* (i.e., the perpetrator does not merit to see the Divine Presence, and he can never remedy his sin through repentance; *Zohar*, Genesis 38:10; *Zohar*, Leviticus 21:15; *Zohar*, Genesis 47:29) virtually like the many other "exaggerated" statements intended to serve a purely didactic function: "to keep one far from the forbidden act." All similar rabbinic assertions are to be treated in like manner: "umimenu taqish'el kol domehu . . . asher mimenu taqish gam ken el kol ka-yoṣe' bo."

9. See *Mishneh Torah*, *Hilkhot Isurei Bi'ah* 21:18; and cf. B. Niddah 13a–b. Regarding the nature of the excommunication, see Maggid Mishneh loc. cit. Azariah, having found support in Maimonides' *Commentary*, ignores Maimonides' juristically formalized statement of the matter in the *Mishneh Torah*. In his revision of chap. 20, Azariah eliminates the entire discussion of "the effusion of

seed in vain" but retains, however, a very shortened version of Maimonides' statement in the *Commentary*. With its specific intent now conveniently deleted, Azariah uses Maimonides' phrase about language intended "to intimidate and frighten" as a general support of his own view regarding rabbinic hyperbole. In revising the chapter Azariah also replaced the controversial illustrations with several that had already been used by the fourteenth-century Isaac ben Sheshet Perfet to demonstrate "the custom of the sages to exaggerate, through the magnification of iniquities, in order that one be on his guard not to stumble with respect to them" (*M.E.* 1:235. The citation is from the responsa of Perfet, no. 171). The authority of this leading halakhist no doubt helped to make Azariah's revised statement of the matter more palatable to his critics. Azariah himself, when he already felt compelled to concede with respect to the disputed passages, added "halo be-khol zot lo tishaḥet kavanat ha-pereq meumah" (Mehlman, *Genuzot Sefarim*, 38f.). The fact remains that he had to reformulate his position so as to remove the shadow of doubt from the literal intent of certain obviously sensitive areas of rabbinic discourse, irrespective of how he personally continued to perceive them. He was in effect constrained to acknowledge, at least officially, that the range of authoritative teaching contained in the corpus of rabbinic lore exceeded the bounds of the criteria that he had set forth (see pp. 115f. above). See too Cassel, *M.E.* 1:ivf. The Bodleian Library copy of *M.E.* (Mantua, 1574), for example, pp. 87a–b, reflects the revisions that Azariah had been forced to make in chap. 20. These pages correspond to the text as Cassel has it in his edition (*M.E.* 1:235f.).

10. *Epistle to Yemen*, ed. Abraham S. Halkin and trans. Boaz Cohen (New York: American Academy for Jewish Research, 1952), ix and 44–47 of Hebrew and Arabic texts. This is Maimonides' version of the aggadah in Sifrei Deuteronomy, sec. 343; Mekhilta Ba-Ḥodesh chap. 5 (in the Lauterbach edition, 2:234ff.), and more briefly in the Talmud, B. 'Avodah Zarah 2b. The many more rabbinic references for this aggadah are given by Louis Ginzberg, *The Legends of the Jews* (Philadelphia: Jewish Publication Society, 1954), 6:30f. n. 181. In substituting Rome for the original "children of Esau" in the midrashic text Maimonides is of course following the frequent rabbinic identification of the two. Similarly, he substitutes Arabs for "children of Ishmael."

11. *Mishneh Torah, Hilkhot 'Avodat Kokhavim* 1:3; and see Salo W. Baron "The Historical Outlook of Maimonides" in *History and Jewish Historians*, (Philadelphia: Jewish Publication Society, 1964), 118. Like some geonim, Maimonides was critical of many scientifically or philosophically objectionable aggadot, but both "rather uncritically accepted any semilegendary reconstructions of the Jewish past" (Baron, p. 110). Maimonides' "rejection of the authority of the Aggadah when it contradicts his logical or theological convictions" contrasts with his historical outlook, which "is wholly determined by the aggadic elaborations of past events. Here, too, he rejects all legends which appear rationally impossible, but not those which lack confirmation in the original sources" (Baron, p. 404 n. 204). If Maimonides omitted the specific midrashic reference to the fiery furnace from which Abraham was miraculously rescued, he nevertheless apparently found the

aggadic record of the deliverance, however construed, as evidence of the miraculous and yet rationally conceivable. See also the important discussion, based on an autograph responsum of Maimonides from the Cairo Genizah, in M. Lutzki, "Ve-Khatav Mosheh-ḥamesh Teshuvot, . . ." in *Ha-Tequfah* 5 (1946): 699–702. In the sensitive area of eschatology, as for example with respect to the messianic age, Maimonides of course urges in his *Mishneh Torah* a very restrictive posture toward aggadic formulations. See the concluding lines of *Hilkhot Melakhim* 12:2.

12. *Mishneh Torah*, Introduction; and see Baron, "Outlook of Maimonides," 152f., and n. 186. Regarding Ahijah, see 1 Kings 11:29ff. Although the Ravad of Posquières challenged Maimonides on this point (*Hasagat ha-Ravad*; and cf. Isadore Twersky, "Rabbi Abraham ben David of Posquières: His Attitude to and Acquaintance with Secular Learning," in *Medieval Jewish Life*, ed. Robert Chazan [New York: Ktav, 1976], 173), Azariah's sixteenth-century contemporary in Safed, the distinguished rabbinic authority Joseph Caro, apparently had no problem with its historicity (see *Kesef Mishneh* to Maimonides' introduction). And even a philosophically oriented Italian Jewish contemporary like Obadiah Sforno appears disposed to treat such aggadic reconstructions of the past as quite tenable. Noting the unusual longevity of Phinehas, Sforno goes on to refer without qualification to the alternative rabbinic views that place him in the days of Jephthah or even identify him with Elijah, a view much earlier dismissed by Abraham ibn Ezra. See the Sforno and Ibn Ezra commentaries to Numbers 25:12; and cf. *M.E.*, chap. 18, where, apropos of the rabbinic telescoping of three Persian kings into one ("hu' Koresh, hu' Daryavesh, hu' Artaḥshastah"), Azariah addresses similarly problematic assertions including the Phinehas-Elijah identification.

13. *M.E.* 1:224ff. Azariah notes (p. 226) Maimonides' view in the *Guide*, that it was only the particular individuals mentioned in scripture who attained phenomenal age, whereas others lived the normal life-span. Azariah, however, has previously rejected this in favor of the view—"more in keeping with the meaning of the Torah"— of Augustine (!), which "you will also find in Nahmanides" (p. 221; and see pp. 55f. above).

14. *Mishneh Torah*, Introduction; and see Baron, "Outlook of Maimonides," 140, and n. 131.

15. The relevant discussion is contained in much of chaps. 30–40 of the *Me'or 'Einayim*; and see 2:363, e.g., regarding the tradition of thirty-four years for the Persian period.

16. See *M.E.* 2:309, 316. Azariah comments on Maimonides' reference to Simeon the Just, a tradition also included in the latter's Introduction to his *Commentary on the Mishnah*. He cites others, too, like Ibn Daud, who followed this tradition. As Azariah approvingly notes, Abraham Zacuto disputed the presumed high priesthood of Ezra (*M.E.* 1:2 n.); but Zacuto nevertheless assumed, quite unlike Azariah and even contra Rashi, that Simeon the Just was indeed Ezra's contemporary (*Sefer Yuḥasin* 11, col. a).

17. *M.E.* 2:316; and cf. 1:199. The reference to the *Guide* is to Pt. 3, chap. 48 (Pines, 2:600) and to the *Mishneh Torah, Hilkhot Tefillah* 9:7. W. G.

Braude ("Maimonides' Attitude to Midrash," in *Studies in Jewish Bibliography . . . in Honor of I. Edward Kiev*, ed. Charles Berlin [New York: Ktav, 1971]), 78, 81, speaks of Maimonides' "utter inconsistency" with respect to midrash and concludes that his real attitude toward it is to be found not in the *Guide* but in the "eloquent statement" in the "introduction to the *Mishnah*": "Should an utterance of the Sages appear to us farfetched then we must train ourselves in the disciplines of wisdom. . . . After all . . . our intelligence is weak . . . whereas all the Sages had to say is clear, precise and contains no dross . . . whatsoever." Braude is much too categorical in his resolution of this issue, but he does attempt to demonstrate its complexity. Cf. Reuven Bonfil ("Some Reflections on the Place of Azariah de Rossi's *Me'or 'Einayim* in the Cultural Milieu of Italian Renaissance Jewry," in *Jewish Thought in the Sixteenth Century*, ed. B. D. Cooperman [Cambridge: Harvard University Press, 1983], 44 n. 8), who says Maimonides "formulated the question clearly in his introduction to Pereq Ḥeleq." He describes Azariah's method as "at worst, a disputable position on an already controversial issue," it being moreover "superfluous to mention here the terms of the debate upon this issue starting with Maimonides" because "the evidence adduced by De Rossi himself (chapters 14–16) is sufficient." (Bonfil, p. 24 and n. 8). The evidence in those chapters, however, omits some of the important post-Maimonidean opinion on the issue, as Azariah knew (see pp. 97–101 above), and the thrust of those chapters in the *Me'or 'Einayim* (notably 14 and 15) is far less intended to reflect the continuing controversy as to the nature of midrashim and aggadot than to convince contemporaries that, after all, the most widely recognized authorities—both pre- and post-Maimonidean—had always argued against a literal approach to this material and that nevertheless the priority and honor of the sages had not been compromised. Indeed, insofar as controversy is concerned, it is primarily with respect to certain of his own contemporaries that he refers to any, and this presumably is what leads him to elaborate a point of view that at least the enlightened reader already takes or ought to take for granted ("'ad sheha-maskil yukhal le-hitpale' 'alenu ve-lomar zo vadai enah ṣerikhah le-fanim deqa'ari lah 'amai qa'ari lah umai kule hai asher ki rokhlah kaḥashiv va-azel . . . odi'a el ha-qore' eikh qin'at soferim asher hiṣikatni ve-yelaḥamuni ḥinam hikhriḥatni va-tikaḥeni be-ṣiṣat roshi la-vo' 'atah le-kabeṣ pezurei ha-maḥloqot ha-nizkarot min ha-aḥaronim 'al ha-rishonim"; *M.E.* 1:200, and see 219, for reference to contemporary criticism). As for the evidence in chap. 16, the terms in which Azariah analyzes the talmudic and midrashic story of Titus's death are new relative to the long history of interpreting aggadah (consideration of textual variants and divergence of detail, skepticism toward what purports to be an eyewitness account, use of non-Jewish historical and medical evidence, etc.). With the exception of a brief concluding reference, again, to the *Guide*, the chapter reflects above all the person and mind of Azariah.

18. In the course of his elaborate discussion in the *Maṣref la-Kesef* demonstrating the late origins of the traditional calendrical system, Azariah deals at length with an apparent discrepancy on this point between the *Guide* and the *Mishneh Torah*. The relevant passage in the *Guide* that rejects the views of certain

sages with respect to the sequence of creation presumably sustains Azariah's own position, even though it involves some biblical exegesis to which he objects (see *Maṣref la-Kesef*, 72–75, esp 75: "Ve-im be-devarim mah zulat eleh timṣa ha-Ram ha-nizkar soter be-yeter sefarav . . . ha-nimṣa' lo be-ḥibburav ha-talmudiyim kemo she-zakharnu sof pereq lamed-zayin [i.e., *M.E.* 2:316], ha-amen ki ba-derush ha-zeh asher lefi ha-nir'eh hararim gedolim teluyim bo hayah me'od nizhar bi-devarav ha-aḥaronim af ki n'omar bi-veḥinat ha-derush ha-zeh shelo yitakhnu"). In *M.E.* 1:199, Azariah uses the same passage from the *Guide* (Pt. 2, chap. 30) to demonstrate that Maimonides, like other medieval authorities, did not necessarily accept the midrashic interpretations of the sages where these were of a purely homiletic nature. But there Azariah does not refer to the serious implications of this passage for the traditional calendrical calculations and its incongruence with Maimonides' discussion in the *Mishneh Torah*.

19. Jacob Katz observes that in Ashkenazic Jewry, "Certainly, no sentence or dictum even of the 'Aggadah would have been discarded as representing merely the opinion of its author in talmudic times. It is true that such an attitude was adopted by Spanish Jewish authorities in order to refute the accusations of Christian opponents and as part of a genuine criticism of certain details of the tradition. Among Ashkenazi Jews, however, such an approach would have been considered as bordering on heresy" (*Exclusiveness and Tolerance* [New York: Schocken, 1962], xiii). By the late middle ages and early modern period the observation may be extended to non-Ashkenazic spokesmen as well.

20. Aboab, *Menorat ha-Ma'or* (Vilna: Romm, 1884), 9, 12, 96. See the introductory, rhymed section (p. 7). To illustrate the punishment to be meted out in the next world for derision of any dictum of the sages, Aboab refers, among others, to the fate of Titus as described in B. Gittin 56b–57a. See *Menorat ha-Ma'or*, 96, and also 46 ("ve-lamadnu gam ken onshei ha-rasha' mi-ma'asiyot ha-ketuvim ba-aggadot"), where the Titus and Onkelos bar Kalonikus story is cited more fully. Regarding the fourteenth- or fifteenth-century authorship of this work, see n. 10 above. There is an interesting and revealing progression in this religiously conditioned response to geonic limitations on the authority of aggadah. At about the turn of the eighteenth century when Moses Frankfurter of Amsterdam translated Aboab's ethical treatise into Yiddish, he deleted entirely the references to Sherira and Hai, apparently out of concern that the simple faith of the popular reader not be disturbed. And in his Hebrew commentary to Aboab's text, presumably addressed to the more learned reader, he went even further than Aboab himself in an effort to invalidate the obvious intent of Sherira's assertion and to uphold the sanctity of aggadah: he disregarded the literal meaning of the term *umdanah* and instead endowed it with a moralistic interpretation (*Menorat ha-Ma'or*, 12, Yiddish translation, and the Hebrew commentary *Nefesh Yehudah*). To this increasingly pietistic attitude toward aggadah—inclusive of both Ashkenazic and Sephardic rabbinic spokesmen—and with particular regard to the earlier geonic view of the matter, one should add Azariah's own contemporary and bitter critic, the famous Judah Loew of Prague. See below, chap. 8, esp. pp. 143f.

21. See pp. 34f. above. Zacuto, for example, includes the story, already reported by Sherira, about the Persian king, Yazdegerd II, who had been swallowed by a dragon for having interfered with the practice of Jewish religion (see p. 90 above; and Zacuto's *Sefer Yuḥasin*, 202a).

22. *She'elot u-Teshuvot ha-Radbaz* (Warsaw, 1882), pt. 3, responsum 405, pt. 4, responsum 232, pt. 3, responsum 641. See also Israel M. Goldman, *The Life and Times of Rabbi David Ibn Abi Zimra* (New York: Jewish Theological Seminary, 1970), 68ff.

23. *She'elot u-Teshuvot ha-Radbaz*, pt. 4, responsum 232. See too Cassel's n. 1 to *M.E.* 1:209. Abi Zimra refers here also to the pitfalls of limited understanding of aggadah, exemplified for him "in these generations she'osin bema'amarei raza"l perushim asher lo khen."

24. *M.E.* 1:209f.

25. *She'elot u-Teshuvot ha-Radbaz*, pt. 4, responsum 232; *M.E.* 1:210, 211, 212; and cf. the talmudic usage, e.g., B. Ḥagigah 14a: "elu ba'alei aggadah she-moshkhin libo shel adam."

26. The language used by Abi Zimra to distinguish between the apparent and hidden meaning in aggadah (*nigleh-nistar*) occurs long before in Maimonides' *Introduction to Pereq Ḥeleq* in his commentary to Mishnah Sanhedrin, chap. 10: ("she-divreihem yesh lo nigleh ve-nistar ve-khi hem be-khol mah she'omrim min ha-devarim ha-nimna'im dibru bahem be-derekh ḥidah u-mashal"). Maimonides, however, referred to the metaphor as that in which the intent is not in its outer imagery but rather is its inner (i.e., "hidden") meaning ("ki ḥidah hu' ha-davar sheha-mekhuvan bo be-nistar lo' be-nigleh mimenu." See also Pines, *Guide* 1:11: "Now consider the explicit affirmation of [the Sages] . . . that the internal meaning of the *words of the Torah is a pearl* whereas the external meaning of all parables *is* worth *nothing*" That Azariah's concern in *M.E.* was not with the esoteric appears to have elicited the praise of one of his contemporaries. A highly laudatory letter addressed to him, perhaps by his close friend Abraham Provençal, reads in part: "Kol yamai niṣta'arti 'al ha-rishonim, bir'oti ka'asher lo maṣ'ah yadam pishrin le-mifshar ve-qitran le-mishrah, 'amdu ve'amru vehi sod, umi 'amad be-sod ha-shem? *Atah ben adam ein lekhah 'eseq be-nistarot raq asher timṣa' ekhol*, ekhol et ha-megillah" (emphasis added). See S. J. Halberstam, "Sheloshah Ketavim 'al Devar Sefer Me'or 'Einayim u-Mikhtav ehad el Rabbi Azariah Min ha-Adumim ve-'od Mikhtav 'odotav," in *Festschrift zum Achtzigsten Geburstage Moritz Steinschneider's* (Leipzig: Otto Harrassowitz, 1896), 7; and see chap. 2, n. 39 above.

27. *M.E.* 1:213, 218, 2:339; and see *Bereshit Rabbah* 64:8, regarding Joshua ben Hananiah and the fable of the lion and the partridge.

28. The late-eighteenth-century Italian Rabbi Hananel Neppi, in discussing the ban of the rabbis in Safed against the *Me'or 'Einayim*, explained that it was not at all because of any "blemish of heresy and disbelief" in it (a very questionable interpretation; see below, n. 36). But even he conceded their concern that "this book might get into the hands of some unworthy student and he would

drink the *evil waters* (emphasis added) of many diverse opinions of certain authors whom he [Azariah] cites in matters such as these, and they would make an impression on his [the student's] mind leading him to stray from the tradition of the sages . . . and to deny the principles of our holy Torah. And therefore, it appeared in their eyes appropriate to remove a stumbling block from the path of our people" (Halberstam, "Sheloshah Ketavim 'al Devar Sefer Me'or 'Einayim," 4, from manuscript material in Neppi's biographical and bibliographical lexicon *Zekher Ṣadiqim li-Verakhah*).

29. *M.E.* 1:206.

30. Ibid., 208.

31. Cf. for example the view of Maimonides in his *Guide* to the effect that the midrashim "have the character of poetical conceits whose meaning is not obscure for someone endowed with understanding. At that time this method was generally known and used by everybody, just as poets use poetical expressions" (Pines, *Guide* 2:573).

32. This is the characterization given by Cassuto, *Ha-Yehudim be-Firenze bi-Tequfat ha-Renesans*, trans. M. Hartom (Jerusalem: Kiryat Sefer Press, 1967), 275.

33. *Minḥat Qena'ot*, ed. David Kaufmann (Berlin, 1898), 14. Jehiel Nissim was taking issue with the position affirmed in the previous century by Jedaiah Bedersi. See chap. 6, pp. 98f., nn. 47–48, and n. 35.

34. See Cassuto, *Ha-Yehudim be-Firenze*, 277, and 278, concerning the great esteem in which Jehiel Nissim was held as a talmudic scholar and the weight his opinion carried in some of the most complicated halakhic issues. But see Bonfil, "Reflections," 28, for his description of the rabbis who signed the 1574 manifesto and the reference only to "some Rabbis of Ferrara"; cf., however, Bonfil, *Ha-Rabbanut be-Iṭalyah bi-Tequfat ha-Renesans* (Jerusalem: Magnes Press, 1979), 33, 183, the discussion of Jehiel Nissim's major place among Italian Jewish thinkers of the period. Among the Pesaro signatories was Jehiel Trabot, who was, according to some, one of the leading Italian rabbinic decisors (see Meir Benayahu, *Haskamah u-Reshut bi-Defusei Veneṣiyah* [Jerusalem: Ben-Zvi Institute, 1971], 97). Regarding the then fifty-three-year-old rabbi in Venice, Samuel Judah Katzenellenbogen (see *Encyclopaedia Judaica* [1972], s.v. "Katzenellenbogen"), who initiated the campaign against the *Me'or 'Einayim*, cf. Bonfil, "Reflections," 26f.; and cf. Bonfil, *Rabbanut*, 190, 197ff. The text of the 1574 ban is in David Kaufmann, "Contributions à l'histoire des luttes d'Azaria de Rossi," *Revue des études juives* 33 (1896): 83ff.

35. See the discussion in Bonfil, *Rabbanut*, 195, and also his article "Perush R. Mosheh Provençal le-Khaf-He Haqdamot ha-Rambam," *Kiryat Sefer* 50 (1975): 158, where the text of Provençal's response to Yehosef Hazak is quoted. Bonfil describes Provençal as "a dogmatic scholastic" who "forced dogmatic faith on the scholastic philosophy to which he adhered" (*Rabbanut*, 195). That Provençal believed in "aggadot ḥaza"l ki-feshutan" even though they appeared to contradict empirical knowledge would be consistent with his theological stance,

given his encompassing view of the Sinaitic character of rabbinic tradition. See p. 73 and n. 13 above, regarding his serious criticism of Azariah on the chronology issue, in which he invoked virtually the same theological position. In the later sixteenth-century, the view that the opinion of physicians and naturalists was to be rejected insofar as it ran counter to certain aggadic assertions was also expressed by Judah Loew of Prague. He refers to those individuals who offer naturalistic opinions, in this instance with respect to an aspect of human anatomy, as charlatans who know nothing of the wisdom whereby creation was effected (see Loew, *Be'er ha-Golah* [New York: Talpiyot, 1953] sec. 3, p. 35). The aggadic statement in question had been cited earlier by Maimonides to illustrate midrash as "poetical conceit," and Loew without referring to him was in effect refuting that view. See Pines, *Guide*, 2:513 and Jacob Elbaum ("Rabbi Judah Loew of Prague and His Attitude to the Aggadah," *Scripta Hierosolymitana* 22 [1971]: 33), who refers to the "veiled" criticism of Maimonides. Loew's open and unrestrained criticism of Azariah will be dealt with further on.

36. "Deshafakh ḥamimei deḥamimei 'al rabbenu ha-meḥaber be-khol pinah u-finah . . . ḥamato ba'arah bo ve-qara' 'alav devarim qashim ke-gidim." This is reported by Hananel Neppi, who described Provençal's reaction on the basis of a manuscript of "objections to the *Me'or 'Einayim*" that he found in a collection in Reggio ("hasagot 'al sefer *Me'or 'Einayim* . . . bekh"y [i.e., bi-khetav yad] mekhuvanot le-Mahara"m Provençal deshafakh ḥamimei deḥamimei" [see Halberstam, "Sheloshah ketavim 'al Devar Sefer Me'or 'Einayim," 5]. Joseph Yarei's version of the text reads: ". . . hamimei ve-hamimei dehamimei . . ." See "Liquṭim me-Kitvei ha-Rav Ḥananel Neppi," in *Zikaron le-Avraham Eliyahu Harkavy* [St. Petersburg, 1909], 479). Bonfil ("Reflections," 31) merely quotes Neppi to the effect that he himself found not even "a morsel of heresy or unbelief" in Azariah's work and that "all this flurry stirred up by those excellent scholars and foundations of the world (i.e., the rabbis in Safed) was probably a result of their apprehension that the book might perhaps come into the hands of some unworthy student" (cited from Halberstam, p. 4). Whether Neppi himself was correct in assuming that these "excellent scholars" in Safed found no "blemish of heresy and disbelief" in the *Me'or 'Einayim* is extremely doubtful. Those rabbis, notably Joseph Caro, did after all consider that the work deserved to be burned and expressed amazement that the local rabbis had allowed its printing (see pp. 58f. above). That Caro died before he had an opportunity to sign the ban against the *Me'or 'Einayim* that he had directed his pupil to prepare, and that the ban was therefore not disseminated and only became known about two hundred years later is explained by Neppi as providential (Halberstam, p. 5). This explanation is, however, irrelevant and in any event merely confirms Neppi's own opinion of *M.E.*, not that of the sixteenth-century rabbis in Safed. Neppi's interpretation of the text of the ban is also open to question: the proposed ban referred to the need to extirpate the work "because of the honor of the Torah and its principles"—which they believed Azariah had desecrated. Neppi ("in my humble opinion") takes the intent of the phrase to be that "some unworthy student" might be adversely affected by the work. This was

no doubt a concern, but in the first instance the Safed rabbis were condemning Azariah's own views. And even Neppi's interpretation presupposes that the *Me'or 'Einayim* did indeed contain "the noxious waters of varied opinions of certain authors whom he [Azariah] cites." Neppi's assumption that the Safed rabbis were stirred up *only* because Azariah had brought the creation era chronology into question is also extremely unlikely. It is inconceivable that in this prominent center of talmudic learning and the focal point of contemporary Jewish mysticism the scholars (who since about 1559 included David ibn Abi Zimra, who apparently died in 1573) would not have been absolutely scandalized by Azariah's attitude toward aggadah, not to speak of his frequent recourse to non-Jewish works in dealing with many of its problems.

CHAPTER 8

Aggadic Exegesis: Between Azariah's Critical Analysis and Maharal's Denunciations

As significant as Azariah's overall perception of aggadah, and his exposition of its relationship to the rabbinic tradition as a whole, is his specific handling of problematic aggadot, particularly those that present historical difficulties. He undertakes to dissect aggadah and either to extract, where feasible, the historical kernel that had often become garbled in the process of transmission or to demonstrate its moralistic intent, which had often been transmitted in a miraculous and therefore historically indefensible medium. Thus Azariah frequently finds it necessary to confront differing versions of a particular aggadah in order to harmonize them or at least to reconstruct the most reasonable course of events or the identity of the principal individuals involved. These reconstructions may not always be quite accurate but they are usually imaginative and reflect the best sources and techniques he has at his disposal. Where the investigation reveals not only discrepancies between the versions but, even more seriously, an underlying account that cannot, according to historical and rational criteria, possibly have transpired, Azariah rejects it as a factual representation despite alleged eyewitness testimony in the aggadah. These efforts accord him a unique position in the tradition of aggadic exegesis and result in paradigms of aggadic analysis.

In historical matters generally Azariah assumes that as an account was passed on it never quite retained its original form, having undergone changes as each author drew on the available tradition: "even an event that transpires before our eyes results in differing versions with those who report it, whether with additions or deletions."[1] As for the historical information that aggadah provides, Azariah also assumes that it may be imprecise or incomplete, although here he attributes these limitations to the nonchalant attitude of the sages toward history. History was incidental to the sages' abiding preoccupation with the Law, and they passed on whatever historical traditions they had before them without much scrutiny.[2] In accounts of profane matters they concerned themselves with generalizations with little concern for details; therefore, Azariah declares, whoever is determined to acquire a knowledge of things as they really occurred can be expected to give greater credence to one recognized as a more expert authority (than the sages).[3] Of course, such lack of historical reliability in the rabbinic aggadah is more than adequately compensated for by the religious benefit deriving from it—at least so Azariah would like his most severe critics to believe. For with respect to rabbinic accounts he says, "many times foolishness in them is [really] wisdom, and deficiency is [really] completeness in that our heart will [thus] not be enticed because of them [i.e., profane matters] to turn aside from the essential matters to the pursuit of vanity."[4] Surely this is not Azariah hankering after closeted pietism. Rather it is a combination of irony and an attempt to put the best possible face on his own exposure of a good many follies, errors, and inconsistencies in the aggadic material in the process of reconstructing it.

At the heart of this process is the art of textual criticism, in which Azariah proves himself to be the most accomplished Jewish practitioner of the period.[5] He is forthright in addressing the problem of textual interpolations in aggadic works and other Jewish classics. He observes in passing that even halakhic works need to be scrutinized for textual errors.[6] Nonetheless, Azariah deems it judicious to invoke a talmudic dictum to justify correcting traditional texts[7] and for good reason, for it was undoubtedly a delicate undertaking to question sacred classics. Those for whom all versions were equally sacred and in need of only casuistical resolution would consider it irrelevant, and worse yet, irreverent to call attention to factual and stylistic discrepancies between multiple versions of talmudic and midrashic accounts and to collate variant, often anachronistic readings. Yet Azariah proceeds to introduce numerous historical, literary, and linguistic considerations, often on the basis of non-Jewish sources; frequently he is motivated less by the desire to confirm the particular account than to engage in critical analysis that may even lead to its refutation. There is far greater specificity, critical intent, and consequence here than in the general comparison, previously noted, that he draws between the didactic purpose of aggadic metaphor and of Greco-Roman mythology.[8] Such analysis of detail and formulation and comparison with internally discrepant parallels or external sources of information yields an especially great potential for erosive impact on the authority of the received texts of the Oral Tradition.

For all his undoubtedly sincere desire to make the best possible sense of these rabbinic sources, Azariah is by the very nature of his analytical procedure in some degree challenging their integrity. Having made the distinction in principle between the normative halakhic *and* the aggadic components of the hallowed tradition there was no assurance that one could successfully reintegrate its respective segments and restore that integrity. In Azariah's work the tenability of the aggadic component was now often dependent upon new, external approaches including an acknowledgment of factually superior outside sources,[9] even Christian ones. Azariah is no adversary of Judaism. But his approach, coming precisely at a time of growing emphasis on the unique, qualitatively different, even superior and spiritually self-sufficient qualities of Jewry and Judaism,[10] goes a long way to explain the strong opposition to the *Me'or 'Einayim*. The pietism of the age, the mysticism that permeated Jewish society, and the pervasive preoccupation with messianic anticipation militated against a positive reception to Azariah's quest for rational and historical verification of aggadic narratives, except in the most limited circles.

The sense of identification with tradition and its sacred sources, including the aggadic ones that especially lent themselves to the exposition of Jewish spiritual distinctiveness, became pronounced as the sixteenth century progressed. The Italian qabbalists, for example, turned increasingly to the aggadic sources in their elaboration and dissemination of mystical doctrine, and they and the conservative element among Italian Jewish scholars generally reacted sharply even to the allegorizing of aggadah by preachers such as Judah Moscato.[11] In Ashkenazic circles, such an outstanding spokesman as Judah Loew of Prague, the only comprehensive Ashkenazic thinker in the early modern period, personified the cultural isolation of Jewry from the larger society. Despite his knowledge of secular studies, his awareness of Renaissance developments, and his contact with Christian scholars and theologians, he viewed Jewry as a species unto itself in whose unique nature he found metaphysical significance.[12] His attitude toward aggadah, to the interpretation of which he devoted an immense intellectual effort, was extremely conservative. He viewed it to be as authoritative and true as the halakhic pronouncements of the ancient rabbis and believed that it embodied the inner, esoteric wisdom known to the sages from received tradition reaching back to Moses himself. For meddling with and misconstruing the dicta of the rabbinic sages, as, from Loew's point of view, Azariah had done, one would surely be punished and have to "offer his soul in restitution." It is not surprising that what Loew perceived as a challenge to the status of aggadah as Torah should therefore take on doctrinal consequence: he who asserted that aggadic dicta were not "words of Torah" like the rest of the Torah forfeited his share in the world to come.[13] Nothing in the rabbinic tradition itself nor in the vast majority of medieval aggadic exegesis comes close to this extreme assertion.

Loew directed a particularly sharp attack against Azariah's work in his *Be'er ha-Golah*, a defense of talmudic tradition and aggadah against various categories of critics, written some years after the *Me'or 'Einayim*. Loew expressed deep chagrin that *Me'or 'Einayim* had been published—without anyone voicing protest, according to him—for in his opinion it was worse than the works of heretics and sorcerers; like them it deserved to be burned. Loew found no more fitting appellation for the non-Jewish sources that are so prominent in the *Me'or 'Einayim* than that they are the "works of idolators" ("sifrei ha-'aku"maz").[14] Confident though he was that no believer in the Law of Moses would "drink of his evil, accursed waters," Loew nonetheless elaborated his denunciation of Azariah. He condemned the latter for having challenged the reliability of various aggadic statements and for having dared to enlist the aid of gentile authors, with the result that "the major part of his structure" was often based on these profane sources.[15]

According to Loew, aggadot—"words of Torah" and thus of Sinaitic origin—had been reduced in Azariah's scheme to nothing more than "fantasies intended to mislead the masses." Azariah's serious suggestion that the ancient rabbis had devised aggadot in order to impress certain religious values on the populace was paraphrased by Loew as "invention and a plot to entice the multitude." Loew condemned Azariah for such "words of mockery," for his derisive attitude toward "the words of the living God" as if they were in vain and useless. Indeed, Loew was astounded that a Jew should have made such statements, for although religious zeal might have led someone of another faith to make disparaging remarks concerning Jewish sanctities, nothing of this kind had ever before been perpetrated by a member of the Jewish faith: it had never occurred to anyone that Jewry had such a one in its midst.[16] As for the charges themselves, whatever other failing Azariah may have been guilty of from the traditional Jewish standpoint of his age, he was not guilty of mockery of the rabbinic lore nor the attitude that it was worthless.[17] It was the novelty of the *Me'or 'Einayim* that was so disturbing to the late-sixteenth-century Jewish cultural milieu. Loew must certainly have been aware of some of the more extreme, post-Maimonidean opinion regarding aggadah, yet he considered Azariah's position as shockingly different, qualitatively separate, and hitherto unknown in Jewish circles. Azariah had not feared to speak about the sages as if they were his contemporaries and colleagues, something Loew said had never happened in Jewish society "until this generation."[18]

Among other things Loew was specifically distressed by the unconventional approach to aggadic materials in chapter 12 of the *Me'or 'Einayim*. Here Azariah finds it of consequence to compare and analyze over half a dozen rabbinic texts in order to clarify a narrative about Alexandrian Jewry. These sources contained conflicting detail as to the identity of the ruler who presumably destroyed this Jewish community. Azariah first "reveals" that in the *Tosefta*, the protosource of the narrative, there is no mention whatsoever of the massacre, this being an apparent addition of the Talmud itself. The Palestinian and Babylonian versions of that talmudic account are, however, in disagreement, and the latter itself gives two discrepant reports concerning the ruler in question.[19] Azariah dismisses Alexander of Macedon and Hadrian, those mentioned in the Babylonian Talmud, because on historical and chronological grounds, substantiated from various non-Jewish authors, they could not possibly have been related to the events.[20] Despite his high regard for the distinguished Isaac Abravanel, Azariah categorically rejects his suggestion that the Roman ruler intended in the Babylonian Talmud was Severus Alexander—the rabbinic sages who related the narrative concerning Alexandrian Jewry had preceded Severus by about a century! Moreover non-Jewish historical sources that Azariah had consulted (Eutropius and Platina) report nothing about exploits of Severus Alexander against Alexandria or its Jewish community. The fuller discussion in Abravanel's introduction to his commentary on 1–2 Kings makes the contrast between him and Azariah even clearer. Despite the differing versions, Abravanel was convinced that both Talmuds had meant the same thing and that "there is nothing perverted and twisted in them." According to him there had been two destructions of Alexandrian Jewry in Roman times: under "Tragynus" and, at a much later date, under the twenty-fourth Roman emperor (Severus) Alexander. Although Abravanel refers to and presumably consulted "chronicles of the Roman kings," he is simultaneously determined to preserve the integrity of the tradition in the Babylonian Talmud, and its reference to "Alexander." However, in substituting (Severus) Alexander for the obviously impossible "Alexander of Macedon," he still ends up with a hopelessly anachronistic explanation of the events in question. He emerges here, as well as in his discussion of other historically problematic rabbinic texts, as a far less exacting interpreter of the Jewish past than Azariah; unlike Azariah he is not disposed to grant the possibility of contradictory historical traditions in the rabbinic literature.[21]

Azariah himself follows a different procedure in dealing with the narrative in question. He attempts to resolve the orthographic problems presented by the names "Tragynus" and "Trakhynus," which occur in the Palestinian Talmud and the related Midrash Rabbah sources, respectively. These are obviously variants of the same name. And Azariah, noting the problem of ascertaining the correct reading due to the lack of vowel signs but also the relationship between the consonants *g* and *kh* in the usage of the Palestinian literature, concludes that the reference is obviously to the Roman ruler Trajan[us].[22] He also relies on the ancient Roman and Christian authors for their accounts of Trajan's campaigns and seeks historical corroboration in Petrus Messia's then recently published *Los cesares*, which mentions a revolt by the Alexandrian Jews that Trajan violently suppressed.[23] Azariah, in short, does a commendable job of attempting to piece together and interpret obscure aggadic material concerning an aspect of the Jewish insurrection during Trajan's reign, a set of events that are inadequately treated even by ancient non-Jewish authors such as Eusebius and that have only relatively recently been further reconstructed with the aid of papyrological materials.[24]

Azariah's purpose is to eliminate contradictions in the rabbinic sources that relate to well-known historical events and to prevent the reader from being misled.[25] He presupposes that there is often a significant historical element in the aggadah—even if historical narrative was not the rabbis' major concern—but that it may often have been garbled. Judah Loew faulted Azariah on both scores. He viewed as madness Azariah's suggestion at the end of chapter 12 that the sages may have received and then passed on erroneous historical information. If there was any error it was Azariah's, none of whose comments were worthy of a wise and intelligent scholar. To attribute contradiction and error to the sages was to Loew's way of thinking an unforgivable act. Azariah could instead have followed the traditional procedure of suggesting another reading of the text to remove the difficulty of certain names. Loew concluded that the intent and result of Azariah's fraud and error was to darken all the divine sources of illumination in the world.[26]

In his discussion, Azariah himself may have made a token effort to resolve one of the talmudic passages relating to Alexandrian Jewry in accordance with the tosafists. But since this required accepting a patently erroneous version that referred to Alexander of Macedon, Azariah rejects their approach.[27] In matters of historical concern at least, Azariah does not feel constrained to defend or accept the view of even the most distinguished Jewish spokesman of the past: that is, mere precedence in time does not necessarily assure infallible opinions.[28]

For Loew, by contrast, the reference to Alexander of Macedon presented no problems. He considered it a correct version. That it conflicted with another version in the Babylonian Talmud (i.e., Hadrian) had been adequately explained by the tosafists: Alexandrian Jewry may have experienced destruction under both these rulers.[29] Loew's reverence for aggadic tradition was such that difficulties arising from the rabbinic record were in effect inconsequential. After all,

> even though it seems clear that there is no difficulty whatever, I declare that the words of the sages are not a historical work in which authors write about events that have transpired. For had it been their intent to describe who inflicted destruction in Betar and what happened concerning Trajanus [etc.], the matter would be difficult. However, it was the intent of the sages to relate only what befell Israel and the Holy Land, which rulers destroyed. . . . To sum the matter up, this man [Azariah] has taken it into his mind, Heaven forbid, to substitute falsehood for truth, but everyone who is a believer and a person of understanding will know that these words of the sages are trustworthy.[30]

Underlying Loew's isolation of rabbinic dicta from historical reality was his conviction that the sages did not address material issues, natural causation, or the concrete aspects of events in their aggadic statements: they were concerned only with the inner essence and hidden meaning of things.[31] In other words, there was nothing historically problematic since history itself was of no issue. Therefore, to impose historical considerations and Azariah's brand of historical investigation on sources for which historical perspective, explanation, and evidence were irrelevant (and whose sanctity defied error) was at best folly, at worst transgression against the authoritative assertions of the ancients.

This polarization between Azariah and Judah Loew is also

evident when Azariah moves from historically obscure aggadah to aggadah that he regards as historically unreliable and purely "an invention and means of edification." Azariah's essay concerning the strange affliction suffered by the Roman emperor Titus poignantly exemplifies his analysis of aggadic narrative contrived and embellished by the sages as though the events had actually taken place in the manner related.[32] Here too Azariah notes at the outset the problem of multiple versions of the Titus story and emphasizes that whoever compares the various sources will easily discover the many discrepancies among them. This itself will arouse the enlightened person's attention, "for if the story were true the aforementioned narrators would be inclined to greater agreement."[33] For Azariah then, with an aggadic narrative as unusual as this, one vital consideration in determining credibility is whether the relevant parallel texts are reasonably similar and compatible.

In this instance, however, the more critical factor is that the basic elements of the story are legendary, not historical. Especially notable therefore are the erudition and analytical skills that Azariah marshals against the most incredible point, on which all the versions agree: Titus, the despoiler of Jerusalem and its Temple during the Judeo-Roman War, had supposedly been divinely punished for his destructive acts and blasphemous utterances. A gnat entered his nostril and pecked away at his brain for seven years. At his death it was found that the gnat had grown into something the size of a sparrow or young pigeon. There is also the report of a rabbinic sage who gave firsthand testimony to these postmortem findings; and a somewhat later talmudic "tradition" even vividly described its beak of brass and claws of iron. Predictably, Azariah views this strange combination of circumstances as riddled with impossibilities from the point of view of nature,[34] and he proceeds to analyze the relevant anatomical and related scientific data. Regarding the historical matter, Azariah is convinced that the various classical and more recent non-Jewish authorities whom he introduces to controvert the rabbinic account should be recognized, at least by those who acknowledge the truth, as being in greater control of the details than the sages. By all reliable accounts not only were there chronological discrepancies in the rabbinic sources, but Titus had either died of malarial fever or been poisoned by his brother Domitian.[35] Azariah is also clearly determined to respond to Italian Jewish contemporaries from whom he seems to have expected a greater degree of intellectual sophistication: "For in this matter I have heard, especially from those whom I too consider learned in Jewish tradition, that they believe the words [of the Titus story] as written. And they are intense in speaking evil of those who do not believe it."[36] Azariah's words suggest at least disappointment with—perhaps disdain for—the *ba'alei Torah* to whom he refers. We have here, moreover, further indication of that contemporary climate of opinion hostile to any appraisal of aggadah that appeared to compromise its sacrosanct character.

It is his concern regarding this literalist position in the Jewish camp, Azariah tells us, and his consequent concern for the coreligionist "who thirstily drinks the words of our sages but who is also drawn by human reason" that led him to address the Titus story. In so doing, he attempts to resolve the dilemma of rationally oriented Jewish contemporaries who, although steadfast in their commitment to the tradition, cannot, as he says, bring themselves to believe such aggadot.[37] In their interest and despite prevailing religious sentiment to the contrary, he feels intellectually compelled to challenge an essentially metahistorical approach to aggadic material, particularly where such material is, as here, patently absurd in its literal sense. For Azariah the Titus story is "pure fiction" intended merely to imbue the masses with the awareness that "our Lord is great, and mighty in power" to mete out punishment to those who rise against Him, even through the minutest of His creatures. Characteristically, he reminds the reader that metaphorical device is universally employed by "the enlightened" to reinforce religious conviction.[38] Azariah has not abandoned the classical Jewish theological position with respect to belief in divine retribution, but he is determined to demonstrate that the classical aggadic *expression* of how such doctrine may have been implemented is entirely imaginative. Although the sages displayed "great wisdom" in applying their aggadic "invention" to the wicked Titus,[39] that imaginative "invention" has no relationship to the actual facts of Titus's death. The invention itself does not stand the test of historical analysis nor, from Azariah's point of view but contrary to many of his Jewish contemporaries, was it ever intended to.

Azariah urges the favorably disposed reader to exercise discretion in applying his method of dealing with the Titus story—not all aggadot can be explained in the same manner. To employ this method indiscriminately could be a disservice to both reader and author. Azariah may be legitimately concerned with setting limits to metaphorical interpretation of aggadah, but he obviously is also concerned with being personally compromised before hostile public opinion.

> Behold I will not refrain from informing you, my dear reader, that when what I have written concerning [the story of] the gnat of Titus became known to some of the learned among our people, they raised their voices against me saying that I brought discredit upon

> the sacred words of our sages. . . . But I nevertheless have not refrained from recording this in the work.[40]

Not only has he seen fit to put these views into print despite their unpopularity in certain quarters; in his explanation there is also an implicit irony in his reference to those who take every rabbinic dictum literally. This chapter of the *Me'or 'Einayim*, Azariah assures his audience, is entirely neutral in its effects on such individuals, but he has in the meantime given them the dubious distinction of assuming that the honor of heaven is served whenever they attempt to make the inconceivable seem reasonable.[41]

Azariah sees a parallel between what he has set forth here and a discussion in Maimonides' *Guide*. Maimonides had distinguished between the individual able to grasp that various biblical terms (i.e., seeing, vision, looking) refer to intellectual apprehension of God *and* the "individual of insufficient capacity" who "should not wish to reach the rank to which we desire him to ascend" and instead views all such words as "indicative of sensual perception of created lights—be they angels or something else." Maimonides concludes by saying of the latter type that "there is no harm in his thinking this"[42] since presumably this involves no anthropomorphism with respect to God. If Maimonides, however, views such an individual as intellectually and spiritually inferior, Azariah is even more explicit in his disparagement of the literalist and in his approval of the individual who, being unable to make rational sense of a problematic aggadah, "wisely" applies Azariah's exegetical method.[43]

Judah Loew sharply contested Azariah's rationalistic-historical approach to the Titus story, insisting that a "miraculous event"[44] could not be explained in this manner. To be sure, Loew's definition of the miraculous with respect to such aggadic accounts was more symbolic than literal. He repeatedly emphasized that the aggadic wisdom of the ancient sages expressed an inner essence of things, not outer material form or sense experience, and that there had been no gnat in actual substance.[45] Nevertheless, Loew was certain that it symbolized a destructive power, a deleterious force that was the essence of the gnat in the abstract and that had actively brought about Titus's physical ruin and demise.[46] The aggadic formulation, then, presented in perceptible form what the sages in their profound and unchallengeable wisdom believed to have been the actual fate of the Roman ruler, as due punishment for his destructive deeds. Loew insisted that it was totally inappropriate to consult gentile works, as Azariah had done, to clarify the Titus story. To do so was to acknowledge the authority of such sources or, as Loew put it, to oblige one to respond to everything gentile writers had said that might have had some bearing on rabbinic tradition.[47] Under no circumstances was Loew prepared to grant this, since aggadah transcended all considerations of verification. From this point of view Loew even rejected information about Titus in the popular and highly regarded Jewish historical work *Josippon*—long but mistakenly regarded as the authentic Hebrew version of Josephus—when it appeared to contradict rabbinic sources. Moreover, although there was good reason to be skeptical about *Josippon*'s excessive praise of Titus and the author's attempt to exonerate him from any responsibility for the destruction of the Temple during the Judeo-Roman war, Loew's refusal to accept this characterization of the Roman general was based purely on moralistic, not historical, considerations inspired by the talmudic account.[48]

Convinced as he was that the words of the sages represented a higher, prophetically inspired and transmitted order of wisdom, Loew could declare in a strikingly confident tone that the circumstances of Titus's death as described by some non-Jewish authors presented no difficulty at all.[49] Whatever element of accuracy there was in such descriptions was for him merely the outer manifestation of the events, whereas the aggadic "secrets of the Torah and wisdom" embodied the inner and abiding truth of the matter. This view of wisdom (*ḥokhmah*) with respect to aggadic lore was metahistorical in nature and thus in total conflict with Azariah's radically different frame of reference. For him "wisdom" might indeed inhere in aggadah; but aggadah itself was not necessarily endowed with theological certainty, doctrinal authority, or historical accuracy. In turn, Loew viewed as anathema the suggestion that in the process of its crystallization, aggadah had often been subject to the flights of fancy of the ancient sages, the limitations of their knowledge, their casual neglect of historical detail, or at times a combination of all these circumstances. He consequently cursed the day on which the *Me'or 'Einayim* had appeared and in several of his works warned his coreligionists against its vain and misleading views. Azariah, he declared, had spoken arrogantly against the words of the sages in a work "abounding in blasphemies."[50]

His great dismay with Azariah's handling of aggadah even led Loew to raise serious questions regarding one of the main geonic foundations on which Azariah had rested his case from the very outset. Although the gaon Sherira had described aggadot derived from the exegesis of scripture as *umdanah*, he had not at all meant supposition or guesswork as Azariah, who "wanted to attach himself to a great, pious authority," had misunderstood it. Rather, Loew asserted, *umdanah* meant that which reason and logical argument dictated. Sherira in other words had said, according to Loew, that were various aggadic interpretations of scripture not logically compelling, the sages would not have given support to them by reference to biblical verses. Loew then saw the issue as quite "plain." And having thus further demonstrated Azariah's ignorance and arrogance to his own satisfaction, he went one step further, suggesting that perhaps Sherira had never said any such thing to begin with: "Mar bereh de-Ravina" (i.e., a great talmudic dignitary), he caustically observed, had not affixed his signature and authenticated the definition of aggadah that Azariah had sought to make the mainstay of his position.[51]

Notes

1. *M.E.* 1:132. Azariah does not mention but was perhaps aware of contemporary discussion in Europe regarding the reliability of historical evidence. Charles de la Ruelle, for example, rejects the possibility of an accurate eyewitness account. He notes the difficulty of any certitude regarding events in the distant past when "we are uncertain and in disagreement about things that have occurred almost before our eyes and happened in our days." (*Succintz adversaires contre l'histoire et professeurs d'icelles* [Poitiers, 1574], 16). In the 1560s historian-jurists like François Baudouin had occasion to deal with the problem of historical evidence: "I say the newer and more recent a narration of the past, the more mendacious it normally becomes. . . . a history, which has been tossed about in many repetitions, and besprinkled with the words of many versions, will often be at last contaminated, and thus degenerate to fable." (*De institutione historiae universae*, quoted in Julian H. Franklin, *Jean Bodin and the Sixteenth-Century Revolution in the Methodology of Law and History* [New York: Columbia University Press, 1963], 129.) With respect to "current events," Azariah once refers to David Reuveni, the mysterious sixteenth-century visitor from the East who claimed to represent a kingdom of descendants of the lost tribes of ancient Israel. Azariah here too evinces at least a healthy degree of skepticism when he speaks of the possibility of there having been a grain of truth in Reuveni's story (*M.E.* 1:194: "mah *she'ulai* hayah bo *shemeṣ emet*"; emphasis added). He clearly does not accept Reuveni's story in toto. Cf. Baron's biographical sketch of Azariah in the Hebrew encyclopedia *Eshkol* (1929), s. v. "Adumim, Azariah Min": "ve-hu ma'amin ba-kol le-Eldad ha-Dani vela-Re'uveni"; but see the revised English translation of this essay in Baron, "Azariah de' Rossi: A Biographical Sketch," in *History and Jewish Historians* (Philadelphia: Jewish Publication Society, 1964), 167–173. With regard to Eldad, Baron elsewhere notes that Azariah "has few compunctions about assuming his usual critical posture toward the stories, primarily non-mystical, told by Eldad the Danite" ("Azariah de' Rossi's Historical Method," in *History and Jewish Historians*, 224, and n. 113, referring to M.E. 2:460). Azariah writes: "Ve-im sefer Eldad ha-Dani . . . yesh qeṣat emun bo" ("And if Eldad the Danite's work . . . despite all that Ibn Ezra had written about it . . . can somewhat be trusted . . .").

2. *M.E.* 2:265.
3. Ibid., 1:246 n.
4. Ibid., 2:266.
5. The Renaissance development of documentary criticism is described, for example, in Peter Burke, *The Renaissance Sense of the Past* (New York: St. Martin's Press, 1970), chap. 3. Baron ("Historical Method") has demonstrated many aspects of its influence on Azariah, indicating his strengths and weaknesses.
6. *M.E.* 1:233; and see the reference here to Avtalyon da Modena. Avtalyon's nephew, the famous Leone Modena, noted Azariah's *many* references to his uncle in the *Me'or 'Einayim*. In fact there appear to be only two (*M.E.* 1:233, 2:323). More serious is Leone's description of the *M.E.* as largely "flour that he (Azariah) ground in my uncle's millstone"—supposedly Azariah's main source of inspiration and material was Avtalyon. (See *Sefer Ḥayyei Yehudah*, ed. A. Kahana [Kiev, 1911], 12.) Mordecai Samuel Ghirondi and Hananel Neppi, *Toledot Gedolei Yisra'el u-Ge'onei Iṭalyah ve-Zekher Ṣadiqim li-Verakhah* (Trieste: Tipographia Marenigh, 1853; reprint, Israel, 1968), 26 also cites this from *Ḥayyei Yehudah*. However, in the long entry on Azariah and the controversy surrounding the *Me'or 'Einayim* in his autobiographical dictionary, Neppi himself says nothing about Azariah's supposed indebtedness to Avtalyon. See S. J. Halberstam, "Sheloshah Ketavim 'al Devar Sefer Me'or 'Einayim u-Mikhtav eḥad el R. Azariah Min ha-Adumim ve-'od Mikhtav 'Odotav," in *Festschrift zum Achtzigsten Geburstage Moritz Steinschneider's* (Leipzig: Otto Harrassowitz, 1896), 4–6. But Ghirondi, who was very critical of Azariah, omitted that entire entry when he prepared Neppi's work together with his own for publication in the nineteenth century. (See Halberstam, p. 4 n. 1; and Ghirondi and Neppi, p. 82: "sifro ha-mekhoar . . . he-Adom asher halakh aḥar anshei Sedom ha-megaleh panim be-sifro shelo ka-halakhah ve-qabbalat rabbotenu".) There is no reason or evidence that I am aware of to take Leone Modena's statement seriously, nor the description of Avtalyon as one to whose learning there was no match in his generation. Leone's personality would seem to suggest that he was not above exaggeration regarding his own achievements or those of other family members. (See too Moses A. Shulvass, *Ḥayyei ha-Yehudim be-Iṭalyah bi-Tequfat ha-Renesans* [New York: Ogen, 1955] 294.) Leone after all also claimed that in his youth, Avtalyon bound Elijah the prophet by an oath, and he revealed himself to the rabbi (*Ḥayyei Yehudah*, 12).
7. *M.E.* 1:229. The passage from B. Ketubbot 19b that Azariah cites forbids one to retain *an uncorrected copy of scripture* in his possession ("sefer she'eino mugah . . . asur lishhoṭo").
8. See p. 121 above.
9. In describing the period "between the old and the new" in his history of modern Jewish thought, Eliezer Schweid deals briefly with post-Spanish expulsion intellectual developments in Italy (see *Toledot he-Hagut ha-yehudit ba-Et ha-ḥadashah* [Jerusalem: Keter, 1977], 87). Here he refers to Azariah as the outstanding representative of that approach in which the condition laid down for the understanding of Torah sources was the introduction of a discipline of inves-

tigation exterior to those sources themselves. This was undoubtedly a "qualitative innovation" that was similar, as Schweid notes, to what Judah Abravanel achieved in the realm of philosophy. But it can hardly be described, as Schweid does, as approaching the critical position of Spinoza, whose total and absolute rejection of Jewish tradition and its religious foundations is well known. Schweid indeed underscores that Azariah did not intend to undermine the authority of the Torah but adds that he could not have been unaware of the problem implicit in the nature of his undertaking, and he found it necessary to defend its legitimacy (p. 89). In fact, the reality implicit in this awareness and concern even apart from the total posture of Azariah is such that one may describe him as light-years away from Spinoza. That Azariah considered it unnecessary to submit to the concepts of the past *or rather*, as Schweid readily qualifies, to particular realms of the Jewish cultural heritage (p. 88), does not cogently demonstrate "despite the qualitative difference between them" how close he is to the author of the *Theological-Political Tractate* (p. 88). The novelty of the *Me'or 'Einayim* and even the problems it poses or gives rise to are, after all, a reflection of an intellectual and religious ally of Judaism (albeit not a wholly conventional one), not an adversary.

10. See the discussion in Reuven Bonfil (*Ha-Rabbanut be-Iṭalyah bi-Tequfat ha-Renesans* [Jerusalem: Magnes Press, 1979], 186, nn. 91–94, 199f.), regarding the increasingly pronounced sense of Jewish distinctiveness in sixteenth-century Italy, and the very significant impetus given to this development by the mysticism of the qabbalists. Jehiel Nissim da Pisa (see p. 122 above) was among the leading exponents of this view. It later also found expression in the sermons of the leading rabbi-preachers. There is a parallel to this in sixteenth-century Ashkenazic Jewry, especially in the work of Judah Loew of Prague, Azariah's fierce adversary. He emphasized the fundamental dichotomy between Jewry and other nations based on the conception of Jewish spiritual superiority (see Jacob Katz, *Exclusiveness and Tolerance* [New York: Schocken, 1962], the chap. on ghetto segregation, esp. 135–142, 146–148. Katz's emphasis on Jewish indifference to the Christian world in the early modern period is disputed by Haim Hillel Ben-Sasson in the long critique-review of Katz's *Tradition and Crisis*. See "Musagim u-Meṣiut ba-Hisṭoriyah ha-yehudit be-Shelahei Yemei ha-Beinayim," *Tarbiz* 29 [1960]: 297–312. Katz's position is nonetheless compelling).

11. Bonfil, *Rabbanut*, 197f.

12. See Katz, *Exclusiveness and Tolerance*, 136, 139, 142; and see n. 10 above. Katz refers to Loew as a "medieval thinker" (p. 142), part of the period from the sixteenth to eighteenth centuries, which Katz describes as one of "ghetto segregation" when "Judaism now became, more than ever, a closed system of thought" (p. 136). Gershom Scholem strongly underscores the qabbalistic character of Loew's works in which he "appears to have renounced the Kabbalistic vocabulary only in order to give the widest possible range of influence to Kabbalistic doctrine" (*Major Trends in Jewish Mysticism* [New York: Schocken, 1946], 339). See Jacob Elbaum, "Rabbi Judah Loew of Prague and His Attitude to the Aggadah," *Scripta Hierosolymitana* 22 (1971): 39 n. 36; and *Encyclopaedia Judaica*

(1972), s. v. "Judah Loew ben Bezalel." Cf., however, André Neher, *Le puits de l'exil* (Paris: Albin Michel, 1966), 98, for his characterization of Loew, and 47, for his characterization of Azariah.

13. Elbaum, "Rabbi Judah Loew of Prague," 32, 47; *Be'er ha-Golah* (New York: Talpiyot, 1953), 92, 5, 134f.

14. *Be'er ha-Golah*, 126. Loew refers to his acquisition and reading of *Me'or 'Einayim* (p. 125); from the tone of his complaint it sounds as if Azariah's work had appeared in print fairly recently. Moreover, although his own *Be'er ha-Golah* was not published until 1598, Loew makes reference to it in another of his treatises, which appeared in 1582 (see *Gevurot ha-Shem* [Lublin, 1875], 55, 62). Given his extreme reaction to *Me'or 'Einayim*, this suggests that he formulated his position regarding that work relatively soon after its publication. Even if we assume that the text of *Be'er ha-Golah* was not yet in its final form, the challenge presented by Azariah's views and the gravity with which Loew perceived them would certainly have been among his primary and earliest concerns in writing this treatise. It is also hardly likely that he would have waited a quarter of a century before making his position known to contemporaries and to those over whom he could bring his great influence to bear, including, of course the enlightened Jewish circle in Prague and its intelligentsia (see p. 37 above). The article in *Encyclopaedia Judaica* ("Judah Loew ben Bezalel") merely refers to Loew's "defense of oral tradition against its Italian critics" (p. 375).

15. *Be'er ha-Golah*, 135, 130f.

16. Ibid., 134, 133, 141, and also 136, regarding distortion of Jewish religious truth by someone of another faith, a situation that Loew can understand, since it results from diverse views ("ki ḥiluf ha-datot gorem hester ha-emet ve-lir'ot ha-yashar me'uvat").

17. In his analysis of *Be'er ha-Golah* and of Loew's debate with Azariah, Neher's view is that Azariah, by his frequent references to non-Jewish authors alongside Jewish ones, had obliterated *all* distinctions and somehow trivialized Jewish tradition. Neher also finds a "guarded, sometimes jocular and disdainful manner, with which Azariah treats the Midrash" (*Le puits de l'exil*, 104f.).

18. *Be'er ha-Golah*, 125. In his study of Loew, A. Gottesdiener views the concluding line cited here from *Be'er ha-Golah* as an entirely fitting assessment of *M.E.* and quite correctly notes that Loew sensed the danger of the "new spirit" represented by Azariah's work and responded to it. I doubt however that Azariah really failed to understand the esoteric wisdom considered by Loew to be implicit in aggadah ("umi-veḥinat 'sitre ḥokhmah' . . . ṣodeq beheḥlet ha-Maharal be-omro . . . 'ish asher lo yada' le-havin divrei-ḥakhamim af davar eḥad' "). Azariah undoubtedly understood this approach but concluded that it did not represent the true intention of the rabbinic sages in their dicta. See "Ha-Ari shebe-Ḥakhmei Prag," in the Rav Kook memorial volume *Azkarah: Qoveṣ Torani-Mada'i*, ed. J. L. Fishman (Jerusalem: Mosad ha-Rav Kook, 1937), 402. Problematic too is Gottesdiener's characterization of Loew as being more than once "a total rationalist" with respect to aggadah, as for example in his handling of the Titus story (p. 296, and n. 80; and see below, pp. 139–143).

19. *M.E.* 1:180ff.

20. Ibid., 183f, 187f. The talmudic reference to Hadrian as the perpetrator of the events in Alexandria (B. Gittin 57b) is, like the simultaneous reference to Vespasian as the destroyer of Betar, considered by Azariah to be entirely erroneous. This view is upheld quite independently by Gedalyahu Alon, *Toledot ha-Yehudim be-Ereṣ Yisra'el bi-Tequfat ha-Mishnah veha-Talmud*, 3d ed. (Tel Aviv: Ha-Kibbutz ha-Meuḥad, 1958), 1:249, and n. 122, in his analysis of the aggadic material relating to the situation in Alexandria.

21. The talmudic passage in B. Sukkah 51b refers to "Alexander Mokdon," and Abravanel views the second word as an erroneous scribal addition, taking Alexander to mean Severus. See *M.E.* 1:184f.; and Abravanel's *Perush 'al Nevi'im Rishonim* (Jerusalem: Torah ve-Daat, 1955), introduction, 425. Abravanel's view of the chronology of the Persian period also suggests a far less critical perception than Azariah's, for Abravanel insisted on a span of "fifty-four years more or less" from Cyrus to Alexander. Since Josephus had followed other than rabbinic tradition on this point, Abravanel was extremely critical of him. "The conclusion of the matter is that one ought not to raise any difficulties with respect to the words of the sages from what Josephus says because during the period of the Second Temple, they were as great as he, and wiser and more pious. And they did not seek to flatter the Romans as he did, therefore their words are true" (*Ma'ayenei ha-Yeshu'ah* 10:7 [Jerusalem, 1960], 375f.). In historical awareness and its bearing on critical analysis of rabbinic sources Azariah is far in advance of Abravanel. Yitzhak Baer briefly notes Abravanel's limited critical analysis of the second commonwealth period, which preceded the work of Azariah, but he emphasizes that Abravanel's interpretations of rabbinic texts are largely of an allegorical nature and very far removed from critical evaluation ("Don Yiṣḥak-Abravanel ve-Yaḥaso el Beʿayot ha-Hisṭoriyah veha-Medinah," *Tarbiz* 8 [1937]: 257 n. 40). Cf. Baer, *Galut*, trans. R. Warshow (New York: Schocken, 1947), 60f. The limitations in Abravanel's treatment of aggadic traditions did not, however, preclude his own readiness to report that some midrashic views had not become generally accepted rabbinic opinion (see introduction to the commentary on Joshua in *Perush*, 13). See too his discussion in *Yeshu'ot Meshiḥo* (Königsberg, 1861) of how problematic aggadot had previously been dealt with and his reservations concerning philosophic interpreters like Maimonides and Abraham ibn Ezra (pp. 16b–17b, 39a–40a). Even so, Abravanel himself was bitterly condemned for his handling of certain aggadot by the late-fifteenth-century Elijah Hayyim ben Benjamin of Gennazano in the latter's work on the Qabbalah, *Iggeret Ḥamudot*, ed. A. W. Greenup (London, 1912), 7, 13–16.

22. *M.E.* 1:181, 182, 185f. Regarding orthographic usage in the Palestinian Talmud and the spelling of Trajan's name, see Zacharias Frankel, *Mevo ha-Yerushalmi* (Breslau, 1870), 8a; *'Arukh ha-Shalem*, ed. A. Kohut (1878–1892; reprint, New York: Pardes, 1955), 4:74, 82; M. Jastrow, *A Dictionary of the Targumim, the Talmud Babli and Yerushalmi, and the Midrashic Literature* (New York and Berlin: Verlag Choreb, 1926), 533.

23. *M.E.* 1:185f. Azariah does not attempt to relate the aggadic account to the larger geographical dimensions of this insurrection (Cyrenaica, Cyprus, etc.). Nor does he make mention here of Eusebius's *Ecclesiastical History* and Dio Cassius's *Roman History*, the two most important of the meager literary sources that refer to this Jewish revolt. He is perhaps especially skeptical toward and possibly offended by Dio's obvious exaggerations, particularly the horrible cruelties that Dio claimed the Jews had perpetrated. See Salo W. Baron, *A Social and Religious History of the Jews* (New York: Columbia University Press and Jewish Publication Society, 1952–1983), 2:96f.; and Alon, *Toledot ha-Yehudim*, 236–239. E. Mary Smallwood, *The Jews Under Roman Rule: From Pompey to Diocletian*, 2d ed. (Leiden: Brill, 1981), appears to give greater credence to Dio's report regarding "the atrocities said to have been perpetrated by the Cyrenaican Jews" (p. 394). "Even if the figure for gentile casualties (in Cyprus, 240,000), like that for Cyrenaica (220,000), is unconvincingly high . . . the severity of the Jews' punishment . . . is a measure of the savagery of their attack" (p. 413).

24. The events and various sources are discussed in Baron, *Social and Religious History* 2:94–97, 370 n. 7; Avigdor Tcherikover, *Ha-Yehudim be-Miṣrayim ba-Tequfah ha-hellenisṭit–ha-romit*, 2d rev. ed. (Jerusalem: Magnes Press, 1963), chap. 6.; Alon, *Toledot ha-Yehudim*, 232–264; Smallwood, *Jews Under Roman Rule*, chap. 15.

25. *M.E.* 1:182, 189.

26. *M.E.* 1:189; *Be'er ha-Golah*, 131. Loew observes that in the matter of a difficult reading in a rabbinic text, "halo raza"l ba'alei ha-tosafot u-she'ar mefarshim ka'asher nir'eh setirah ba-girsah hayu omrim *d'hakhei garsinan* . . . u-mikol sheken be-khiluf shem aḥer shehu ragil harbei me'od."

27. *M.E.* 1:187f.

28. Ibid., 2:507, on the basis of the talmudic passage (B. Bava Batra 142b) in which one of the sages argues that final decision in a *legal issue* depends not on seniority in years but upon sound reasoning. Azariah invokes this passage in the prefatory paragraph to his index of objections raised throughout *M.E.* against various earlier authorities (see his *Luaḥ ha-Hasagot*, 507f.).

29. *Be'er ha-Golah*, 132.

30. Ibid.

31. Ibid., 103f, 111, 137. This notion is common in Loew's treatment of aggadah. See Elbaum, "Rabbi Loew of Prague," 41f. Neher refers to Loew's view of the Torah—inclusive of course of rabbinic lore—as metahistorical. This lore was therefore a domain that had to be approached and understood through the method of qabbalah, of received tradition, not inquiry of the kind used in the study of human wisdom. From Loew's point of view, then, Azariah had profaned rabbinic lore by applying to it the inappropriate method (*Le puits de l'exil*, 112–115).

32. *M.E.* 1:217.

33. Ibid., 215.

34. Ibid., 214ff. Azariah is aware of similar stories reported by his

contemporary Augustinus Ferentillus and in 2 Macc. 9, relating to the Seleucid ruler Antiochus Epiphanes. See also Baron, *Social and Religious History* 2:93, 369 n. 6, for sources regarding the belief in antiquity that desecrators of sanctuaries suffered unnatural death. Azariah introduces the Titus story with the summary version from the supposedly early tannaitic *Pirqei de-Rabbi Eliezer* (chap. 49) apparently because of the specific reference there to God's use of even the smallest object or being as a means to demonstrate that the strength of mighty men is ultimately worthless (see p. 141 above, for Azariah's use of this theme in explaining the Titus legend. Azariah nowhere takes note of the obviously late elements in *Pirqei de-Rabbi Eliezer*, as he sometimes does with other rabbinic works. See Leopold Zunz, *Ha-Derashot be-Yisra'el*, ed. H. Albeck [Jerusalem: Mosad Bialik, 1947], 134–140, regarding the likely eighth-century authorship of the work). However, the main sources for his analysis of this aggadah are the more detailed talmudic version (B. Gittin 56b) and the midrashic ones (Bereshit Rabbah 10:8 and Vayiqra Rabbah 22:2). From these he extracts and fuses the essential elements of the narrative that concerns him. The midrashic account seems to indicate that Titus died *after* these most unusual findings in his brain, but how Azariah understands the midrash on this point is not clear, for having just quoted the talmudic description of a postmortem he is not likely to imply the opposite a few lines later. The meaning of the Aramaic passage from the midrash with which Azariah concludes his composite narrative is somewhat obscure: "kol mahn [or *mah*; Azariah has *mai*] dehava haden shane hava haden shane" ("As the one [i.e., the bird] changed [to its original form?] so did the other [i.e., Titus] change, and when the gnat fled, the soul of the wicked Titus fled [Titus died?].") See *'Arukh ha-Shalem* 8:47, and nn. 3–4, for a different reading and interpretation. This passage is not in the talmudic version; nor with the exception of Qohelet Rabbah 5:9 is it in any of the other midrashic ones, including those cited by Azariah (i.e., Tanḥuma, *Huqat* 1; *Pirqei de-Rabbi Eliezer* 49; and see Bemidbar Rabbah 18:18). It in fact exemplifies the "marked difference" between the midrashic account (Bereshit Rabbah and Vayiqra Rabbah) and the talmudic one (*M.E.* 1:215), and it is only Azariah's conflation of the two that makes the passage appear to be integral to the talmudic version too. Azariah undoubtedly included this passage in order to accentuate still another of the quite extraordinary features of the story. The discrepancies between the various versions are further underscored in Azariah's brief reference to the Midrash Tanḥuma, where "you will find it [related] *most strangely* both with respect to the details of the story and its circumstances, as well as the duration of time" (emphasis added). The Tanḥuma, for example, reports that the postmortem revealed "something resembling a pigeon *and* a sparrow and its claws were as hard as brass." S. Buber has occasion to discuss the printed and manuscript variants of the Titus story as they relate to his edition of the older Midrash Tanḥuma (Vilna, 1885; reprint, Israel, 1946) 2:99f. nn. 24–27, but makes no reference to the problematic passage in Bereshit and Vayiqra Rabbah.

35. *M.E.* 1:216.
36. Ibid., 217.

37. Ibid.

38. Ibid., 217f.

39. Ibid., 217.

40. Ibid., 219. Azariah refers to "qeṣat maskilei 'ameinu" as those who took issue with him.

41. Ibid.

42. *Guide of the Perplexed*, trans. Shlomo Pines (Chicago: University of Chicago Press, 1963), 1:31; and see the commentary in the edition of Yehudah Ibn Shmuel, *Sefer Moreh ha-Nevukhim* (Jerusalem: Mosad ha-Rav Kook, 1959), pt. 1, p. 65.

43. *M.E.* 1:219.

44. *Be'er ha-Golah*, 137.

45. See for example, *Be'er ha-Golah*, 111, 114, 137, 138; *Sefer Neṣaḥ Yisra'el* (Jerusalem, 1970), 35. In defense of his own exposition, even Loew found it necessary to remind his readers that the plain meaning (*peshat*) of the Titus story was not what appeared to be the literal one (*Be'er ha-Golah*, 137), which suggests that there were those who thought so.

46. *Be'er ha-Golah*, 137f; *Neṣaḥ Yisra'el*, 346; *Sefer Ḥiddushei Aggadot Maharal mi-Prag* (London: Honig, 1960), 2:107f., commentary on B. Gittin 56b. Loew had occasion to deal with the Titus story in each of these works, although the point in question is handled much more succinctly in the two latter ones.

47. *Be'er ha-Golah*, 138f.

48. *Ḥiddushei Aggadot*, 105; and cf. *Sefer Yosifon*, ed. H. Hominer (Jerusalem, 1978), 384f., 404.

49. *Be'er ha-Golah*, 139.

50. Ibid., 125; *Neṣaḥ Yisra'el*, 35; and *Ḥiddushei Aggadot*, 108, 117. In the two latter works Loew adds that he had already refuted Azariah's arguments in the *Be'er ha-Golah*.

51. *Be'er ha-Golah*, 133.

CHAPTER 9

Maharal versus Azariah: The Issue of Ancients and Moderns

Fundamentally what Loew found outrageous and what understandably shocked his religious sensibilities was Azariah's disregard of the long interval between himself and those ancient authorities whose dicta he presumed to appraise and pass judgment on. In the Talmud itself, as Loew noted in the introduction to *Be'er ha-Golah*, there was reference to the steady diminution of intellectual capacity from the time of the early sages to the later ones so that the "heart" (i.e., mind) of the latter was open only as wide "as the eye of a very fine needle." If there had been such intellectual deterioration in the relatively short span of time that separated the generations of rabbinic sages, what could one expect by the present age, when all semblance of wisdom had dried up? By reason of this dearth, the words of the ancients were like a sealed book for contemporaries.[1] The present was bereft of all intelligence, making it impossible for "donkeys such as we to stand in the council of the saintly."[2] Successively, or so it appeared to Loew, no spokesmen in any previous generation had dared to take issue with those who had preceded them, being aware of the superiority of the earlier authorities because of their greater proximity in time to prophetic inspiration. "But now, in this generation so inferior and devoid of wisdom, shall an individual arise and direct his tongue against the holy ones who preceded us by more than a millennium and declare: 'Perceive my ways and become wise?' "[3] In his challenge to ancient authority, as revealed in the vagaries of his aggadic exegesis, Azariah had displayed his lack of understanding of even the simplest aspects of rabbinic discourse, a point Loew reiterated again and again.[4]

Azariah had in fact preceded Loew in raising the issue of "ancients" and "moderns"—with the same talmudic passages about the successive diminution of the generations as his point of departure. This constitutes a rather critical juncture in the *Me'or 'Einayim* that can hardly have escaped Judah Loew's attention. Azariah is led to deal with this issue in order to account for the many instances in which post-talmudic commentators and authorities departed from the scriptural exegesis of the ancients. He considers this hardly in need of demonstration, but he tells us that contemporary criticism of himself forced it upon him.[5] We thus encounter a framework of discussion that commences with ostensible approval of the talmudic sentiment and ends in an expression of humility that makes it unimaginable that "we who are [blind as] bats" should see more than those exceedingly sagacious authorities of antiquity.[6]

Although he invokes the talmudic contrast with its emphasis on the disparity between the early and later generations, he simultaneously observes that "indeed, the later spokesmen having been recipients of that which the early authorities comprehended, apart from their own perception itself, it appears that the situation is analogous to the simile of the dwarf seated on the shoulders of the giant."[7] Azariah adopts this well-known medieval aphorism from the work of Zedekiah ben Abraham Anav citing the thirteenth-century talmudist Isaiah di Trani the Elder. The latter had carefully qualified its meaning: The wise insights of contemporaries are entirely predicated on the strength of our early predecessors' wisdom, but by no means are we greater than they.[8] Azariah identifies his source, cites the aphorism, and then informs the reader that one may conclude the following: the advantage that the ancient truly has over the modern is with respect to matters dependent on prophecy and results from his greater proximity to that source of inspiration. The modern, however, has the advantage in matters stemming from reflection and empirical investigation, since he is continually in the process of enlarging his range of understanding until, with the aid of the ancients who *struggled to no avail* in this pursuit, *his* efforts succeed. Azariah's figurative language on this point is telling: the ancients had "unsuccessfully labored in the environs of the rivers to bring forth water." The modern well digger who follows after them can proclaim: "It is *I* who have dug and *I* have drunk."[9]

The aphorism adopted by Azariah, which apparently had originated with Bernard of Chartres,[10] had from the beginning been intended to emphasize high regard for the authority of the past, but it no doubt implied some measure of self-confidence as well. The latter sense tends to be muted in Isaiah di Trani's use of the aphorism. Azariah acknowledges generally that the modern is indebted to those who preceded him, without whom his own achievements would have been impossible. But ancient Jewish wisdom is for him by no means all of the same cloth; and with respect to those pronouncements that are "wholly human" in nature, as is the case with rabbinic aggadah and homilies, he would argue the essential equality of the modern with the ancient. Indeed, he declares in consequence of his analysis of the ancient-modern relationship that the distinction between the sages of antiquity and moderns is similar in dimension to that which separated them from the prophets. Both ancients and moderns rely equally on the instrument of reflection in these speculative matters. He reinforces this argument by attempting to demonstrate from certain geonic discussion that in such speculative matters it is not good to be partial to the ancients, the love of truth having been of such greater importance to the sages than their own honor that they themselves permitted independent reflection. He asks rhetorically: Why should we be insincere with them against their wish and proclaim with our mouth what we reject with our heart?[11]

Azariah does not make explicit just where the rabbinic sages had encouraged such independent investigation by later generations. He does, however, insist that other than in matters of religious law each individual, depending on his gift of intelligence and the strength of his evidence, is free to challenge the sages, provided only that his intent is for the sake of truth and heaven.[12] Azariah's prior emphasis on truth should be noted, for it, rather than ancient authority per se, constitutes his guide to an adequate understanding of the sages' lore and opinion.

As many of his own areas of investigation in the *Me'or 'Einayim* demonstrate, so his circuitous reasoning implies that the modern "dwarf," by standing on his own two feet, may often see a good deal further than the ancient "giant." Having adapted the aphorism to his needs, Azariah has effectively undone his prior affirmation regarding the qualitative disparity between the generations. It is unlikely to have been coincidence that Judah Loew prefaced his defense and exposition of rabbinic lore in *Be'er ha-Golah* by emphasizing the absolute superiority of the early authorities[13]—and this, long before he even mentioned the *Me'or 'Einayim* by name and launched his attack against it. In the sixteenth-century climate of the Renaissance, which for contemporary gentile scholars was so intimately linked with the restoration of ancient classical culture, Loew could even seek to strengthen his refutation of Azariah by insisting that *everyone*, even gentiles, had acknowledged that wisdom was the exclusive preserve of the ancients.[14]

Azariah's outlook, however, suggests that humanist position that acknowledged the grandeur of antiquity but did not believe that truth had been fully realized by the ancients. The early humanists beginning with Petrarch in the mid-fourteenth century had already recognized, for example, the fallibility of the ancient historians, including even the much-venerated Livy (although they did not perceive that history other than that of ancient Greece and Rome might have any value).[15] So great was the veneration of classical antiquity in humanistic circles that for a time it indeed tended to engender a sense of inferiority and futility that stifled the potential for creativity, historical or other. Even Leonardo Bruni, with whom Italian humanist historiography began early in the fifteenth century, could negatively contrast the limitations of the moderns with the great achievements of the ancients and characterize contemporaries as dwarfs who, even if not so in spirit, had "not the stuff needed for lasting glory."[16] However, it was precisely Bruni who within not quite a decade overcame this sense of contemporary inadequacy. In the preface to his important work of around 1418 on the Florentine people, he did not hesitate to insist that the achievements of Florence would in no part appear inferior to those of antiquity.[17] Among Bruni's companions and successors, Poggio Bracciolini too viewed modern times as on a par with the ancient ones; and outside of Florence, the Sienese historian Agostino Dati, for instance, held a similar view.[18] How qualitatively equal with ancient times modern times came to be viewed can also be gauged from Bruni's insistence in the 1430s on the important place of postclassical languages, and notably the Italian vernacular, the "Volgare," as distinguished from Latin. Every language according to Bruni had its "own perfection."[19] Expanding upon earlier efforts to demonstrate the legitimacy of vernacular culture[20] in the face of strident voices that argued the exclusive superiority of antiquity, the influential Bruni helped establish a trend that vigorously supported modern no less than ancient creativity and talents, literary and otherwise. This trend would be given great impetus in the later quattrocento by the statesman and poet Lorenzo de' Medici and others and would continue unabated into the sixteenth century. Thus in the 1540s a leading Paduan spokesman of academic culture, Speroni, argued further the equal value and potential of all languages, as well as the possibility that the modern age too might produce men like Plato and Aristotle.[21]

The view that there was much left for future generations to discover and that progress in knowledge could and constantly had to be made is developed too by the influential sixteenth-century Spanish humanist Vives. Although grateful to the ancients, Vives claimed that "yet they were men as we are, and were liable to be deceived and to err. . . . Neither are we dwarfs, nor they giants, but we are all of one stature, save that we are lifted up somewhat higher by their means." The cause of learning was far better served by critical assessment of the great authors' works than by unquestioning compliance with their authority and implicit reliance on others. "I do not profess myself the equal of the ancients," Vives asserted, "but I bring my views into comparison with theirs."[22]

Azariah's familiarity with these developments in humanistic thought may be assumed, although the degree to which they influence his thinking is obviously conditioned by the limits that he himself sets in the *Me'or 'Einayim*. For example, he does not presume to scrutinize the ancient Jewish sages insofar as their juristic function is concerned, that is, regarding that aspect of Jewish tradition that he, like his coreligionists, views as divinely revealed or derivative thereof. As we have seen, however, he is convinced of the possibility of limitations or even error in their human assertions, and he warns people that admiration for the sages may lead them to read contemporary awareness into the ancient pronouncements where it may not apply.[23] In chapter 11 of the *Me'or 'Einayim*, Azariah deals with aspects of the natural world and science, which exemplifies this position especially well. He seeks to demonstrate that the views of the rabbinic sages in empirical matters represented not divine revelation but human wisdom and speculation, not all of which is tenable in the light of more recent advances and discoveries. Therefore, where it is not possible to sustain their views, "we ought to distance ourselves from falsehood and hypocrisy" and not compel their assertions to yield meaning that one knows full well was not intended by them. Azariah declares that the affirmation of falsehood and the dissemination of nonsense will cause the sages to be, "heaven forbid," an object of derision; according to Azariah's paraphrase of a talmudic dictum, those guilty of such deceptive intent are morally culpable.[24] Respectfully yet adamantly Azariah even takes to task his contemporary, the distinguished talmudist and halakhic authority Moses Isserles. In his 1570 treatise *Torat ha-'Olah*, a philosophical analysis of many aspects of Judaism, Isserles utilized traditional Jewish methods of interpretation in good conscience to resolve some of the same problems Azariah addresses. Concerned that he might be attacked for having departed from the teaching of this great master, Azariah states that he has found it necessary to call attention to flaws in Isserles' efforts to reconcile various rabbinic statements with the present-day consensus concerning the realities of the natural world. Hopeful that truth and intellectual integrity will prevail, he confidently assumes that even his Ashkenazic coreligionists who so rely upon Isserles will acknowledge that "indeed *my* words have not proved false."[25]

Without a doubt Azariah implies that the claim that the sages were bearers of comprehensive superior wisdom cannot be sustained. Lest the reader not fully appreciate why this should be, he explains that in all areas of general knowledge they were not unlike any other person, including the many gentile sages; they all relied on purely human judgment[26]—with all its attendant fallibility. Conveniently, scripture itself provides Azariah with authoritative confirmation of the limits to which even the great Jewish ancients were subject, even though it requires reading intellectual intent into the psalmist's moralistic complaint that "all men are faithless" and into Ecclesiastes' assertion, after Azariah's rearrangement of the verse, to the effect that "there is no man who does not err."[27] Such appropriation of scripture reinforces the belief that beyond the function of presiding over and interpreting this higher biblical wisdom, the ancient Jewish sages were, in all other spheres of knowledge, indeed men. It does not suggest that empirical and reflective pursuits are inconsequential because they are not of the same order of certainty as divinely revealed wisdom. In all, Azariah has introduced reservations about the Jewish ancients not unlike those upheld in humanistic circles. In substance his position is like that of Vives: "When . . . the weights of arguments are equal, it would be impudent for anyone to refuse precedence to the old authors." But otherwise Azariah embraces the urging of those who seek truth to "make your stand wherever you think that she is."[28]

Notes

1. *Be'er ha-Golah* (New York: Talpiyot, 1953), 3f.; and the talmudic passage in B. Eruvin 53a.

2. *Be'er ha-Golah*, 5; *Sefer Neṣaḥ Yisra'el* (Jerusalem, 1970), 51. Loew's characterization of the present generation as donkeys no doubt echoes the similar sentiment of one of the rabbinic sages about his own time (see B. Shabbat 112b, J. Demai 1:3, J. Shekalim 5:1, Bereshit Rabbah 60:10; and see *M.E.* 1:196, and n., although Azariah's reference to the passage in J. Shekalim and Bereshit Rabbah is not precise).

3. *Be'er ha-Golah*, 125f. Determined to demonstrate fully Azariah's audacity in this regard, Loew even appears to have occasionally quoted the text of the *Me'or 'Einayim* in a manner intended to accentuate Azariah's personal culpability. Thus Azariah writes in reference to the aggadah about Titus, that "*you* are able and permitted to say that the story is merely a device and pedagogical technique" (*M.E.* 1:217), and Loew in citing the passage changes "you" to "I" (p. 36).

4. *Be'er ha-Golah*, 125, 126, 127, 134, 136, 139.

5. *M.E.* 1:196f., 200.

6. Ibid. 196, 201.

7. Ibid. 196.

8. See *Sefer Shibbolei ha-Leqet*, ed. S. Buber (Vilna: Romm, 1886; reprint, New York, 1958), 35. The original of Isaiah di Trani's remarks and use of the aphorism is in his responsa, *Teshuvot ha-Ri"d*, ed. A. J. Wertheimer (Jerusalem, 1967), 302.

9. *M.E.* 1:196. The imagery also suggests a qualitative distinction between the somewhat muddied sources with which the ancients had to work, as opposed to the clear spring water that the modern discovers. Equally suggestive moreover is Azariah's adaptation of the language in Isa. 37:24f. (and cf. 2 Kings 19:23f.) in which Sennacherib of Assyria is depicted as self-assuredly proclaiming his victories with a loud refrain in the first person ("It is I who have climbed the highest mountains . . . It is I who have dug and drunk the waters . . ."). Although Sennacherib's haughty tone is roundly denounced by the prophet Isaiah, Azariah nevertheless finds this piece of biblical imagery particularly well suited to celebrate the achievements of the modern. It is unlikely that in this entire analysis Azariah's shift away from the belief in the superiority of the ancient authorities is simply due to an inconsistency of which he himself is unaware. Cf. Salo W. Baron ("Azariah de' Rossi's Attitude to Life," in *History and Jewish Historians* [Philadelphia: Jewish Publication Society, 1964], 200f.). Whatever Azariah's other limitations may be, his intellectual posture makes it highly improbable that he "is not aware that . . . he is giving up most of what he had said previously on the same page and elsewhere" (Baron, p. 422 n. 131, and see n. 128). Azariah's discussion in *M.E.* 2:366f., too, suggests that while he will not depart from established custom in practice, he is fully committed to open-ended analysis of ancient tradition. The contrast between "kol ha-tamim be-libbo vi-derakhav" *and* "kol ha-qarev le-harher aḥar divreihem ve-liṣrof otam ki-ṣrof ha-kesef" should be noted.

10. See Robert K. Merton's *On the Shoulders of Giants* (New York: Free Press, 1965), 37, 40f., 177f., 193f., where the modern literature tracing the aphorism to Bernard of Chartres is cited. Merton also discusses Azariah's use of it (pp. 233–237) and Isaiah di Trani's (pp. 240ff.). Azariah, however, does not say that Zedekiah's quotation of the aphorism was "in a manner" that inspired his own application of it; rather he finds the aphorism analogous to a view that he himself has already assumed, "so that [*be-ofen*] it is proper" to maintain the superiority of the "moderns" in matters dependent upon reflection and empirical investigation (see *M.E.* 1:196). If in such matters the ancients, as Azariah goes on to say, labored

unsuccessfully, the implication then is that the benefit they ostensibly provided for the moderns is inconsequential, and the achievements of the latter are arrived at independently—a position that neither Isaiah di Trani nor Zedekiah ben Abraham would likely have subscribed to. The later-sixteenth-century talmudist and qabbalist Abraham Azulai used the giant-dwarf simile in his commentary to the Mishnah and apparently adopted it from the same source as Azariah had (see Dov Zlotnick, "The Commentary of Rabbi Abraham Azulai to the Mishnah," *Proceedings of the American Academy for Jewish Research* 40 [1973]: 163–167). Zlotnick correctly considers it unlikely that Azulai's source was the *Me'or 'Einayim*, "de Rossi being an anathema in his circles" (n. 102). One may add that for Azulai, the purposes to which Azariah adapted the aphorism were certainly reprehensible.

11. *M.E.* 1:197, 2:270.

12. *M.E.* 1:197; and see 2:496, for another expression of the prior emphasis on truth.

13. See pp. 143, 153f. above.

14. See A. Gottesdiener, "Ha-Ari shebe-Ḥakhmei Prag," in *Azkarah: Koveṣ Torani-Mada'i,* ed. J. L. Fishman (Jerusalem: Mosad ha-Rav Kook, 1937), 398.

15. Cochrane, *Historians and Historiography in the Italian Renaissance* (Chicago: University of Chicago Press, 1981), 16f.

16. Hans Baron, *The Crisis of the Early Italian Renaissance*, rev. ed. (Princeton: Princeton University Press, 1966), 282.

17. Ibid., 283; and see Cochrane, *Historians*, 19. See also Giacinto Margiotta, *Le origini italiane de la Querelle des anciens et des modernes* (Rome: Editrice Studium, 1953), 77. Margiotta notes how Bruni was led to write his history of the Florentine people because of his deep feeling about the grandeur of Florence. In Bruni's view, after its conquest of Pisa, the city had become like a second Rome—following Rome's conquest of Carthage—all Florentine attainments being, according to Bruni, "in no respect inferior to those of antiquity."

18. Cochrane, *Historians*, 29, 132; and H. Baron, *Crisis*, 406ff., regarding the development of Poggio's position.

19. H. Baron, *Crisis*, 344; and see Margiotta, *Origini italiane*, 76.

20. H. Baron, *Crisis*, chap. 15, esp. 332–338.

21. Hans Baron, "The *Querelle* of the Ancients and the Moderns as a Problem for Renaissance Scholarship," in *Renaissance Essays*, ed. Paul O. Kristeller and P. P. Wiener (New York: Harper and Row, 1968), 112f.; idem, *Crisis*, 350ff. Margiotta, *Origini italiane*; Margiotta refers to Lorenzo's conviction, despite the influence of his education in classical culture, that the Italian vernacular was equally capable of giving expression to all matters of consequence, essential for human life (p. 87).

22. The Vives citations (*De disciplinis*) are from H. Baron, "*Querelle*," 105f. and from *Vives: On Education*, trans. F. Watson (Cambridge: Cambridge University Press, 1913), cv, 8f. Regarding the status of the ancients and moderns, see also Jean Bodin, *Method for the Easy Comprehension of History*, trans. Beatrice Reynolds (Reprint, New York: Octagon Press, 1966), 296, 301f.: "No one . . . can

doubt that the discoveries of our men ought to be compared with the discoveries of our elders; many ought to be placed first. . . . They are mistaken who think that the race of men always deteriorates."

23. *M.E.* 1:154.

24. Ibid., 179. Although in this chapter of *M.E.* Azariah appears to interject reservations with respect to ordinary men's limited comprehension of nature (to the effect that human wisdom is foolishness in comparison with God's knowledge; *M.E.* 1:165, 178f.), such reservations, even if they are not partially verbal smoke, cannot except in isolation obscure the main thrust of the chapter. Azariah's ostensible reservation along the same lines in *Qol Elohim* (*M.E.* 1:20) also needs to be considered in context. See pp. 18ff. above. Cf. Baron, "Attitude to Life," 178, 409 n. 28.

25. *M.E.* 1:179f. In his treatment of aggadah, Azariah does not address Isserles' attempt to deal with the problem of anthropomorphism in rabbinic lore. See *Sefer Torat ha-'Olah* (Prague, 1833), 55b–56b.

26. *M.E.* 1:167: "raq ke-khol adam asher le-mar'eh 'einav yishpot o le-mishma' oznav yokhiaḥ ve-rabim gam ken asher itam me-ḥakhmei yeter ha-umot qadmonim o ḥadashim mi-qarov ba'u."

27. Ibid., 167; and cf. Ps. 116:1, Eccles. 7:20.

28. Watson, *Vives*, 9.

Epilogue

Given the nature of the sixteenth-century cultural climate—with its theological presuppositions and its continuing deference to the authority of inherited tradition, which sometimes impeded the progress of knowledge—one does not expect, indeed one does not find, the Jewish historiographical work of Azariah de' Rossi to exhibit inquiry "scientifically" detached from religion, ethical doctrine, or ethnic loyalty. Nor is there in his work that disposition toward a total change of values in Judaism similar to what one first discerns, for example, over a generation later in the quite different scholarly activity of Joseph Shlomo Delmedigo.[1] It certainly will not do to cast Azariah in the role of a freethinker who assumes a pious pose merely in order to disguise irreverent views[2] intended to encourage a line of inquiry, the ultimate purpose of which is to raise doubts regarding Jewish sanctities. He is of course concerned with contemporary religious sensitivities and with the possible impact of his work on the popular perception of Judaism as a whole; he is therefore careful to present his underlying assumptions and conclusions in as positive a manner and as traditional a frame of reference as possible. But the moderation in tone is not merely to serve as apologetics in anticipation of possible censure; nor is it to facilitate a conscious subversion of Jewish tradition. For even those aspects of the Jewish past that Azariah feels free to explore are after all for him as for his contemporaries important sources of Jewish identity, but having transcended their historical innocence and their metahistorical orientation, he seeks to establish a meaningful understanding of such sources.

His effort is accompanied by an extraordinary application of secular learning and critical techniques, and it generated considerable speculation and analysis. It imposed on his readers the need for significant intellectual adjustment in their perception of tradition. Azariah utilized secular learning in a way specifically calculated to realize the greatest possible measure of truth; and when he showed that the ancient rabbinic sources had erred, he in effect set his own findings against those of the sages. Consequently in his work ancient Jewish historical situations are often no longer what the rabbinic classics had described them to be but rather what the "modern" scholar Azariah has attempted to reconstruct after having subjected the relevant sources to critical evaluation. The realization of his objective, then, does not coincide with the integrity of the Jewish sources in the conventional or popular religious sense still pervasive in the sixteenth century.

Azariah deems it perfectly legitimate, indeed worthy of merit, to sort out the historically conditioned elements of the Jewish tradition for critical examination. In so doing, however, he does not intend to exclude those elements and to reconstitute the notion of Torah as only that which is theologically mandated. While the intellectual consequences of this position could be more far-reaching than he seems to imagine, the historically conditioned elements are themselves replete with Jewish religious and ethical values, most of which Azariah himself is essentially committed to, even though he accords those elements or the sources in which they are contained a status that lacks the authority with which scripture and halakhah are invested. The qualitative distinction Azariah draws between the substance of the Jewish juristic or legal teaching *and* rabbinic lore in all its other manifestations is, as has already been made clear, definitive. Yet even the descriptive terminology he employs suggests that he does not therefore envisage the tradition as unalterably dichotomized.[3] He designates the former by terms that spell out their authoritative halakhic status: *ḥoq ha-Torah, miṣvot ha-Torah, dinei ha-Torah, gufei Torah ve-dinim.*[4] In all these terms there inheres the idea of mandatory law and commandment. Yet the nonjuristic material that constitutes the main focus of his studies is, for all of his historical critique of its problematic aspects, variously subsumed under phrases describing the teaching, assertions, or opinion of "our sages": *Toratenu, Torah shelemah shelanu, Torat ḥakhamenu, divrei ḥakhamenu, da'at ḥakhamenu.*[5] The latter describe dimensions of the tradition that from Azariah's point of view are subject to different considerations and criteria than are the binding precepts of the Torah; it should be noted, however, that all these latter terms nonetheless either partake of the notion "our" Torah or imply it. Through such formulations Azariah does not mean to disarm opposition to the twofold distinction he has drawn but rather to make clear that he perceives the entire tradition as an organic unity that contains both diverse elements. Not only is this unity uncompromised by assuming such diversity but the stature of the tradition is enhanced and its moral and theological intent elicited by the illumination of the creative wisdom of the ancient sages, as expressed through their own subjective experience, intellectual effort, and temporal situation.

But this approach to classical Jewish tradition, of which part is endowed with absolute authority and part is open to empirical analysis, was perhaps too novel not to have evoked sharp disapproval by many in Azariah's day and long thereafter. For in traditional Jewish society the ancient sources and cultural heritage were viewed as essentially embodying a totality of eternal and immutable verities in which virtually every area of experience was accounted for. Azariah's historically inspired distinction could only be seen as out of step with the age-old Jewish ideological system, his own personal loyalties to its theological and halakhic foundations notwithstanding.

The resistance to historical argument is perhaps best illustrated by the treatment of the subject of chronology: for Azariah it is historically conditioned and subject to historical investigation; according to the conventional wisdom of the age in its established creation era form it is an aspect of sacred Jewish tradition from time immemorial. For *the many* to whom Azariah refers as engaged in intensive debate with him on this subject, there is no doubt that this chronological system was ancient and already customary among the Israelites in early biblical times. But for the reader whose careful attention he calls upon here, Azariah proposes that inquiry into earliest times "will make it clear to you that the counting of time from creation has only become customary among us from the age long after the redaction of the [Babylonian] Talmud or at most from the time of that redaction." He demonstrates that from biblical times on, specifically since the period of the Exodus, "several beginnings," that is, systems of dating, had been successively initiated. These were determined by momentous events in the history of the Jewish people such as the building and destruction of the Temple in Jerusalem and the reign of foreign monarchs, notably the Persians, Cyrus and Darius. And the Seleucid chronology, adopted by Jewry in the Hellenistic period of Greek domination, continued to be used, as Azariah points out, well into the age of the post-talmudic geonim and even as late as Maimonides' time. Referring to the Jews' usage of the Seleucid chronology Azariah observes that long-established custom takes long to undo, especially among a widely dispersed people, and only very gradually was this system of dating, which had lost its meaning for Jewry, replaced by the creation era chronology.

Azariah perhaps hints at what he views as the generally adverse effects of his coreligionists' ahistorical temperament in stating that "since earlier things are not recalled" (that is, since memory is short) "*many people* think that the dating from creation is Sinaitic and derived from antiquity when in fact it is merely new, of recent origin, as we have indicated." His careful consideration of classical and postclassical Jewish sources may rightly convince Azariah's attentive and sympathetic reader that the evidence of scripture, of the mishnaic and talmudic authorities, and of the medieval halakhic decisors all point to a late date for the introduction of this chronological convention.[6] But *the many* to whom he refers could hardly be expected to respond with enthusiasm to historical argument on this or on other of the religiously sensitive issues that he had addressed. He might perceive an authentic historical record of such matters as a great boon to the integrity of the tradition as a whole; failure to accept it or relying instead upon forced arguments would be, in his opinion, a form of deception.[7] However, the opposing view of the many, not all of whom were by any means obscurantists, was to see the integrity of the whole as ill served by speculation about any of its constituent parts, it being sacrilegious to subject timeless sacred truth to time-bound profane considerations.

Over the next two centuries various Jews and Christians consulted or borrowed from the first edition of the *Me'or 'Einayim*,[8] indeed, the only one available until the end of the eighteenth century. Even Yehiel Halperin, the early-eighteenth-century talmudist and chronicler, included references to *M.E.* in his *Seder ha-Dorot*. Halperin's source, however, does not appear to have been the original of the *Me'or 'Einayim* but rather David Gans's *Ṣemaḥ David*, from which he transcribed a great deal of information, including an abstract of Azariah's account of the 1570 Ferrara earthquake. In the third part of his *Seder ha-Dorot*, Halperin provided a listing of Hebrew books, adopted from the work of the contemporary

Jewish bibliographer Shabbetai Bass. Here, in the entry on *Me'or 'Einayim* (for which Bass's own description of the contents by no means suggests anything of their controversial nature), Halperin noted Judah Loew's displeasure with that work and urged the reader to consult Loew's comments.[9] This suggests that the use of the *Me'or 'Einayim* remained problematic and, as other evidence suggests, often very controversial. That the overall response to it was as unsympathetic as it had been during Azariah's lifetime may also be gauged from the fact that it was not reissued until the Berlin Maskilim did so in 1794.[10]

Azariah himself might have been convinced that with some good will, at least the enlightened reader (*kore' maskil*) would find that "from the beginning of the treatise until its conclusion you will see that my lips have spoken certainty and I have said nothing that, if you read it with deliberation, you will [find it necessary to] reject."[11] Still, well into the eighteenth century, a traditionalist of the prominence and authority of Jacob Emden, who clearly was familiar with and quite positive about various aspects of general knowledge, including history, took a jaundiced view of Azariah's work, considering it not as "the enlightenment of the eyes" (*me'or 'einayim*) but "the blinding of the eyes" (*me'aver 'einayim*). In a rabbinic responsum he takes his correspondent Moses Hagiz to task for having relied on Azariah's opinion that the text of the rabbinic chronicle *Seder 'Olam* contained later, unreliable additions. He goes so far as to say, with obvious derogatory intent, that Azariah himself had "named his work *Me'aver 'Einayim* for he had gone about in darkness that he might delude [others]."[12] The talmudic scholar and native of Jerusalem, Hagiz, who was also at home in secular learning and was especially interested in history, lived for many years in Altona where he made the acquaintance of the Christian Hebraist and bibliographer Johann Christoph Wolf, author of *Bibliotheca Hebraea*. He reports with great enthusiasm his impression of the rich Hebraica collection in Wolf's "upper chamber," to which the bibliographer had invited him. It was perhaps this devotee of Hebrew books and warm admirer of Azariah who familiarized Hagiz with the *Me'or 'Einayim* and discussed it with him.[13] Emden, however, contemptuously refers to Azariah as "that Adumi" (i.e., Azariah Min ha-Adumim, no doubt with the negative connotation of "Edomite"), condemning him in language as extreme as that of Judah Loew two centuries earlier. Indeed, in the same responsum Emden speaks glowingly of Loew, his famous ancestor by marriage, and invokes his *Be'er ha-Golah* with its devastating critique of the *Me'or 'Einayim*.[14]

Yet at a later period, Emden appears to have been prepared to grant at least Azariah's adjustment of the chronology according to the creation era, the relevant calendrical reckoning not being referred to, as he observed, either in scripture or the Talmud. His own relentless campaign against the eighteenth-century heirs of Sabbateanism eventually appears to have made Emden more sympathetic to Azariah's sixteenth-century efforts to defuse messianic speculation. He continued to reject almost everything else in the *Me'or 'Einayim*, especially Azariah's recourse to "gentile vanities" (i.e., non-Jewish works from which, Emden prayed, "God may spare us") since these in particular had led Azariah to deny the validity of talmudic historical traditions such as that pertaining to the supposed thirty-four-year duration of the Persian period of Jewish experience. Emden, however, in defense of Azariah, sharply refuted the opinion of the eighteenth-century Mantuan rabbi and qabbalist Solomon Basilea who, in his *Emunat Ḥakhamim*, had accused Azariah of heresy, of seeking to undermine religious faith and to cause confusion in the tradition.[15] But the fact that with respect to Jewish tradition Azariah had actually "stimulated historical doubt," as the critical theologian Abraham Geiger was to observe complimentarily in the nineteenth century,[16] could hardly be a matter for approval among traditionalists such as Emden in the eighteenth.

By the time the nineteenth-century practitioners of the "Science of Judaism" (*Wissenschaft des Judentums*) began to establish the study of Jewish history and tradition on modern critical foundations they, admittedly, brought to the task a rather different set of ideological presuppositions and scholarly tools. Still, the talents, achievements, and even the inadequately answered but nonetheless challenging questions revealed in the *Me'or 'Einayim* would now be accorded their due, albeit in sometimes overly excessive praise, by scholars like Leopold Zunz and Moritz Steinschneider.[17] And even staunchly orthodox eastern European type talmudists of the stature of Zevi Hirsch Chajes and Mathias Strashun, who combined rabbinic erudition with extensive secular knowledge, could admit Azariah de' Rossi into their discourses and novellae.[18] This despite the often problematic coexistence of the old and the new in the *Me'or 'Einayim* and its not fully resolved ambiguities in establishing an accommodation between historical consciousness and religious tradition.

Notes

1. See Yitzhak Barzilay, "Biqoret shel Yahadut ve-Yehudim be-Kitvei Yosef Shlomo Delmedigo (Yasha"r mi-Candiah), 1591–1655," *Proceedings of the American Academy for Jewish Research* 43(1976): 23.

2. Cf. Israel Zinberg, *Toledot Sifrut Yisra'el*, ed. and trans. S. Z.

Ariel, D. Kennani, G. Karu (Tel Aviv: Sifriyat Poalim, 1955–1960), 2:292ff., who notes that Azariah was cautious in his choice of words in order to disguise "his scientific truths" in pious garb. He adopted a pious posture "so that his heretical views not be recognized."

3. See Isadore Twersky (*Introduction to the Code of Maimonides* [New Haven: Yale University Press, 1980], 220), who in discussing the place of aggadah in Maimonides' work observes that "a clear-cut dichotomy between halakhah and aggadah is a modern scholarly construct and not a reality of Jewish intellectual history."

4. *M.E.* 2:264, 271, 274, 275, 1:208; *M.L.*, 23.

5. *M.E.* 1:3f., 154, 160, 83, 239; *M.L.*, title page.

6. *M.E.* 1:254f.; *M.L.*, 7; *M.E.* 2:259; 1:256f.

7. *M.L.*, 120. Even if his own resolution of the chronological issue appears inadequate, Azariah insists that every maskil ought to pursue further and not ignore the problem: "u-midei heyot shor shaḥut lefanekhah ein lomar kevan she-ein lanu ṣad le-ha'alot lo 'arukhah u-marpe, hekhreḥ hu she-ya'amod ḥai af be-aḥizat 'einayim."

8. See, e.g., Leopold Zunz, "Toledot Rabbi Azariah Min ha-Adumim," in *Sefer Me'or 'Einayim*, ed. I. Benjacob (Vilna: Finn and Rosenkranz, 1863–1865), 3:11–14.

9. See *Seder ha-Dorot*, ed. N. Maskil Le'Etan (Warsaw, 1882–1883), pt. 1, pp. 246f., pt. 3, pp. 61f.; and see, e.g., pt. 1, p. 160, regarding the Bar Kokhba rebellion. Cf. David Gans, *Ṣemaḥ David*, ed. H. Hominer (Jerusalem: Hominer Publications, 1966), pt. I, 54; pt. II, 198. Other references in *Seder ha-Dorot* to *M.E.* include pt. 1, pp. 136f., 141, 144, 145f., 237.

10. Zunz, "Toledot Rabbi Azariah," 15f.; Cassel, *M.E.* 1:x; and see Yosef Hayim Yerushalmi, "Clio and the Jews: Reflections on Jewish Historiography in the Sixteenth Century," *Proceedings of the American Academy for Jewish Research* 46–47 (1979–1980): 636f., to the effect that the republishing of *M.E.* in 1794 had no bearing on the development of modern Jewish historical scholarship, there being no "continuum" between this scholarship and the sixteenth-century historiographical achievement that had "proved abortive." Salo Baron notes the influence of the *M.E.* during the nineteenth-century Jewish historical revival, but due to the virtual oblivion into which the work had previously fallen among Jews, it was now necessary for Jewish Wissenschaft to "start anew," to resume Azariah's "constructive quest" ("Attitude to Life," 204; idem, "Azariah de' Rossi's Historical Method," in *History and Jewish Historians*, 206, 239).

11. *M.E.* 1:90.

12. Jacob Emden, *She'ilat Ya'aveṣ* (Lemberg, 1884), 29a–b, responsum 33, See also Emden's autobiography, *Megillat Sefer*, ed. A. Bick (Jerusalem, 1979), 153–161, regarding Emden's long, close, but troubled relationship with Hagiz, and also 155, for reference to the responsum cited here. And see Baron, "Azariah de' Rossi: A Biographical Sketch," in *History and Jewish Historians*, 172.

13. See Hagiz, *Sefer Mishnat Ḥakhamim* (Wandsbeck, 1733), 4; and

see also Zunz, "Toledot Rabbi Azariah," 13; *Encyclopaedia Judaica* (1972), s.v. "Ḥagiz, Jacob," and s.v. "Wolf, Johann Chistoph"; Azriel Shohet, *Im Ḥilufe Tequfot: Reshit ha-Haskalah be-Yahadut Germanyah* (Jerusalem: Mosad Bialik, 1960), 209f.

14. *She'ilat Ya'aveṣ*, 29b.

15. Zunz, "Toledot Rabbi Azariah," 10f.; Shohet, *Reshit ha-Haskalah*, 229. See Solomon Basilea, *Emunat Ḥakhamim* (Warsaw, 1888), 108: "Ve-hu' adom halakh aḥarei anshei Edom ve-heḥeshivam yoter me-ḥakhmei ha-Gemara . . . bal 'esah shemo 'al sefatai."

16. Abraham Geiger, *Nachgelassene Schriften*, ed. L. Geiger (Berlin: Gerschel, 1875), 2:173.

17. See, e.g., Zunz, "Toledot Rabbi Azariah," 7; Moritz Steinschneider, *Jewish Literature from the Eighth to the Eighteenth Century*, trans. W. Spottiswoode (London, 1857; reprint, New York: Hermon Press, 1970), 207, although Salo Baron has called attention to the very brief consideration Steinschneider actually gave to Azariah (see "Moritz Steinschneider's Contributions to Jewish Historiography," in *History and Jewish Historians*, 314f.).

18. See, for example, *Kol Sifrei Mahara"ṣ Chajes* (Jerusalem, 1958); *Darkhei ha-Hora'ah*, 243f.; *Mevo' ha-Talmud*, 319, 326, 330, 340, 344; *'Ateret Ṣevi*, 354; *Darkhei Moshe*, 448f.; and the *Hagahot ve-Ḥiddushim* of Mathias Strashun to B. Bava Batra 3a, 14a.

GLOSSARY

Important Hebrew Terms and Titles of Works Used in This Book

Aggadah (pl. aggadot), the nonjuristic, anecdotal, homiletical, or narrative component in classical rabbinic tradition, contained in the Talmud and in the midrashic literature.

Gaon (pl. geonim), "excellency" or "glory," the title accorded the heads of the two leading talmudic academies in Babylonia in the post-talmudic period. The geonim exercised authority from about the late sixth to mid-eleventh century.

Gemara, the exposition of the Jewish ceremonial and civil law contained in the Mishnah. The *Gemara* together with the Mishnah came to constitute the Talmud, of which there is both a Babylonian and a Palestinian recension.

Guide of the Perplexed, Moses Maimonides' great philosophical work, written between 1185 and 1190.

Halakhah (pl. halakhot), rabbinic law; the juristic component in classical rabbinic tradition.

Josippon, an anonymous narrative on the Second Temple period, widely read and cited down to early modern times as Josephus's own Hebrew version of his Greek work. It was actually written in southern Italy around the mid-tenth century.

Maskil (pl. maskilim), an intellectually cognizing or enlightened individual.

Midrash (pl. midrashim), having to do with Jewish inquiry into and exposition of scripture, either of scriptural law (midrash halakhah) or of its narrative and moralistic sections (midrash aggadah). This exegesis is contained in various midrashic collections and often in the *Talmud*. The terms *midrashim* or *derashot* also refer to specific individual homilies, anecdotes, or biblical expositions.

Mishnah, the body of orally transmitted halakhic precepts and customs developed from or related to the Torah (i.e., the Pentateuchal law). The present systematization of the material was undertaken, although not yet clearly committed to written form, by Rabbi Judah the Prince around 200 C.E.

Mishneh Torah, Moses Maimonides' comprehensive codification of Jewish law, completed in 1180.

Oral Law (*torah she-be'al peh*), post-biblical Jewish legal and ethical tradition, related to but distinguished from the written, scriptural law (*Torah she-bikhtav*). It was eventually assembled in the form of the talmudic and midrashic literature.

Qabbalah, received or traditional religious law and lore, but also and especially in medieval Jewish experience the oral mystical and esoteric tradition presumably passed down from remote antiquity. In this book it occurs almost exclusively in the latter sense.

Sefer ha-Zohar, the Book of Splendor, for long the major and most influential work in Jewish mysticism. Although traditionally ascribed to the second-century C.E. Simeon bar Yohai, it was actually compiled in the thirteenth century.

Shemonah Peraqim (Eight Chapters), Maimonides' treatise integrating Aristotelian ethics with rabbinic teaching. It is the preface to his commentary to the tractate Avot in the Mishnah.

Talmud (see *Gemara*).

Talmud Torah, a fundamental religious precept of Judaism, to study constantly and be conversant with the law and tradition.

Torah, religious teaching, doctrine, and law in the Pentateuchal sense, but also inclusive of the oral tradition based upon or related to it.

Tosefta, a supplementary, parallel work to the Mishnah, of lesser authority than the latter work and containing halakhic traditions excluded from it.

Tosafists, medieval Franco-German glossarists on the Talmud. Their novellae very often took their point of departure from the eleventh-century commentary of Rashi (Rabbi Solomon ben Isaac).

Bibliography

Primary Sources

Unless otherwise specified, references to the following are from standard printed editions: books of the Bible; the Mishnah; the Tosefta; the Babylonian and Palestinian Talmud and their respective commentaries; midrashim; medieval halakhic compendiums such as Alfasi and Asher ben Jehiel; medieval halakhic codes such as Maimonides' *Mishneh Torah*; and medieval Hebrew commentaries to the Bible.

De' Rossi (Min ha-Adumim), Azariah. *Sefer Me'or 'Einayim*. Edited by D. Cassel. Vilna: Romm, 1864–1866. Reprint. Jerusalem: Maqor, 1970. 3 vols. Cited in notes as *M.E.*

______. *Sefer Me'or 'Einayim*. Edited by I. Benjacob. 3 vols. Vilna: Finn and Rosenkranz, 1863–1865.

______. *Sefer Me'or 'Einayim*. Mantua, 1574. Bodleian Library, Oxford, Opp. 4. 875.

______. The original censored pages from the first Mantua edition of *Me'or 'Einayim* are reproduced in "Saviv *Sefer Me'or 'Einayim* le-R. Azariah

Min ha-Adumim (shetei Mahadurot la-Defus ha-ri'shon, shala"d-shala"h)." In *Genuzot Sefarim: Ma'amarim bibliografiyim* by Israel Mehlman. Jerusalem: National and University Library Press, 1976.

———. *Sefer Maṣref la-Kesef*. Edited by H. Filipowski. Edinburgh, 1854.

———. *Maṣref la-Kesef* and *Ṣedek 'Olamim*. MSS. Bodleian Library, Oxford, in MS Mich. 308.

———. *Maṣref la-Kesef* and *Ṣedek 'Olamim*. MSS. Bodleian Library, Oxford, MS Heb. e. 153.

Abi Zimra, David ben Solomon ibn. *She'elot u-Teshuvot ha-Radbaz*. Warsaw, 1882.

Aboab, Isaac. *Menorat ha-Ma'or*. Vilna: Romm, 1884. Includes the eighteenth-century Hebrew commentary and Yiddish translation of Moses Frankfurter.

Abraham ben Isaac of Narbonne. *Sefer ha-Eshkol*. Edited by B. H. Auerbach. Vol. 2. Halberstadt, 1869.

Abravanel, Don Isaac. *Yeshu'ot Meshiḥo*. Königsberg, 1861.

———. *Perush 'al Nevi'im Ri'shonim*. Jerusalem: Torah ve-Daat, 1955.

———. *Ma'ayenei ha-Yeshu'ah*. Jerusalem, 1960.

Abulafia, Meir. *Kitāb al-Rasā'il*. Edited by Y. Brill. Paris, 1871.

Al-Nakawa, Israel ibn. *Menorat ha-Ma'or*. Edited by H. G. Enelow. New York: Bloch, 1929.

Anav, Zedekiah ben Abraham. *Sefer Shibbolei ha-Leqeṭ*. Edited by S. Buber. Vilna, 1886. Reprint. New York, 1958.

Ashkenazi, Eliezer. *Ma'asei ha-Shem*. Warsaw, 1871.

Astruc, Abba Mari ben Moses. *Minḥat Qena'ot*. Pressburg, 1833. Reprint. Israel, 1967.

Basilea, Solomon Aviad Sar Shalom. *Emunat Ḥakhamim*. Warsaw, 1888.

Benjamin Nehemiah ben Elnathan. *Divrei ha-Yamim shel ha-Apifiyor Paulo Revi'i*. In *Mi-Paulo ha-Revi'i 'ad Pius ha-Ḥamishi*, edited by Isaiah Sonne. Jerusalem: Mosad Bialik, 1954.

Bertinoro, Obadiah di. "Iggrot R. 'Ovadiah mi-Bertinoro." In *Sifrut ha-Hisṭoriyah ha-yisra'elit*, edited by A. Kahana. Warsaw, 1923.

Bodin, Jean. *Method for the Easy Comprehension of History*. Translated by Beatrice Reynolds. Reprint. New York: Octagon Press, 1966.

Capsali, Elijah. *Seder Eliyahu Zuṭa'*. Edited by A. Shmuelevitz, S. Simonsohn, M. Benayahu. 2 vols. Jerusalem: Ben-Zvi Institute and Diaspora Research Institute, 1975.

De la Ruelle, Charles. *Succintz adversaires contre l'histoire et professeurs d'icelles*. Poitiers, 1574.

Delmedigo, Elijah. *Beḥinat ha-Dat*. Edited by I. S. Reggio. Vienna, 1833.

De' Rossi, Solomon. *'Edut ha-Shem Ne'emanah*. In *Meḥqarim u-Meqorot*, edited by J. Rosenthal, vol. 1. Jerusalem: Reuven Maas, 1967.

Emden, Jacob. *Sefer She'ilat Ya'aveṣ*. Lemberg, 1884.

———. *Megillat Sefer*. Edited by A. Bick. Jerusalem, 1979.

Fano, Menahem Azariah da. *She'elot u-Teshuvot*. Duhrenfurt, 1788.

Gans, David. *Ṣemaḥ David*. Edited by H. Hominer. Jerusalem: Hominer Publications, 1966.

Gennazano, Elijah Hayyim ben Benjamin. *Iggeret Ḥamudot*. Edited by A. W. Greenup. London, 1912.

Hagiz, Moses. *Sefer Mishnat Ḥakhamim*. Wandsbeck, 1733.

Halperin, Yehiel. *Seder ha-Dorot*. Edited by N. Maskil Le'Etan. Warsaw, 1882–1883.

Hillel of Verona. *Tagmulei ha-Nefesh*. Edited by S. J. Halberstam. Lyck: Mekiṣe Nirdamim, 1874.

Ibn Adret, Solomon ben Abraham. "Perushei Aggadot la-Rashba'." In *R. Salomo ben Abraham ben Adreth*, edited by J. Perles. Breslau, 1863.

______. "Perush ha-Aggadot la-Rashba' le-Masekhet Bava' Batra'." Edited by Leon A. Feldman. *Bar-Ilan Annual* 7–8 (1970): 138–161.

Ibn Daud, Abraham. *Sefer ha-Qabbalah: The Book of Tradition*. Edited by Gerson D. Cohen. Philadelphia: Jewish Publication Society, 1967.

Ibn Ezra, Abraham. *Yesod Morah*. Prague, 1833.

Ibn Habib, Jacob. *'Ein Ya'qov*. 4 vols. Reprint. New York: Shulsinger Bros., 1944.

Ibn Verga, Solomon. *Sefer Sheveṭ Yehudah*. Edited by A. Shohet. Jerusalem: Mosad Bialik, 1947.

Ibn Yahya, Gedaliah. *Shalshelet ha-Qabbalah*. Warsaw, 1881.

Isaac ben Sheshet Perfet. *She'elot u-Teshuvot Rivash*. Vilna, 1805.

Isaiah di Trani. *Teshuvot ha-Ri"d*. Edited by A. J. Wertheimer. Jerusalem, 1967.

Ishmael Haninah of Valmontone. "Ḥaqirot 'al 'Inyenei ha-Noṣrim." Edited by A. Jellinek. *Ha-Shaḥar* 2 (1870): 17–23.

Isserles, Moses. *Sefer Torat ha-'Olah*. Pt. 1. 1833.

Jehiel of Paris. *Vikuaḥ Rabbenu Yeḥi'el mi-Pariz*. Edited by R. Margaliot. Lvov, n.d.

Jehiel Nissim da Pisa. *Minḥat Qena'ot*. Edited by D. Kaufmann, Berlin, 1898.

Joseph ha-Kohen. *'Emeq ha-Bakhah*. Edited by M. Letteris. Cracow: Faust's Buchhandlung, 1895.

Josippon. *Sefer Yosifon*. Edited by H. Hominer. Jerusalem, 1978.

Kaspi, Joseph ibn. *Guide to Knowledge*. In *Hebrew Ethical Wills*, edited by I. Abrahams, pt. 1. Philadelphia: Jewish Publication Society, 1948.

Loew, Judah (Maharal). *Gevurot ha-Shem*. Lublin, 1875.

______. *Be'er ha-Golah*. New York: Talpiyot, 1953.

______. *Sefer Ḥiddushei Aggadot Maharal mi-Prag*. Vol. 2. London: Honig, 1960.

______. *Sefer Neṣaḥ Yisra'el*. Jerusalem, 1970.

Maimonides, Moses. *Epistle to Yemen*. Edited by A. S. Halkin and translated by Boaz Cohen. New York: American Academy for Jewish Research, 1952.

______. *Sefer Moreh ha-Nevukhim*. Edited by Yehudah Ibn Shmuel. 3 vols. Jerusalem: Mosad ha-Rav Kook, 1959.

______. *Sefer Moreh Nevukhim*. Translated by Samuel ibn Tibbon. Reprint. Jerusalem, 1960.

______. *The Guide of the Perplexed*. Translated by Shlomo Pines. 2 vols. Chicago: University of Chicago Press, 1963.

______. *Mishnah im Perush Rabbenu Mosheh ben Maimon: Seder Nezikin*. Edited and translated by Y. Kafah. Jerusalem: Mosad ha-Rav Kook, 1963.

Modena, Aaron Berechiah da. *Ma'avar Yaboq*. Vilna: Romm, 1911.
Modena, Judah Aryeh (Leone). *Sefer Ḥayyei Yehudah*. Edited by A. Kahana. Kiev, 1911.
———. *Ari Nohem*. Edited by N. S. Lebowitz. Reprint. Jerusalem: Maqor, 1970.
Nahmanides, Moses. *Viquaḥ ha-Ramban*. In *Kitvei Rabbenu Mosheh ben Naḥman*, edited by H. D. Chavel, vol. 1. Jerusalem: Mosad ha-Rav Kook, 1963.
Nathan ben Yehiel of Rome. *'Arukh ha-shalem*. Edited by A. Kohut. Vols. 4,8. 1878–1892. Reprint. New York: Pardes, 1955.
Oṣar ha-Ge'onim: Berakhot. Edited by B. M. Lewin. Haifa, 1928.
Oṣar ha-Ge'onim: Masekhet Yom Tov, Ḥagigah, u-Mashqin. Edited by B. M. Lewin. Jerusalem: Hebrew University Press Assoc., 1931.
Oṣar ha-Ge'onim le Masekhet Sanhedrin. Edited by H. Z. Taubes. Jerusalem: Mosad ha-Rav Kook, 1966.
Shem Tov ibn Shaprut. *Pardes Rimonim*. Edited by E. Zweifel. Zhitomir, 1866.
Sherira ben Hanina. *Iggeret Rav Sherira' Ga'on*. Edited by B. M. Lewin. Reprint. Jerusalem, 1971.
Shishah Sidrei Mishnah: Seder Nezikin. Edited by H. Albeck. Jerusalem: Mosad Bialik, 1953.
Usque, Samuel. *Consolation for the Tribulations of Israel*. Translated by M. A. Cohen. Philadelphia: Jewish Publication Society, 1965.
Vives, Juan Luis. *Vives: On Education*. Translated by F. Watson. Cambridge: Cambridge University Press, 1913.
Zacuto, Abraham. *Sefer Yuḥasin ha-shalem*. Edited by Zvi Filipowski. 2d ed. Frankfurt am Main: Wahrmann Verlag, 1924.

Secondary Sources

Allon, Gedalyahu. *Toledot ha-Yehudim be-Ereṣ Yisra'el bi-Tequfat ha-Mishnah veha-Talmud*. 2 vols. 3d ed. Tel Aviv: Ha-Kibbutz ha-Meuḥad, 1958.
Altmann, Alexander. "*Ars rhetorica* as Reflected in Some Jewish Figures of the Italian Renaissance." In *Essays in Jewish Intellectual History*. Hanover: University Press of New England, 1981.
Assaf, Simhah. *Meqorot le-Toledot ha-Ḥinukh be-Yisra'el*. Vol. 2. Tel Aviv: 1930.
———. *Tequfat ha-Ge'onim ve-Sifrutah*. Edited by M. Margaliot. Jerusalem: Mosad ha-Rav Kook, 1954.
Bacher, W. "Die Agada in Maimunis Werken." In *Moses Ben Maimon: Sein Leben, seine Werke und sein Einfluss*, edited by Jacob Guttmann, vol. 2. Leipzig, 1914.
Baer, Yitzhak. "Le-Biqoret ha-Vikuḥim shel R. Yeḥi'el mi-Pariz ve-shel ha-Ramban." *Tarbiz* 2 (1931): 172–187.
———. "He'arot ḥadashot le-Sefer Sheveṭ Yehudah." *Tarbiz* 6 (1935): 152–179.
———. "Don Yiṣḥaq Abravanel ve-Yaḥaso el Ba'ayot ha-Hisṭoriyah veha-Medinah." *Tarbiz* 8 (1937): 241–259.
———. *Galut*. Translated by R. Warshow. New York: Schocken, 1947.

Baron, Hans. *The Crisis of the Early Italian Renaissance*. Rev. ed. Princeton: Princeton University Press, 1966.

______. "The *Querelle* of the Ancients and the Moderns as a Problem for Renaissance Scholarship." In *Renaissance Essays*, edited by Paul O. Kristeller and P. P. Wiener. New York: Harper and Row, 1968.

Baron, Salo W. "Adumim, Azariah Min." In *Eshkol, Enṣiqlopediyah Yisra'elit*. Berlin: Hoṣa'at Eshkol, 1929.

______. *A Social and Religious History of the Jews*. Vol. 2. New York: Columbia University Press, 1937.

______. *A Social and Religious History of the Jews*. Vols. 2, 6, 8, 9, 14. 2d ed. New York and Philadelphia: Columbia University Press and Jewish Publication Society, 1952–1983.

______. *History and Jewish Historians: Essays and Addresses*. Philadelphia: Jewish Publication Society, 1964.

______. *Steeled by Adversity: Essays and Addresses on American Jewish Life*. Philadelphia: Jewish Publication Society, 1971.

Barzilay, Isaac (Yitzhak). "The Italian and Berlin Haskalah." *Proceedings of the American Academy for Jewish Research* 29 (1960–1961): 17–54.

______. *Between Reason and Faith: Anti-Rationalism in Italian Jewish Thought, 1250–1650*. The Hague: Mouton, 1967.

______. *Yoseph Shlomo Delmedigo, Yashar of Candia: His Life, Works, and Times*. Leiden: Brill, 1974.

______. "Biqoret shel Yahadut ve-Yehudim be-Kitvei Yosef Shlomo Delmedigo (Yasha"r mi-Candia), 1591–1655." *Proceedings of the American Academy for Jewish Research* 43 (1976): 1–27.

Benayahu, Meir. "Maqor 'al Megorashei Sefarad be-Portugal ve-Ṣetam aḥarei Gezerat Rasa"v le-Saloniki." *Sefunot* 11 (1971–1977): 231–265.

______. *Haskamah u-Reshut bi-Defusei Veneṣiyah*. Jerusalem: Ben-Zvi Institute, 1971.

Ben-Sasson, Haim Hillel. *Peraqim be-Toledot ha-Yehudim be-Yemei ha-Beinayim*. Jerusalem: Am Oved, 1958.

______. *Hagut ve-Hanhagah*. Jerusalem: Mosad Bialik, 1959.

______. "Musagim u-Meṣi'ut ba-Hisṭoriyah ha-yehudit be-Shelahei Yemei Ha-Beinayim." *Tarbiz* 29 (1960): 297–312.

Bergmann, J. "Gedichte Asarja de Rossi's." *Zeitschrift fur Hebräische Bibliographie* 3 (1898): 53–58.

______. "Abrabanels Stellung zur Agada." *Monatsschrift für Geschichte und Wissenschaft des Judentums* 81 (1937): 270–280.

Berlin, Charles. "A Sixteenth-Century Hebrew Chronicle of the Ottoman Empire: The Seder Eliyahu Zuta of Elijah Capsali and Its Message." In *Studies in Jewish Bibliography, History, and Literature in Honor of I. Edward Kiev*, edited by Charles Berlin. New York: Ktav, 1971.

Bettan, Israel. "The Sermons of Judah Moscato." *Hebrew Union College Annual* 6 (1929): 297–326.

Bloch, P. "Der Streit um den Moreh der Maimonides in der Gemeinde Posen um die Mitte der 16. Jahrh." *Monatsschrift für Geschichte und Wissenschaft des Judentums* 47 (1903): 153–169, 263–279, 346–356.

Bonfil, Reuven (Robert). "Bituyim le-Yiḥud 'Am Yisra'el bi-Tequfat ha-Renesans." *Sinai* 76 (1974): 36–46.

———. "Perush R. Mosheh Provençal le-Khaf-he Haqdamot ha-Rambam." *Kiryat Sefer* 50 (1975): 157–176.

———. *Ha-Rabbanut be-Iṭalyah bi-Tequfat ha-Renesans*. Jerusalem: Magnes Press, 1979.

———. "Some Reflections on the Place of Azariah de Rossi's *Meor Enayim* in the Cultural Milieu of Italian Renaissance Jewry." In *Jewish Thought in the Sixteenth Century*, edited by B. D. Cooperman. Cambridge: Harvard University Press, 1983.

Bouwsma, William J. *Venice and the Defense of Republican Liberty*. Berkeley and Los Angeles: University of California Press, 1968.

Braude, W. G. "Maimonides' Attitude to Midrash." In *Studies in Jewish Bibliography, History, and Literature in Honor of I. Edward Kiev*, edited by Charles Berlin. New York: Ktav, 1971.

Breuer, Mordechai. "Qavim le-Demuto shel R. David Gans Ba'al *Ṣemaḥ David*." *Bar-Ilan Annual* 11 (1973): 97–118.

———. "Modernism and Traditionalism in Sixteenth-Century Jewish Historiography: A Study of David Gans' *Tzemah David*." In *Jewish Thought in the Sixteenth Century*, edited by B. D. Cooperman. Cambridge: Harvard University Press, 1983.

Burke, Peter. *The Renaissance Sense of the Past*. New York: St. Martin's Press, 1970.

Cassirer, Ernst. *The Individual and the Cosmos in Renaissance Philosophy*. Translated by M. Domandi. New York: Harper and Row, 1964.

Cassuto, Mosheh David. *Ha-Yehudim bi-Firenze bi-Tequfat ha-Renesans*. Translated by M. Hartom. Jerusalem: Kiryat Sefer, 1967.

Chajes, Zevi Hirsch. *Kol Sifrei Mahars Chajes*. Vol. 1. Jerusalem, 1958.

Chazan, Robert. "A Medieval Hebrew Polemical Mélange." *Hebrew Union College Annual* 51 (1980): 89–110.

Cochrane, Eric, ed. *The Late Italian Renaissance, 1525–1630*. London: MacMillan, 1970.

———. *Historians and Historiography in the Italian Renaissance*. Chicago: University of Chicago Press, 1981.

Collingwood, R. G. *The Idea of History*. New York: Oxford University Press, 1957.

Cotroneo, Girolamo. *I trattatisti dell "Ars Historica."* Naples: Giannini, 1971.

David, Abraham. "Le-Toledot ha-Polmos Saviv ha-Sefer *Me'or 'Einayim*." *Kiryat Sefer* 59 (1984): 641–642.

Elbaum, Jacob. "Rabbi Judah Loew of Prague and His Attitude to the Aggadah." *Scripta Hierosolymitana* 22 (1971): 28–47.

Elon, Menahem. *Ha-Mishpaṭ ha-'ivri*. Vol. 1. Jerusalem: Magnes Press, 1973.

Epstein, Jacob N. "R. Mosheh Taku ben Ḥasdai ve-Sifro *Ketav Tamim*." In *Meḥqarim be-Sifrut ha-Talmud uve-Leshonot shemiyot*, edited by E. Z. Melamed. Jerusalem: Magnes Press, 1983.

Febvre, Lucien. *Life in Renaissance France*. Edited and translated by Marian Rothstein. Cambridge: Harvard University Press, 1977.

———. *Le Probleme de l'incroyance au XVIe siècle: La religion de Rabelais*. Paris: Albin Michel, 1968.

Fox, Marvin, "Nahmanides on the Status of Aggadot: Perspectives on the Disputation at Barcelona, 1263," *Journal of Jewish Studies* 40, no. 1 (Spring, 1989).

Frankel, Zacharias. *Mevo' ha-Yerushalmi*. Breslau, 1870.

———. *Darkhei ha-Mishnah*. Reprint. Warsaw, 1923.

Franklin, Julian H. *Jean Bodin and the Sixteenth-Century Revolution in the Methodology of Law and History*. New York: Columbia University Press, 1963.

Friedenwald, Harry. *The Jews and Medicine: Essays*. Vol. 2. Baltimore: Johns Hopkins Press, 1944.

Geffen, David. "Insights into the Life and Thought of Elijah del Medigo, Based on His Published and Unpublished Works." *Proceedings of the American Academy for Jewish Research* 41–42 (1973–1974): 69–96.

Geiger, Abraham. *Nachgelassene Schriften*. Edited by L. Geiger. Vol. 2. Berlin: Gerschel, 1875.

Ghirondi, Mordecai Samuel, and Neppi, Hananel. *Toledot Gedolei Yisra'el u-Ge'onei Iṭalyah ve-Zekher Ṣadiqim li-Verakhah*. Trieste: Tipographica Marenigh, 1853. Reprint. Israel, 1968.

Gilbert, Felix. "The Renaissance Interest in History." In *Art, Science, and History in the Renaissance*, edited by Charles Singleton. Baltimore: Johns Hopkins University Press, 1967.

———. *Machiavelli and Guicciardini: Politics and History in Sixteenth-Century Florence*. Princeton: Princeton University Press, 1965.

Gilmore, Myron P. "The Renaissance Conception of the Lessons of History." In *Humanists and Jurists*. Cambridge: Harvard University Press, 1963.

Ginzberg, Louis. *Students, Scholars, and Saints*. Philadelphia: Jewish Publication Society, 1928.

———. *The Legends of the Jews*. 7 vols. Philadelphia: Jewish Publication Society, 1954.

Ginzburg, Carlo. *The Cheese and the Worms: The Cosmos of a Sixteenth-Century Miller*. Translated by J. Tedeschi and A. Tedeschi. New York: Penguin Books, 1982.

Goez, Werner, "Die Anfänge der historischen Methoden—Reflexion in der italienischen Renaissance und ihre Aufnahme in der Geschichtsschreibung des deutschen Humanismus." *Archiv für Kulturgeschichte* 56 (1974): 25–48.

Goldman, Israel M. *The Life and Times of Rabbi David Ibn Abi Zimra*. New York: Jewish Theological Seminary, 1970.

Gottesdiener, A. "Ha-Ari shebe-Ḥakhmei Prag." In *Azkarah: Koveṣ torani-mada'i,* edited by J. L. Fishman. Jerusalem: Mosad ha-Rav Kook, 1937.

Graetz, Heinrich. *Divrei Yemei Yisra'el.* Translated by S. P. Rabinowitz. Vol. 4. Warsaw, 1890–1899.

Green, Yosef. "Mishpaḥat Trabot." *Sinai* 79 (1977): 147–163.

Guenée, Bernard. *Histoire et culture historique dans l'occident médiéval.* Paris: Aubier Montaigne, 1980.

Guttmann, Julius. "*Yerushalayim* le-Mendelsohn *veha-Masekhet ha-teologit-ha-medinit* le-Spinoza." In *Dat u-Mada',* translated by S. Esh. Jerusalem: Magnes Press, 1955.

———. *Philosophies of Judaism.* Translated by D. W. Silverman. London: Routledge and Kegan Paul, 1964.

Halberstam, S. J. "Sheloshah Ketavim 'al Devar *Sefer Me'or 'Einayim* u-Mikhtav eḥad el R. Azariah Min ha-Adumim ve-'od Mikhtav 'odotav." In *Festschrift zum achtzigsten Geburstage Moritz Steinschneider's.* Leipzig: Otto Harrassowitz, 1896. Includes previously unpublished material relative to *Me'or 'Einayim* from Hananel Neppi's *Zekher Ṣadiqim li-Verakhah.*

Halkin, A. S. "Yedaiah Bedershi's Apology." In *Jewish Medieval and Renaissance Studies,* edited by A. Altmann. Cambridge: Harvard University Press, 1967.

Jastrow, Marcus. *A Dictionary of the Targumim, the Talmud Babli and Yerushalmi, and the Midrashic Literature.* New York/Berlin: Verlag Choreb, 1926.

Katz, Jacob. *Masoret u-Mashber.* Jerusalem: Mosad Bialik, 1958.

———. *Exclusiveness and Tolerance.* New York. Schocken, 1962.

Kaufmann, David. "Contributions à l'histoire des luttes d'Azaria de Rossi." *Revue des études juives* 33 (1896): 77–87.

———. "The Dispute About the Sermons of David Del Bene of Mantua." *Jewish Quarterly Review,* o.s. 8 (1896): 513–524.

———. "La defense de lire le *Me'or 'Einayim* d'Azaria dei Rossi" *Revue des études juives* 38 (1899): 280–281.

Klempt, Adalbert. *Die Säkularisierung der universalhistorischen Auffassung. Zum Wandel des Geschichtsdenkens in 16. und 17. Jahrhundert.* Göttingen: Musterschmidt Verlag, 1960.

Kristeller, Paul O. "The Unity of Truth." In *Renaissance Concepts of Man and Other Essays.* New York: Harper and Row, 1972.

Lieberman, Saul. *Sheqi'in.* Jerusalem: Bamberger, 1939.

———. "The Alleged Ban on Greek Wisdom." In *Hellenism in Jewish Palestine.* New York: Jewish Theological Seminary, 1950.

Lutzki, M. "Ve-Khatav Mosheh-ḥamesh Teshuvot otografiyot me'et ha-Rambam." *Ha-Tequfah* 5 (1946): 679–704.

Maccoby, Hyam. *Judaism on Trial: Jewish-Christian Disputations in the Middle Ages.* Rutherford: Fairleigh Dickinson University Press, 1982.

Mann, Jacob. *Texts and Studies in Jewish History and Literature*. Vol. 1. New York: Ktav, 1972.

Marcus, Ralph. "A Sixteenth-Century Hebrew Critique of Philo." *Hebrew Union College Annual* 21 (1948): 29–71.

Margiotta, Giacinto. *Le origini italiane de la Querelle des anciens et des modernes*. Rome: Editrice Studium, 1953.

Merton, Robert K. *On the Shoulders of Giants*. New York: Free Press, 1965.

Modona, L. "Une lettre d'Azaria de Rossi." *Revue des études juives* 30 (1895): 313–316.

Momigliano, Arnaldo. *Studies in Historiography*. New York: Harper and Row, 1966.

______. *Essays in Ancient and Modern Historiography*. Middletown: Wesleyan University Press, 1977.

Neher, André. *Le puits de l'exil*. Paris: Albin Michel, 1966.

Neuman, Abraham A. "Abraham Zacuto, Historiographer." In *Harry Austryn Wolfson Jubilee Volume*. Vol. 2. Jerusalem: American Academy for Jewish Research, 1965.

Pirotti, Umberto. "Aristotelian Philosophy and the Popularization of Learning: Benedetto Varchi and Renaissance Aristotelianism." Translated by E. Cochrane. In *The Late Italian Renaissance, 1525–1630*, edited by E. Cochrane. London: MacMillan, 1970.

Rabbinovicz, Raphael Nathan. *Sefer Diqduqei Soferim*, vol. 9, Sanhedrin. Munich, 1867–1886.

Roth, Cecil. *The History of the Jews of Italy*. Philadelphia: Jewish Publication Society, 1946.

______. *The Jews in the Renaissance*. Philadelphia: Jewish Publication Society, 1959.

Ruderman, David B. *The World of a Renaissance Jew: The Life and Thought of Abraham ben Mordecai Farissol*. Cincinnati: Hebrew Union College Press, 1981.

Saperstein, Marc. *Decoding the Rabbis: A Thirteenth-Century Commentary on the Aggadah*. Cambridge: Harvard University Press, 1980.

Sasson, David. *Me'at Devash*. Oxford, 1928.

Scholem, Gershom. *Major Trends in Jewish Mysticism*. New York: Schocken, 1946.

______. "Yedi'ot ḥadashot 'al R. Yosef Ashkenazi, ha-Tana' mi-Ṣefat." *Tarbiz* 28 (1958): 59–89, 201–235.

Schweid, Eliezer. *Toledot he-Hagut ha-yehudit ba-'et ha-ḥadashah*. Jerusalem: Keter, 1977.

Shalem, N. "Una fonte ebraica poco nota sul terremoto di Ferrara del 1570." *Rivista geografica italiana* (1938): 66–76.

Shohet, Azriel. *Im Ḥilufei Tequfot Reshit ha-Haskalah be-Yahadut Germanyah*. Jerusalem: Mosad Bialik, 1960.

Shulvass, Moses A. *Roma vi-Yerushalayim: Toledot ha-Yaḥas shel Yehudei Iṭalyah le-Ereṣ Yisra'el*. Jerusalem: Mosad ha-Rav Kook, 1944.

______. "Knowledge of Antiquity among Italian Jews." *Proceedings of the American Academy for Jewish Research* 18 (1948–1949): 291–299.

———. *Ḥayyei ha-Yehudim be-Iṭalyah bi-Tequfat ha-Renesans*. New York: Ogen, 1955.

———. "'Al ha-Hitraḥashut ha-hisṭorit veha-Maḥshavah ha-hisṭorit." In *Bi-Ṣevat ha-Dorot*. New York: Ogen, 1960.

Simonsohn, Shlomo. *History of the Jews in the Duchy of Mantua*. Jerusalem: Kiryat Sefer, 1977.

Smallwood, E. Mary. *The Jews under Roman Rule: From Pompey to Diocletian*. 2d ed. Leiden: Brill, 1981.

Sonne, Isaiah. *Mi-Paulo ha-Revi'i 'ad Pius ha-Ḥamishi*. Jerusalem: Mosad Bialik, 1954.

Spini, Giorgio. "Historiography: The Art of History in the Italian Counter-Reformation." Translated by E. Cochrane. In *The Late Italian Renaissance, 1525–1630*, edited by E. Cochrane. London: MacMillan, 1970.

Steinschneider, Moritz. *Jewish Literature from the Eighth to the Eighteenth Century*. Translated by W. Spottiswoode. London, 1857. Reprint. New York: Hermon Press, 1970.

Stow, Kenneth R. *Catholic Thought and Papal Jewry Policy, 1555–1593*. New York: Jewish Theological Seminary of America, 1977.

Strashun, Mathias. *Hagahot ve-Ḥiddushim*. In the *Talmud Bavli*. Vilna: Romm, 1908.

Tamar, David. *Meḥqarim be-Toledot ha-Yehudim be-Ereṣ Yisra'el uve-Iṭalyah*. Jerusalem: Reuven Maas, 1970.

Tcherikover, Avigdor. *Ha-Yehudim be-Miṣrayim ba-Tequfah ha-hellenisṭit-ha-romit le-Or ha-Papirologiah*. 2d rev. ed. Jerusalem: Magnes Press, 1963.

Tchernowitz, Chaim. *Toledot ha-Halakhah*. Vols. 1, 2. 2d ed. New York: Jubilee Committee, 1945.

———. *Toledot ha-Posqim*. Vol. 2. New York: Jubilee Committee, 1946–1947.

Tishby, Isaiah. "Ha-Polmos 'al Sefer ha-Zohar ba-Me'ah ha-shesh esreh be-Iṭalyah." *P'raqim* (1967–1968): 131–182.

Twersky, Isadore. "Some Non-Halakic Aspects of the *Mishneh Torah*." In *Jewish Medieval and Renaissance Studies*, edited by A. Altmann. Cambridge: Harvard University Press, 1967.

———. "Rabbi Abraham ben David of Posquières: His Attitude to and Acquaintance with Secular Learning." In *Medieval Jewish Life*, edited by Robert Chazan. New York: Ktav, 1976.

———. "Joseph ibn Kaspi: Portrait of a Medieval Jewish Intellectual." In *Studies in Medieval Jewish History and Literature*, edited by Isadore Twersky. Cambridge: Harvard University Press, 1979.

———. "Yeda'ayah ha-Penini u-Perusho le-Aggadah." In *Studies in Jewish Religious and Intellectual History Presented to Alexander Altmann*, edited by S. Stein and R. Loewe. University, Ala.: University of Alabama Press, 1979.

———. *Introduction to the Code of Maimonides*. New Haven: Yale University Press, 1980.

Vajda, Georges. "Hesber raşiyonalisti bilti yadu'a mi-Yemei ha-Beinayim al ha-Nissim." In *Hagut 'ivrit be-Eiropah*, edited by M. Zohari and A. Tartakover. Tel Aviv: Brit Ivrit Olamit, 1969.

Vogelstein, Hermann. *Rome*. Translated by Moses Hadas. Philadelphia: Jewish Publication Society, 1940.

Vogelstein, Hermann, and Paul Rieger. *Geschichte der Juden in Rom*. Vol. 1. Berlin: Mayer and Müller, 1896.

Walsh, P. G. *Livy: His Historical Aims and Methods*. Cambridge: Cambridge University Press, 1961.

Weinberg, Joanna. "Azariah dei Rossi: Towards a Reappraisal of the Last Years of His Life." *Annali della Scuola Normale Superiore di Pisa*, 3d ser. 8 (1978): 493–511.

———. "Azariah de' Rossi and Septuagint Traditions." *Italia* 5 (1985): 7–35.

Weiss, Isaac Hirsch. *Dor Dor ve-Dorshav*. Vol. 4. Vilna: Romm, 1904.

Wilcox, Donald J. *The Development of Florentine Humanist Historiography in the Fifteenth Century*. Cambridge: Harvard University Press, 1969.

Yarei, Joseph. "Liquṭim me-Kitvei ha-Rav Hananel Neppi." In *Zikaron le-Avraham Eliyahu Harkavy*. St. Petersburg, 1909.

Yerushalmi, Yosef Hayim. *The Lisbon Massacre of 1506 and the Royal Image in the Shebet Yehudah*. Cincinnati: Hebrew Union College Press, 1976.

———. "Clio and the Jews: Reflections on Jewish Historiography in the Sixteenth Century." *Proceedings of the American Academy for Jewish Research* 46–47 (1979–1980): 607–638.

———. "Messianic Impulses in Joseph ha-Kohen." In *Jewish Thought in the Sixteenth Century*, edited by B. D. Cooperman. Cambridge: Harvard University Press, 1983.

Zinberg, Israel. *Toledot Sifrut Yisra'el*. Translated and edited by S. Z. Ariel, D. Kenaani, and G. Karu, vols. 2, 3. Tel Aviv: Sifriyat Poalim, 1955–1960.

Zlotnick, Dov. "The Commentary of Rabbi Abraham Azulai to the Mishnah." *Proceedings of the American Academy for Jewish Research* 40 (1973): 147–168.

Zunz, Leopold. "Toledot Rabbi Azariah Min ha-Adumim." *Kerem Ḥemed* 5 (1841): 131–158 and (1843): 119–124. Reprint. In *Sefer Me'or 'Einayim*. Edited by I. Benjacob. Vol. 3. Vilna: Finn and Rosenkranz, 1863–1865.

———. *Ha-Derashot be-Yisra'el*. Edited by H. Albeck and translated by M. A. Zak. Jerusalem: Mosad Bialik, 1974.

Index